Dred Scott's
Revenge

A LEGAL HISTORY OF RACE
AND FREEDOM IN AMERICA

OTHER BOOKS BY ANDREW P. NAPOLITANO

Constitutional Chaos:
What Happens When the Government Violates Its Own Laws

The Constitution in Exile:
How the Federal Government Has Seized Power by
Rewriting the Supreme Law of the Land

A Nation of Sheep

Dred Scott's *Revenge*

A LEGAL HISTORY OF RACE AND FREEDOM IN AMERICA

Andrew P. Napolitano

THOMAS NELSON
Since 1798

NASHVILLE   DALLAS   MEXICO CITY   RIO DE JANEIRO   BEIJING

Published in Nashville, Tennessee, by Thomas Nelson. Thomas Nelson is a registered trademark of Thomas Nelson, Inc.

Thomas Nelson, Inc., titles may be purchased in bulk for educational, business, fund-raising, or sales promotional use. For information, please e-mail SpecialMarkets@ThomasNelson.com.

Library of Congress Control Number: 2009923245

ISBN: 978-1-59555-265-5

Printed in the United States of America

09 10 11 12 13 QW 6 5 4 3

This book is dedicated
to all who suffered
at the hands of any government
because of the color of their skin.
It has been written with the belief
that with knowledge of history,
hatred shall lose its grip on all governments in America.

Can the liberties of a nation be thought secure when we have removed their only firm basis, a conviction in the minds of the people that these liberties are of the gift of God? That they are not to be violated but with his wrath? Indeed I tremble for my country when I reflect that God is just: that his justice cannot sleep for ever: that considering numbers, nature and natural means only, a revolution of the wheel of fortune, an exchange of situation, is among possible events . . . The spirit of the master is abating, that of the slave rising from the dust, his condition mollifying, the way I hope preparing, under the auspices of heaven, for a total emancipation, and that this is disposed, in the order of events, to be with the consent of the masters, rather than by their extirpation.

—THOMAS JEFFERSON,
Notes on the State of Virginia, June 1785

Now hatred is by far the longest pleasure;
Men love in haste, but they detest at leisure.

—LORD BYRON,
Don Juan (canto XII, st. 6)

Contents

CONTENTS

Introduction

When Thomas Jefferson wrote in the Declaration of Independence that "all Men are created equal, that they are endowed by their Creator with certain inalienable Rights, that among these are Life, Liberty, and the Pursuit of Happiness," he could not have meant then what we understand these words to mean today.

When the framers of the government wrote in the Constitution that "No person shall be . . . deprived of life, liberty, or property, without due process of law," and that the Constitution is "the supreme Law of the Land," they conveniently omitted a definition of the word *person*.

And when presidents from Abraham Lincoln to Woodrow Wilson to Franklin Delano Roosevelt, who either appointed judges who upheld and enforced slavery, enforced two sets of laws themselves (one that treated whites fairly and one that treated blacks unfairly) or permitted the government to conduct gruesome medical experiments on poor, ignorant black men, what did they think of their oaths to uphold the Constitution?

The history of the government's behavior in the relationship of blacks to whites in America is one of utter rejection of the very principles upon which the nation was founded and for which it has publicly stood for over two hundred years. It is this sad history that

I shall recount, analyze, and explain from a legal and political perspective here.

When Jefferson wrote the immortal words of the Declaration, he attached the new nation's soul irretrievably to what lawyers and judges call the natural law. When he bought and sold slaves, he rejected the natural law for himself, in favor of what lawyers and judges call positivism.

Natural law teaches that our rights come from our humanity. Since we are created by God in His image and likeness, and since He is perfectly free—or, if you prefer, since we are creatures of nature born biologically dependent but morally free—freedom is our birthright. Thus, the natural law informs that freedom comes from our humanity, not from any outside source like, for example, the government. Under the natural law, therefore, freedom to exercise your own free will; to develop your personality; to think as you wish, say what you think, publish what you say; to worship as you feel; to protect yourself from all others (including the government); to be free from arbitrary restraint; to own, use, and enjoy private property as you see fit; to enjoy consensual personal intimacy; to have the right to be left alone are as natural as our arms and faces and cannot be taken away by law or command but only by due process, which is also guaranteed.

And the natural law is color-blind. We know this because one of its principal expositors, St. Augustine, was black; its other principal proponent, St. Thomas Aquinas, was white.

Due process means that the laws one has been accused of violating have been written down (so there is no dispute over the law's language); are basically fair (laws, for example, that protect a person's natural rights, like laws against murder or theft); are not in violation of the Constitution; and do not violate the natural law. Under our constitutionally mandated due process, only legislatures may write the laws. Presidents and governors enforce them, and judges decide what the laws mean.

Thus a law enacted by the president alone is no law, since under the Constitution all federal legislative powers are vested in Congress. As well, a law enacted by Congress punishing speech is no law at all, since the law itself violates the Constitution and the natural right to speak freely. The framers of the Constitution fully understood this as they wrote in the First Amendment: "Congress shall make no laws . . . abridging *the* freedom of speech." I have italicized the word *the* to make my point. The framers accepted the natural law premise that freedoms come with and from our humanity. *The* freedom of speech obviously preexisted the constitutional amendment, insulating it from government abridgement, and the use of the article *the* reflects the framers' unmistakable acceptance of that truism.

Due process also means that the procedure by which liberty or property are interfered with by the government or guilt as adjudicated by the courts is fair; is presided over by a neutral judge; is based on the findings of a neutral jury with no interest in the outcome; permits challenges to and confrontation of evidence and witnesses; allows a freely chosen, totally loyal attorney; and permits the outcome to be appealed to other neutral judges.

Had the framers and their successors truly adhered to these beliefs for all persons—black as well as white—there could have been no slavery, no Jim Crow, no public segregation, and none of the evils they spawned.

Unfortunately, positivism reared its ugly head. This is the name for laws that reject the natural law and the belief in natural rights. Positivism teaches that the law is whatever the lawgiver says it is, providing it is written down. Under positivism, so long as the legislature in a democracy was validly elected and followed its own rules in enacting a law, the law is valid and enforceable no matter what it says. Thus, under this wretched theory, the Congress or a state legislature could abolish free speech or even free will (as the Congress and state legislatures did for blacks) and the law would be valid, subsisting, and enforceable.

Under positivism, in a democracy the majority always gets its way, and Heaven help the minority. Under the natural law, everyone's rights are guaranteed, and the will of the majority can be frustrated when it seeks to abridge anyone's natural rights—even a minority of one—without due process.

From the beginning of the settlement of the American colonies, the government sometimes enforced the natural law for whites and almost always enforced laws based on positivism for blacks. From slavery to war, to Reconstruction, to Jim Crow, to more war, to official public segregation, to accepted prejudicial cultural norms—the government presumed to pick and choose whose rights to respect and whose to reject, and it did so based on race.

The ultimate positivist rejection of the natural law happened to Dred Scott, a slave who sued for his freedom and lost. The sophomoric ratiocinations, moral contortions, and collectivist absurdities articulated by the Supreme Court of the United States as it purported to justify legally human slavery in *Dred Scott v. Sandford* spawned 150 years of government-sponsored horrific treatment of blacks that destroyed lives, suppressed freedom, and wrecked our American culture with a vengeance.

Natural law and positivism, of course, disagree on the role of the individual in our society. The natural law teaches that the individual is immortal because of our immortal souls. It also teaches that the government is an artificial creation (it has no soul) based on force. When the government protects freedom and respects natural rights, it is doing its job. When it ceases to protect freedom and when it violates natural rights, it is the duty of the people to alter or abolish it. That duty is articulated not only in the Declaration of Independence, but also in federal law.

Positivism rejects the primacy of the individual and embraces instead the troublesome idea of collectivism. Collectivism believes that humans are merely grapes to be crushed and fermented into the wine that meets the needs of the government. Persons may be enslaved, incarcerated, and denied all rights without due process in order to enhance the temporal well-being of those in power. This doctrine permits the government to regulate humans on the basis of groups to which they belong by virtue of their birth; race, gender, age, nationality, place of origin, sexual orientation, and other such attributes may form the basis for valid laws under the collectivism of the positivists.

This book tells the unhappy story of the rejection of the natural law and the embracing of positivism by the government in America at every level, based on the ugliest of collectivist positivist ideology: This ideology is that of *hatred based on race.*

Let me warn you that this is not your grandfather's American history book. I will tell the stories of those whom other writers have hoped you will not learn; of humans like you and me demeaned worse than cattle, denied basic free will, crushed or impeded by the government even up to the present day. You will see that Lincoln's racism was no less tempered than other whites of his day; his Emancipation Proclamations (both of them) did not free the slaves; and he once proposed an amendment to the Constitution that would have guaranteed the right to own slaves. Your grandfather's history has probably distorted these truths.

The real culprit throughout our racial history has been the government. The government—local, state, and federal—at virtually every turn, in every generation, and in innumerable ways, selectively chose to enact and enforce laws based on the natural law or on positivism, depending on race. Relying on the laws of positivism, the government permitted, condoned, and protected the most horrific abuse imaginable to blacks, and to some of the whites who protested.

But on January 20th 2009, the government began anew.

1

———

Slavery Comes to
the New World

All humans are inherently free and equal creatures. Equality and freedom act as common bonds that transcend nationality, ethnicity, and race. Yet since the beginnings of civilization, humans have conquered and enslaved one another time and time again, effectively extinguishing the God-given rights we possess. While there are certain components peculiar to American slavery, every case of human trafficking in history suffers from the inevitable natural repercussions of creating a class of humans defined as things.

The institution of slavery can be found in the histories of the Egyptian, Roman, and Greek civilizations in ways that seem to have foreshadowed the American system. The ancient Greeks believed that no healthy, lasting society could prosper without slaves.[1] Slavery was thus an integral part of common culture and, similar to the inherent contradiction of American slavery, was predominant in those cities where individual liberty for some was at its highest.[2]

The most obvious example was Athens. In order to devote one's true capabilities to the city-state, one could not be consumed by manual or domestic labor. Consequently, it was thought that the freedom to target one's efforts in areas that would benefit society could only come about with the existence of slavery. Democracy and slavery, apparent opposites, were united in Athens.

The number of slaves in ancient Greece was proportionately similar to the number in the American South in 1860, but the distribution of slave ownership was greater in Greece than in the United States.[3] However, the vital social distinction in Greece was not that of slave and freeman, but rather aristocrat and commoner. Generally, the Greeks considered slaves and laborers as members of the same social class and carefully defined a slave as a kind of *possession with a soul*. Slaves were often able to secure their freedom and even become politically and economically powerful due to mercifully lenient Greek law.

According to Jack Hayward, the English writer and academic, "if slavery was an important institution in Greece, it became the *all-important* institution in Rome."[4] Rome's urban, rural, and domestic economies were driven by slave labor. The defining characteristic of the Roman institution was its sheer size: From 65 BC to about 30 BC, one hundred thousand new slaves were needed each year on the Italian peninsula, and from 30 BC to AD 150, a staggering five hundred thousand new slaves were needed *each year* to feed the empire's commercial needs.[5] In comparison, the African slave trade at its peak would bring an average of sixty thousand slaves per year to the New World. At the height of the Roman Empire, it is estimated that one-third of the entire population were slaves.[6]

Slavery in Rome grew almost proportionately to the empire's persistent expansion. The primary supply of slaves came from the enslavement of its conquered enemies and, as any student of history is aware, Rome was not short of enemies. For centuries at a time, Rome was in almost perpetual conflict, the result of which was the eventual control of the entire Mediterranean, Northern Africa, and almost all of modern-day Europe. When conquering an enemy's territory, the Roman military machine would enslave its entire population. The conquest of the Etruscan city of Veii, the siege of Aspis, the destruction of Carthage, the campaign against the Salassi Alpine tribe, and the destruction of the city of Ctesiphon in the war against the Parthians produced approximately 225,000 slaves for the Romans through the system of enslaving their enemies *en masse*.[7] After these conquests, slaves—who had been citizens and denizens of the conquered territories—would be shipped back to the Roman peninsula and auctioned off at slave markets in ways similar to the American slave trade centuries later.

The role of the slave was vital in every conceivable corner of Roman society. In addition to acquisition from war, the system was perpetuated by reproduction, just as American slaves inherited the status of their mothers as slaves in the antebellum South centuries later. Greece would even breed slaves for Rome, just as Virginia and Maryland would later do for other Southern states. Despite the many horrors that Roman slaves faced, they also participated in family religious worship and seasonal feasts, often socially mingling with their masters as apparent equals.[8]

In the Arab world, racial distinctions were more important than in Rome and Greece. This tended to occur as Arab civilization extended deeper into Africa. Arabs actually regarded Africans as a race born to be slaves. China also attached racial significance to slavery, especially between the seventh and tenth centuries AD. The Chinese regarded Koreans, Indonesians, Persians, and Turks as less than human and imposed strict laws to prevent sexual relations between the free and slave populations as a means of maintaining the purity of their race.[9]

Babylonia, Assyria, India, and Russia were all home to slaves. Visigothic Spain was divided into two classes, the free and unfree. The Franks made use of slaves as merchants, and slaves as manufacturers were common during the early Middle Ages. Christians and Muslims enslaved each other during their centuries of wars. The Black and Mediterranean Seas were the highways of an international slave trade during the thirteenth, fourteenth, and fifteenth centuries.[10]

But amidst slavery's historical prevalence, rarely, if at all, can one hear so much as a peep about its immorality, calls for its eradication, or revelations of its patent violation of the natural law. Nearly all ancient civilizations accepted slavery as a natural occurrence of the human condition. People were born into various class and caste systems of which slavery was commonly one. Civilizations relied on the institution as a source of free labor, and it was simply too good a luxury even to think about wrestling with its immorality.

Nor did this in any way cease to exist when notions of individual rights and liberty were at their highest. We have already seen that slavery coexisted with Greek ideas of liberty over two thousand years ago. The Reformation came and went without any change in attitude toward human bondage; so did the Enlightenment.

This hypocrisy even permeated the philosophy of John Locke, one of the pioneers of the Enlightenment whose philosophy is imbedded in the American Constitution. Perhaps the greatest English defender of the inalienable rights of man—he argued that one's fundamental rights should be preserved and protected from "the inconstant, uncertain, unknown, arbitrary will of another man" even upon entering into the social contract (the consent individuals grant to the government that gives government the authority to govern). Locke was an investor in the Royal African Company, a major slave importer, and had no qualms justifying slavery along with his revolutionary notions of individual liberty.[11] To Locke, slavery represented the continuation of the state of war and was free from the obligations otherwise imposed by the social compact. These are but examples of slavery's seductive ability to coexist with seemingly contradictory philosophies over the centuries.

Nonetheless, American slavery has a peculiar horror all its own. The existing evidence leads to the conclusion that slaves throughout history were exposed to similar brutality. Turning a human into a thing, a form of conveyable chattel stripped of natural rights and free will, operates as the same contradiction whether it occurs in ancient Rome, medieval China, or antebellum Virginia. Humans in bondage suffer equally in any civilization or century. Yet in no ancient society was the distinction between slave and freeman so sharply drawn as in America. There is a unique tragedy behind the existence of slavery in what would later become known as the free world.

How could a country founded upon such revolutionary philosophical principles of the primacy of the individual over the state possibly perpetuate humanity's ultimate sin? How could the author of "We hold these Truths to be self-evident, that all Men are created equal, that they are endowed by their Creator with certain unalienable Rights, that among these are Life, Liberty, and the Pursuit of Happiness" be a slaveholder? How could a country that personifies such a declaration permit the existence of legal slavery? True, slavery existed alongside opposing ideologies in the past, but not alongside one as explicit, impassioned, and utterly profound as the Declaration of Independence.

There are no satisfactory answers to these questions. The modern study of American slavery is certainly not intended to justify it. Rather, it is a means of discovering a solution to its continuing negative effects on contemporary American society. Virtually all Americans experience these effects every single day. We experience it when we attend a top-notch school that is 99 percent white and come upon someone who is in the other 1 percent. We experience it when we hear that over a third of all prison inmates in America are black, when blacks make up only 13 percent of the country's population.[12] And we experience it when we pass a member of another race on the street and automatically cast judgment upon that person. This is the inescapable reality of a country that for nearly two centuries perpetuated revolting notions of racial inferiority under the color of law.

THE SEEDS OF AMERICAN SLAVERY:
THE AFRICAN SLAVE TRADE

Slavery existed in Europe when Christopher Columbus made his voyages across the Atlantic Ocean. At that time the Spanish held many groups of people in bondage, including Muslims, Slavs, Africans, and even other Spaniards.[13] King Ferdinand of Spain, who financed Columbus's voyage, even gave Pope Innocent VIII one hundred Moors, which he, in turn, distributed among his cardinals and nobles in 1488.[14]

It was Columbus himself who initiated the transatlantic slave trade when he returned from his first voyage to the New World, bringing Native Americans from what is now Haiti to present to the Spanish royal court.[15] Recognizing the potential for exploiting the native population for labor, he commented, "From here one might send, in the name of the Holy Trinity, as many slaves as could be sold."[16]

The primary European supply of slaves, however, came from the African continent. The Portuguese prince Henry the Navigator obtained the title to undiscovered African lands from the Pope in 1441.[17] The subsequent decades witnessed a steady increase in trafficking Africans, and the Portuguese led the way. The Portuguese would dominate the African slave trade and operate the enterprise under an effective monopoly for decades to come, sending millions of slaves to Europe every year. Without a doubt, the African slave trade was well on its feet at the beginning of the sixteenth century.

However, the 1493 founding of the first Spanish colony of Hispaniola (modern-day Haiti and the Dominican Republic) marked a tragic turning point in the evolution of slavery. The establishment of sugar plantations created a vast and immediate need for cheap labor at an unprecedented level. While slaves were accustomed to operating in an existing civilization in Europe, they were suddenly needed to build a new civilization from scratch in the Americas. Slaves began to be seized from the African continent in increasing numbers; the vast majority was sent to the expanding colonies. As the colonies grew in number, so did the slaves. The huge profit potential eventually enticed the Dutch, French, and English to join the trade.

Government played a major role in the perpetuation of the trade. While private contractors were responsible for much of the trade, the European governments facilitated this through the use of taxation, subsidization, and monopoly contracts. The state was needed to subsidize the trade in almost every case in order to get it organized.[18] The Portuguese would eventually grant state monopolies in the seventeenth century when underdeveloped colonies lacked the money to finance the trade. The infamous Dutch West India Company owed its prominence to a Dutch monopoly of the slave trade. The explicit goal of numerous European governments was to get the slave trade on its feet so as to spur the growth of their respective colonies.

Considering the historical context, this comes as no surprise. The slave trade came to exist at a time when the European powers were beginning their race for colonial prominence. Slavery was only one component of this race, as the Europeans sought to extract every conceivable natural resource from African lands. The effects of this ambition upon the modern world are profound, as a simple observation of the Western languages spoken on the African continent reveal. This competitive atmosphere would usher in the cultural, linguistic, and geopolitical framework of the modern globalized world.

The majority of slaves seized in the seventeenth century came from West Africa.[19] Because the region consisted mainly of warring and competing tribes and civilizations, obtaining slaves was accomplished with great ease. There was no single African identity and no common language binding the African people.[20] Cultural, political, and ethnic differences perpetuated regular conflict, which provided a steady flow of prisoners of war. Africans were also enslaved by their own governments as punishment for crimes and for failure to pay debts.[21]

Regardless of the reasons for the initial servitude, these black men and women were sold by their respective black political captors to the white Europeans. While raids were common as well, the majority of slaves were purchased in a way that created profit on both sides and incentivized the perpetuation of the business. Traders would arrive on the West African coast bearing gifts for the chief or king. The going rate for a healthy slave in 1600 was approximately $60 for a male and $15 for a female (in contemporary American dollars), although the price was usually satisfied with guns, gunpowder, textile products, pots, pans, and alcohol.[22]

It is important to note that the fractiousness on the continent did not mean that Africans lived lives of savagery or barbarism, as was often the common belief and even a stated justification for slavery. Though the political entities were numerous, they operated under their own systems of government and custom. Religion, cultural expression such as music and oral literature, and other signs of civilized life were widespread.[23] Moreover, the market for slavery was very limited in size before the arrival of the Europeans. Their arrival created a demand for human trafficking at an unprecedented level and spurred the turmoil on the continent.

Once the slaves were sold, they were literally branded with the mark of the owner and placed on ships for the colonies.[24] This grueling and horrific journey became known as the Middle Passage: This was the middle leg of the triangular trade route that took the slave ships to Africa for purchase, to the colonies for shipment, and back to Europe with various goods produced by slave labor and with the proceeds of the sales of the slaves.

It is difficult to imagine the horror that slaves faced on a slave ship; it was truly a world unto itself.[25] As William Wilberforce, the great English abolitionist, once said: "Never can so much misery be found condensed in so small a place as in a slave ship."[26] Slaves were chained and leg-ironed in small quarters for anywhere from five to eight weeks, provided that the trip went well.[27] The conditions were abhorrent. Sanitation was virtually nonexistent, and death and disease were rampant. Traders would consciously overpack the quarters, believing that any resulting death would be offset by the large cargo. One out of every eight kidnapped Africans did not survive the journey.[28] It is estimated that three million Africans perished aboard the vessels over the course of the slave trade's history.

If slaves rebelled, they were whipped, branded with hot irons, thrown in cages, and left to die. For fighting for their freedom, slaves had their body parts cut off one by one and thrown to the sharks, a deliberate attempt by slave ship commanders to keep sharks close in order to quell any desire the slaves might harbor to jump overboard.[29] The ships also carried thumbscrews, chains, whips, and mouth-openers.[30] Mouth-openers were metal braces used to force-feed those slaves who tried to starve themselves. As suicide became a more common method of escaping the horrors of the present and future for the slaves, the traders kept a closer eye on their cargo and often would practice a ceremony called "dancing the slaves," which required the prisoners to jump and move about to the sound of a fiddle, harp, or bagpipes.[31] Despite precautions against depression and insurrection, mutiny was still a common occurrence for the traders. In fact, almost all ship owners purchased "revolt insurance."[32] Over time, *barricados* (barriers behind which the crew could retreat in the event of an uprising) were added to the vessels.

At the end of this journey, what was it that awaited the enslaved? A strange new world thousands of miles from their homes and families. They arrived in the colonies robbed of any sense of their own humanity. The vast majority ended up in the Caribbean Islands. The islands were rich in many popular commodities including cotton, ginger, tobacco, hides, coffee, and, most important sugar.[33] The sugar industry almost solely dictated the distribution of the slaves and created a larger demand for slave labor than all other industries combined. As sugar became more and more popular in Europe, the plantation became the destination for more and more slaves. Due to the unique climate of the islands, slaves had to be "broken in" before being sent to the plantation. This lasted up to three years and included conditioning, teaching the trade and language, and ridding them of any suicidal tendencies—a process that would leave them worth financially double their original cost, but with a minimal sense of self-worth.[34]

The immediate brutality created almost immediate rebellion. Uprisings became common on virtually every island in the West Indies on which slavery was present. Some of these were very successful. The so-called Maroons who escaped servitude would often settle in remote areas of the island and conduct occasional violent raids for food. In several cases, the colonies were forced to sign treaties with the "rebels," guaranteeing them freedom in exchange for peace.[35]

Slavery's fate in the West Indies was intertwined with the fate of the sugar industry. By the nineteenth century, the sugar industry in the West Indies succumbed to fierce competition from other parts of the world. As the demand for West Indies sugar fell, so did the demand for slaves on the islands. The focus of the institution then shifted to England's American Colonies, who were growing dependent on slave labor in ways that would shape the history of the modern Western world.

WHAT BEGAN IN JAMESTOWN

The first English colony of Jamestown, Virginia, was founded in 1607. In 1619, the first Africans arrived there as indentured servants, the precursors to race-based slavery in America.[36] Indentured servants promised to work for their master for an agreed period of time in exchange for paid passage to the colonies and the provision of clothing, money, and often a plot of land after the agreement terminated.[37] This system of free labor would last until the turn of the eighteenth century and was not unique to Africans, as white Europeans and Indians were also indentured servants in early Virginia.

England eventually seized primary control of the slave trade, creating a large supply of black slaves for import. Coupled with the rising costs of indentured servitude and the lesser costs and greater benefits associated with slave labor, the institution of slavery eventually tightened its grip on the Southern economy, although it was widespread across the Northern colonies prior to the Revolution.[38]

Blacks were sought after, as they were thought to be easily identifiable and more suited to field labor because of their skin color.[39] (Incredible as it sounds today, it was commonly believed that God or nature selected the black race to do the labor in the harsh conditions of the Southern climate.) Toward the end of the seventeenth century, a significant number of the English settling in the Carolinas came from Barbados and brought black slaves and personal experience with the West Indies slave legal code with them to the mainland.[40]

Yet there were other reasons for the rise of black enslavement in the American colonies. One was the discontent among the poor and unfree in general, both black and white. Because this group outnumbered authorities, dividing the group along racial and ethnic lines aided in controlling the masses, just as it does today.[41] Additionally, mistreating Africans—news that might create a fear that could curb future slave importation—didn't run the risk of being relayed back to England.

Thus, laws slowly began to emphasize social distinctions between the races. As the seventeenth century progressed, the colonial courts began to punish whites more and more frequently for having sexual relations with blacks.[42] Explicit policies began to take shape that sought to limit the level of assimilation of the black race. Blacks were singled out in the churches and in the taverns. Eventually, laws were passed that forbade blacks from giving orders to whites or owning white indentured servants.[43] Slowly but surely, previously free blacks became slaves for life and passed their statuses on to their children.[44] This was a deliberate choice made by the all-white colonial governments and not a result of some natural progression of control that was gradually tightened over blacks.[45] These laws were the foundations of the social hierarchy that would develop and die naturally in the North and develop, prosper, and die only after great violence throughout the South in the next two hundred years.

Slavery became institutionalized much quicker in other American colonies, even in the North. New Netherlands, which today encompasses the coasts of Maryland, Delaware, New Jersey, New York, and Connecticut, was founded by the slave-trading Dutch West India Company. The English recognized the lawfulness of slavery in New York and New Jersey in 1684 after obtaining the territory in the Second Anglo-Dutch War.[46] William Penn felt obligated to permit slavery in Pennsylvania and Delaware because blacks already resided in the territory.[47] Slavery was also present in parts of New England beginning in the early years of settlement.

The dawn of the eighteenth century brought the beginning of the massive forced migration that would last until the slave trade would be prohibited at the beginning of the next century. Over four hundred thousand Africans were ripped from their homes and brought to the New World during this time.

Slavery's grip grew tighter as the eighteenth century pushed forward. More and more laws were passed by Southern colonial governments cementing the status of blacks as slaves. And just as in other civilizations throughout history, there was an absence of any palpable public moral discomfort concerning the institution. The English colonists in America found solace not only in the fact that the Dutch, French, Portuguese, and Spanish partook in the enterprise, but that it had been around for millennia. They accepted the ancient notion that the laws of nature placed some human beings in irreconcilable servitude.

This is precisely the real irony of American slavery: The colonies brought this ancient evil to the New World, a world that would simultaneously nurture truly revolutionary ideas of individual rights and the antediluvian institution of human bondage at the same time.

2

American Slavery

Race relations in America today stem from the institution of slavery. While there was certainly a cultural divide between Africans and the European colonists in the early colonial era, their similarities as human beings could have made legal and political assimilation a reality within one or two generations, not centuries.[1] Instead, the conscious steps by the framers to create an inferior race through constitutional mandate perpetuated a racial divide that continues to this day.

The nineteenth century witnessed the consistent maturation of the slave system. Northern states abandoned their slaves gradually but peacefully, and Southern states fiercely fought to maintain and tighten their collective grip on the institution. Southern lawmakers (initially colonial and eventually state and federal) thought that the institution was theirs as a matter of right and took explicit steps to ensure the survival of the system as a fundamental and inseparable component of the republic. Of course, slavery went against every principle upon which the republic was founded; liberty, equality, natural law, and democracy were strange and unfamiliar notions for American slaves. But by the time the Civil War was on the horizon, the institution was at its peak: A rigid component of antebellum culture and a vital part of its thriving agrarian economy.

14

THE LIFE OF A SLAVE

Most slaveholders understood that slaves were not actually born into bondage and thus focused on breaking them in, a process that can best be understood as ripping the slaves from their natural state of freedom. This included establishing strict codes of discipline, instilling them with a sense of the master's enormous power, incentivizing their labor, and implanting within the slaves a cognizance of their own inferiority and helplessness that created a habit of complete dependence upon their masters.[2] Slaveholders also indoctrinated their slaves into Christianity, selectively quoting from the Bible to justify slavery. These methods may have seemed the models for creating the perfect slave but, as we will see, such an ideal was rarely achieved.

There were several generally accepted rules that were typically followed by all slaveholders. Slaves were not to be out of their cabin after "horn-blow." They could not leave their masters' estates without a pass explicitly providing for their destination and time of return. They could not marry or work with free blacks or whites. They could not sell anything without permits, have alcohol in their quarters, fight, or use foul language.[3]

In the South, the slaves' primary tasks revolved around the cultivation of cotton. The early months of the year required the ginning and pressing of cotton from the previous season's batch and preparing it for shipment. Spring was spent replanting. It took about three slaves to plant a row of cotton; one drove a mule and plowed the dirt; another followed, planting the seeds; and a third followed with another mule to cover up the seeds.[4] The summer months were spent plowing and hoeing primarily to keep the land free from weeds and grass. The picking season was brutal, lasting from August through the following January.[5]

After field work was done, the men typically chopped fire-wood while the women made clothes and prepared meals. The labor was no less constant for females who worked within the master's home, as they were forced to do the cooking, cleaning, sewing, and washing for both the master's family and their own families.[6]

In general, even the most humane slaveholder, as paradoxical as the phrase is, could not afford to be too nice if he hoped to perpetuate his enterprise. The human condition dictates that the loosening of the shackles was a precursor for slave revolt or escape. Southerners knew that humane slaveholders paid a price in the end. Nonetheless, many struck a balance. Slaves were incentivized in many different ways. Some plantation owners gave their slaves their own small plots of land where they could cultivate their own crops and allowed the slaves to exchange them for tobacco, sugar, coffee, and other luxuries. Slaveholders distributed gifts and compensated slaves for extra work. They would make teams and profit-sharing agreements.[7] These minimal benefits are recounted here not to diminish the plight of the slaves, but rather to demonstrate the utter insignificance of being a slave.

While the great majority of slaveholders claimed to use as little violence as possible, this was essentially a myth that slave owners used to perpetuate the system. The slaveholders thought carefully about the treatment of their slaves, and they saw benefits and incentives. Injuring and abusing slaves was costly from a business perspective, as the quality of the labor would be lessened and the desire to escape would be intensified.

But it was the State that conferred upon owners the power to punish, and without this power the slave system could not exist. Many punishments were the simple denial of the incentives that were offered. Some slaves were forced to work longer or on Sundays, and others were given smaller food rations. There were also systems of demotion from more respectable work to field labor that slaves typically sought to avoid. However, it is doubtless that the most common form of punishment was the whip, and almost every slave-holder used it to one degree or another.[8]

Unfortunately, there was no screening process in place to ensure that slaveholders were relatively sane. Slaves would typically end up with the slaveholder with the deepest pockets. This meant that even people lacking mental stability could own slaves and expose them to the extreme brutality that has come to define the institution. Cases of flogging that resulted in the crippling, maiming, or killing of slaves; salting wounds; washing cuts with brine; and pulling toenails with pincers are all documented.[9] Cases of pure brutality were most common on plantations in newly settled regions that were prone to fierce economic competition.

Vigilante justice became a hallmark of the American South with the rise of lynching. If a slave were ever accused of murder or rape, angry mobs would often break into courtrooms and seize the prisoners for summary execution. Some were hanged, while others were burned to death in the presence of other slaves who were forced to watch.[10]

The only wages ordinarily paid the slaves were the provision of food, shelter, clothing, and medical care. This certainly wasn't a gratuity, but rather the required maintenance to keep slaves productive. The slaves' diet consisted mainly of cornmeal and pork.[11] While portions were substantial, the dietary balance was not and resulted in widespread cases of nutritional deficiency. Slaves were generally responsible for preparing their own food and were usually forced to eat sitting on the ground using their hands. Because clothing cost the slaveholders money, the slaves were clad with mere scraps that were often insufficient; they became sick easily during the winters.

Slaves typically lived in their own family cabins near the master's house, but the quality of the quarters mirrored the quality of the food and clothing.

While most slaveholding Southerners believed that blacks were genetically prone to deal with the harsh conditions of the Deep South, disease and illness was widespread among the slaves. They suffered from fevers, malaria, Asiatic cholera, pleurisy, pneumonia, mental and nervous disorders, and Cachexia Africana (dirt eating).[12] Strange as it seems, the last often helped slaves obtain the nutrients lacking in their everyday diet.

Slaves were certainly caste conscious and showed loyalty to one another. It was rather rare for a slave to betray a fellow slave. However, the engineered societal hierarchy created by slaveholders also created an internal class struggle between the slaves.[13] Humans naturally try to give their existence meaning and seek an appreciation of their worth. In many cases, this dominated the slaves' relationships among one another. Each slave in a community looked up to one or two members who showed a degree of leadership, wisdom, or strength.

Domestics, artisans, and foremen constituted the aristocracy of slave society.[14] The foreman was typically the highest-ranking slave in the hierarchy, as he was handpicked by the master for his trustworthiness, sound judgment, and physical prominence.[15] Known as the driver, he was the right-hand man of the overseer, the plantation's superintendent.

The foreman's unique responsibilities led to certain privileges, such as an exemption from field labor, better rations, more clothes, or the inherent respect from the other slaves that comes with a position of power.[16]

Culturally, the slaves lived in a virtual twilight zone. Having been ripped from their homeland, blacks could not find a suitable replacement for their traditions and cultural heritage. Rather, they were forced to accept the customs and traditions of the particular white man to whom they answered. But the cultural system imposed upon them was always qualified to fit their status as slaves. For instance, marriage applied differently to slaves than to whites, the specifics of which were determined solely by the master him-self.[17] With the added pressures of the slave family's minor economic and social significance, the threat of forced sale and encouraged sexual promiscuity, slave families became highly unstable. As this chapter will later address, sexual promiscuity was encouraged by slaveholders for the purpose of breeding additional slaves to sell through the domestic slave trade.

While most slaves sought to forget as much of their African past as possible in order to make their transition smoother, a sort of hybrid oral culture emerged from the early years of bondage, encompassing Protestant hymns and traditional African culture. These songs and folklore have become ingrained in American culture as the heroic sounds of life as a slave and provide an emotional glimpse into just how it *felt* to be in bondage.

> I got a right – we all got a right,
> I got a right to the tree of life.
>
> Go down, Moses,
> Way down in Egypt's Land,
> Tell ole Pharaoh
> To let my people go.
>
> O Mary, don't you weep, don't you mourn,
> Pharaoh's army got drownded,
> O Mary, don't you weep.[18]

In 1825, a Virginia court explained: "Slaves are not only property, but they are also rational beings, and entitled to the humanity of the Court, when it can be exercised without invading the rights of property."[19] This highlights the impossible challenge of morally rationalizing and legally justifying the idea of American slavery.

In virtually every American colony, and in almost every Southern state after the Revolution, slaves were legally regarded as personal property. Slaves were bartered, deeded, devised, pledged, seized, auctioned, awarded as prizes for lotteries and raffles, and wagered at gaming tables and horse races.[20] If the State executed a slave for a capital crime, it would usually reimburse the slave owner for his loss. Thus, much of the study surrounding the institution of slavery focuses on the inherent contradiction of *human property*. Humans naturally cannot be owned by anyone. Property can.

Most slave states adopted the principle that all black people were slaves unless they could prove that they were free. A black man found in the South without any freedom papers was presumed to be a slave and was therefore arrested as a fugitive.

The status of a slave of mixed race depended on the mother. The child of a white mother and a black father was free. The child of a white father and a black or mixed-race mother was a slave. The Texas Supreme Court once held that the child of a slave mother was a slave, no matter how remote the black ancestry.[21] Thus some slaves looked completely white.

Virtually every slave State had a standard slave code, the essence of which required slaves to submit to their masters and forbade them from being at large without a pass.[22] The forbidding of slaves to read or write came from the State as well. This was due to the fear that literacy could lead to organized rebellion or insurrection.[23] Further, slaves could not possess liquor or guns, administer medicine to whites, trade without a permit, gamble, raise cotton or farm animals, or be on the streets after curfew. Violations of this code would lead to flogging. Some of the kinder states limited the number of lashes a slave could receive in one sitting to thirty-nine.[24]

States had separate criminal codes for whites and blacks. Some acts that were misdemeanors when committed by whites were felonies when committed by blacks. If a slave struck his master or a member of the master's family, he or she was legally liable to be put to death. Slaves also received the death penalty when committing murder of any degree, attempted murder, manslaughter, rape or attempted rape upon a white woman, rebellion or attempted rebellion, poisoning, robbery, or arson.[25]

While all slave states outlawed the killing of slaves by the 1850s, there were some important exceptions and differences in actual practice. An accidental death of a slave after receiving "moderate correction" was not a homicide. In actual practice, whites were rarely executed for killing their slaves; most escaped without any punishment whatsoever. Blacks were forbidden to testify against white offenders, and white witnesses were reluctant to testify on behalf of black defendants for fear of the mob. Moreover, getting an all-white jury to convict white slaveholders for killing their slaves was a nearly impossible task.[26] Blacks could not serve on juries, and white juries would almost always acquit the slaveholders out of hatred for the black race or fear for their own lives.

THE DOMESTIC SLAVE TRADE

The African slave trade became illegal in 1808, after the constitutional provision guaranteeing to the states the right to permit human trafficking expired. Nonetheless, estimates of slaves imported to the United States between 1810 and 1820 range as high as sixty thousand.[27] Not until Congress authorized the use of armed cruisers and imposed the death penalty for trade piracy (in 1820) did the African trade effectively begin to cease.[28] While a black market remained for some time, an open and legal interstate slave trade replaced the international slave trade system in the South for the rest of slavery's days. However, the government was not concerned with eradicating the trade from a moral perspective. Rather, the government sought to control the African population on American soil, for reasons associated with both racial purity and fear of rebellion.

As the country developed and expanded, a mobile labor force became convenient. Labor was most needed on the frontier, where new colonies and communities were springing up. Virginia alone exported three hundred thousand slaves to other states from 1830 to 1860.[29] The huge demand for slaves inevitably led to slave breeding. Masters encouraged sexual promiscuity among female slaves, sanctioned the breakup of marriages if sterility were present, and promised rewards to females who were "fruitful." Lawsuits arose if a slave purchaser received a female incapable of reproduction, just as a farmer might seek to void a contract to purchase a female cow that turned out to be infertile.[30] This practice reduced the slaves to a status similar to farm animals.

The interstate slave trade constituted interstate commerce and thus arguably fell within clear striking distance of congressional regulation. Northern abolitionist groups lobbied to get Congress to enact legislation that would ban the trade. They lobbied in vain.

One of the tragedies of the interstate slave trade was the breaking up of families.[31] Family was often the only positive component to a slave's life, so the greatest fear was to be put up for sale. If a master died or his business took a turn for the worse, a slave could be torn from his or her family and friends and taken to a new life of complete uncertainty. Quite often, speculators would purchase whole families, promising to keep them intact, then sell the slaves individually once reaching the Deep South, the states where plantation agriculture called for the most backbreaking labor.[32] In many ways, the trade became the domestic equivalent of the African experience centuries earlier.

Slavery was more than a system of economic exploitation. It was a means of regulating race relations, establishing white superiority, and providing a system to measure affluence and status among Southerners. Slaveholders often held more slaves than efficient labor required in order to enhance their status among their peers. Fear of blacks doubtlessly played a role as well. Southerners sought to gain as much profit and stature from the enterprise with as little sacrifice to the racial and cultural homogeneity of the country as possible.

NORTHERN COMPLICITY IN SLAVE LABOR

But if Southerners jealously guarded their right to keep slaves and to profit from their labor, Northerners were just as guilty of fostering and encouraging the use of slave labor. The economies of the Northern states all depended to some degree on the agricultural output of Southern slave labor. Mills in the North processed textiles from Southern cotton, Northern ships transported Southern cotton overseas, and Northern factories manufactured goods for the Southern market. The wealth generated by slave-based agriculture flowed directly into Northern hands even as many Yankees pressured the South to free its slaves.

The North had an even blacker mark on its conscience, however, and it was far worse than making a profit from Southern slave labor. Slave ownership had, in fact, been quite widespread in the Northern colonies in the seventeenth and eighteenth centuries.

From Pennsylvania to Connecticut to Vermont, nearly every Northern colony had a slave population prior to the Revolution. Even New Hampshire, which proudly adopted the motto "Live Free or Die," had been the main arrival point for slaves coming to New England, as it was one of the few colonies that did not impose an import tax on slaves.[33] In 1771, just prior to the Revolution, New York had the largest northern slave population, with 20,000 slaves in a population of only 168,000,[34] and New Jersey had a special system of courts reserved for slaves, with punishments that were more severe than those accorded white residents of the colony.[35]

Perhaps Northerners felt they could sweep this shameful history under the carpet as they attacked the South for engaging in the very same practices. Slavery was almost completely eradicated in the North by the beginning of the nineteenth century, with most slaves having been given their freedom during the Revolutionary War, though slaves have been documented in New York and New Jersey as late as 1850. Although many Northern slaves were undoubtedly freed in the spirit of liberty and freedom that was common rhetoric before and during the war, both the colonists and British sympathizers shrewdly offered freedom to slaves willing to go into battle, which amounted to thousands of slaves gaining liberty. But to those blacks who were descended from Northern slaves, it must have seemed the height of hypocrisy for the North to preach about the evils of human bondage.

THE PURSUIT OF FREEDOM

It is indisputable that slaves were treated brutally. Slavery as an institution is inherently evil and is contrary to our existence as the human species. However, it is important to note that what made slavery irretrievably cruel was not solely the whipping, the maltreatment, and the denial of the liberty to which we all are entitled. The most evil component of the institution was that it was geared toward making slaves believe that they *should* be slaves—that it was somehow ingrained in their reason for being. This was needed also as justification for slavery's existence in a land themed by freedom and equality. Blacks were considered worthless, subhuman, and ill-prepared for freedom. They were seen as childlike, in need of direction, lazy, and cursed by God.[36] Slavery was thus God's punishment for the shortcomings of the black race, and slaveholders made sure to make this clear to both the slaves and the general public.

However, Southerners understood that the system could not survive if it were fueled by sheer brutality. Slaveholders feared rebellion and were most concerned with the system being one of effective labor. They were careful not to mistreat slaves too much in order to keep them productive. In order to accomplish this, it was necessary to strike a delicate balance between discipline and incentive. Slaveholders sought to make slaves both fear and love their masters; to make them completely dependent on their masters for their own existence; and to come to understand their so-called natural place in the world as slaves.

But the human spirit proved too difficult to crush. There is an instinctive inclination for freedom within the human makeup that no ingrained system of servitude can quell. Masters did not always have their way.[37] The continuous natural human yearning for freedom is the essence of the natural law; it is hardwired into us. We all have it, and we all know it—whether free, imprisoned, or enslaved.

Slaves knew very well that the Southern slave system was one of labor extortion. They understood that slavery was morally wrong. While slaves often focused on obtaining the immediate benefits of kinder discipline, they were never satisfied with simply a lighter form of slavery. As Frederick Douglass once said: "Give him a bad master, and he aspires to a good master. Give him a good master, and he aspires to become his own master."[38] How true.

Slave resistance was always a looming threat for slaveholders. Most slaves seized any opportunity for even the slightest bit of additional freedom. But they were also realistic. They often knew the futility associated with rebellion when capture, lashing, and potential execution were inevitable. They understood that an entire nation saw them as inferior; they had no political rights anywhere in the country. Free blacks in the North were exposed to the same horrors of government-sponsored racism and did not have a master to protect them from the mob. If you were a slave in early nineteenth century America, freedom—as we understand it today—was not attained simply by escaping your master's plantation.

The number of runaway slaves was not very large in a relative sense. The slaves who suffered from drapetomania, the so-called "disease" that caused slaves to run away, often carried scars of severe brutality.[39] When slaves escaped, slaveholders often hung posters portraying the slaves as ignorant of just how good their lives had been. Slaveholders believed their property was well cared for, even happy. One poster read that the slaves were "well cloathed, work easy, and have all kinds of plantation produce." Such a flagrant mischaracterization of the slave lifestyle often came less from outright lies than from a genuine belief that slaves really did have the life the poster portrayed. Needless to say, such beliefs could only exist if the fundamental assumption was that slaves were less than human, undeserving even of such minimal necessities as being well-clothed, fed, or free, and somehow susceptible to the denial of the essence of humanity: The ability to exercise one's own free will.

Both the federal and state governments took explicit steps to bring fugitive slaves to justice. The federal fugitive slave law allowed a master to claim a runaway slave even if he were found in a free State.

If slaves ran away from the Upper South (those states closer to the free states), they were often sent to the more brutal conditions of the Deep South as punishment. The hopes of escape from the Deep South were bleak and the threat of being sent there as punishment was enough of a deterrent for many slaves. The threat of being sold was also a potential nightmare that slaves did not want to risk. Generally, state governments facilitated the institution by leaving punishment to the private sphere. President Andrew Jackson once offered a $50 reward for the capture of his fugitive slave and $10 extra for every hundred lashes any person would give the slave, to the amount of $300.[40] Hunting of runaways with dogs was defended and justified by the courts, and mauling by the dogs was permitted as extrajudicial punishment.

But suffering from drapetomania was not the exclusive province of grossly mistreated slaves. No matter how well slaves were treated (in a relative sense), no matter how much easier their lives than their fellow slaves on the neighboring plantation, they could not help but wish for liberty. The yearning for self-determination, self-sufficiency, and the natural state of freedom acts as an unquenchable thirst in all humans, regardless of color or indoctrination. It is simply the understatement of all time to assert that there is no suitable substitute for freedom.

A runaway making an escape from the Deep South had little likelihood of success without assistance; it was simply too far to go. The Underground Railroad was a heroic system initiated by abolitionists that aided runaways. A network of way stations to which the runaways would be brought by a "conductor," the Underground Railroad provided food, shelter, and a place to rest until the next night's journey. During the day, travelers were concealed in barns, caves, sail lofts, or hayricks.[41]

Of these conductors, the most famous was Harriet Tubman. A

former slave and runaway herself, Tubman visited the slave states nineteen times and personally conducted more than seventy slaves to the Northern states and Canada. She also served in the Civil War as a spy, a scout, and a nurse. She was never captured.[42]

The moving tale of Harriet Tubman and the Underground Railroad represents one of those rare heroic stories in human history that can only arise in a time plagued by such injustice as in the antebellum South. Dedicated abolitionists who ran the railroad saved the lives of approximately twenty-five hundred slaves per year from 1830 to 1860.

PEACEFUL ERADICATIONS

In the North, white labor was considered more valuable than slave labor. The institution of slavery thus threatened to undermine white supremacy and led to gradual emancipation laws in New York, Vermont, Pennsylvania, and Massachusetts. In reality, emancipation of Northern slaves was geared to bolstering the economic conditions of whites. We'd better get rid of slavery, Northern white legislators reasoned, so that there will be jobs for white folk.

Somersett's Case in 1772 held that slavery was unlawful under the laws of England. Somersett was a slave who escaped when his master was visiting England; he was discovered on a ship bound for Jamaica and imprisoned. His family petitioned the court for a writ of *habeas corpus*,[43] and Somersett was subsequently brought before the court. The Chief Justice, Lord Mansfield, agreed with Somersett that while slavery was permitted in the colonies, it could not be justified by English common law or by any acts of Parliament. Sommersett was released and slavery was prohibited in England, though this had no effect on the British colonies, of course.

In Brazil, the slave trade was peacefully abolished in 1850, the sons of slaves were freed in 1871, and slaves over sixty were freed in 1885. The Paraguayan War played a major role in the emancipation of slaves in Brazil, as slaves were granted freedom in exchange for their service in the military. Popular resistance—in the form of emancipation societies and public resentment—as well as drought also quickened the pace, although Brazil was technically the last nation to abolish slavery, doing so in 1888. However, the institution was actually already in decline due to a huge new labor force arriving in the form of European migrants. These immigrants filled any existing labor void left by the freed slaves.

SLAVERY IS *ALWAYS* WRONG

A man awakens one night to the sound of strange noises coming from downstairs. Grabbing his gun from his nightstand drawer, he slowly proceeds down the stairs and sees an intruder holding a gun just feet from his oldest son's head. Fearing for his family, the man shoots the intruder, killing him instantly.

In Berlin in early 1945, a soldier patrolling a neighborhood known to be a refuge for Nazi holdouts notices a masked man in a German Army uniform on a rooftop with a weapon. The soldier aims his weapon and kills the Nazi without giving him a chance to surrender.

These represent situations where the killing of another is not *always* wrong. While the above examples are somewhat ambiguous, it is perfectly conceivable that both were legitimate, lawful acts of self-defense in one's home and on the battlefield. However, the intentional killing of a baby, for example, can never be right; a baby is the embodiment of innocence and is in no position to have his or her right to life stripped. The same may be said for anyone known to be innocent: It is always wrong to administer any punishment to the known innocent.

It is plain that in the sometimes-wrong versus always-wrong framework, slavery is always wrong. Some who rely on human nature to justify actions argue that slavery's existence throughout human history reflects its natural inclination to exist and is neither right nor wrong but simply a component of human existence, for better or worse. That history is replete with countless examples of slavery is indisputable. Yet the essence of our God-given rights as humans is one of freedom; forced labor, absent personal fault, is the antithesis of that freedom. If we are to labor, it is to be of our own choice unless our liberty is justifiably taken away for infringing upon another's in a way that violates a legitimate, known, and fair criminal code.

There is an important distinction to be made between natural law and positive law. At its minimum, positive law must comport with the ideas of natural law, and natural law thus operates as the best restraint of positive law.[44] In this manner, despite the proper implementation of slavery through positive law (laws legally enacted at the time), its violation of natural law (because it steals the core natural right: freedom) makes it inherently and profoundly unlawful, regardless of the perfection of the democratic processes that are responsible for it. (This concept is discussed in greater detail in the next chapter.)

The teachings of St. Thomas Aquinas provide guidance in the moral debate concerning slavery. The fundamental premise is that a well-formed conscience will naturally seek good and avoid evil. His theory places much faith in human nature—that the truth is available to all people through informed human reasoning and recognition of divine revelation. Of course, the libraries are not short of moral theories that find the institution of slavery abhorrent. Yet

Aquinas did not stop there. He wrote that because unjust laws are not within the power of government to enact, only just laws need to be obeyed. Moreover, unjust laws carry with them a *duty of disobedience*. If laws do not seek and promote goodness, they are unjust and in violation of natural law—and our cognizance of this requires us to disobey them. From this perspective, Harriet Tubman and every other Underground Railroad conductor, abolitionist, and runaway slave were not criminals, but heroes who refused to give in to government-created, government-sustained, and government-enforced injustice.

Prominent American figures have shown support for the theories of natural law. Justice Clarence Thomas once said: "Without such a notion of natural law, the entire American political tradition, from Washington to Lincoln, from Jefferson to Martin Luther King, would be unintelligible." He said that he subscribes to this principle because it guarantees equality, even if the words of the Constitution do not. "Natural rights and higher law arguments are the best defense of liberty and of limited government."[45]

The founders, especially Thomas Jefferson, believed in natural law, which positive law could not lawfully contradict. "A strict observance of the written laws is doubtless one of the high duties of a good citizen, but it is not the highest," Jefferson wrote. "The laws of necessity, [and] of self-preservation, . . . are of higher obligation."[46] And in the Declaration of Independence he wrote that we are "endowed by our Creator" with certain inalienable rights. For Jefferson and his fellow founders, natural law was necessarily discovered.

The great Martin Luther King Jr., in his "Letter from a Birmingham Jail," explained that "an unjust law is a human law that is not rooted in eternal law and natural law." In arguing that government-enforced segregation is morally wrong because it "distorts the soul and damages the personality," King utilized the teachings of St. Thomas Aquinas to urge men to disobey the unjust segregation laws.

Throughout humanity's existence, we have, through trial and error, progressed philosophically, politically, spiritually, and morally. Much of human existence has been spent wrestling with the morality of our inner inclinations as humans. There are certain elements of human nature that societies find repulsive and repugnant to the perpetuation of human civilization: All enlightened societies penalize murder and rape as always wrong, although they are frequent occurrences in human existence. Slavery and its repercussions must also be permanently regarded as always wrong in order to prevent its reemergence in the future.

But it did reemerge in countless government-sanctioned ways throughout the North and South in the United States. It is the purpose of the following chapters to show the myriad ways this happened and the myriad sufferings it has caused, and to expose the governments that made this happen.

3

Ratifying and Interpreting the Constitution

The ratification of the American Constitution is one of the most significant events in human history. After centuries of monarchies and empires that created classes of citizens to which the rule of law did not apply equally, a group of some of the most enlightened individuals ever assembled forged what they hoped would be an eternal (and what they claimed was an impartial) document that was designed to bind the future of the country to a set of fundamental and revolutionary principles and to ensure that nobody was above the law.

However, where the Constitution succeeded, it also failed. The document created a class of people who were not above the law, but below it. The revolutionary protections that the Constitution afforded all persons were simply inapplicable to those whose freedom the law stripped because of immutable conditions of their birth: Skin color and personal ancestry.

The bedrock of the new government, as expressed in the Declaration of Independence, was that "all men are created equal, that they are endowed by their Creator with certain unalienable rights, that among these are Life, Liberty, and the Pursuit of

Happiness." Nevertheless, the Constitution contained express provisions that recognized the existence of slavery, protected it as a legal institution, and insulated it from regulation or interference by the federal government. This specific recognition of slavery was in sharp contrast to the Articles of Confederation, the original pact that governed the United States after independence. The American government thus operated with a most basic and fundamental contradiction embedded in its laws for nearly a century.

It is indisputable that American slavery and its repercussions owe their existence to the government. American race relations today are the offspring of constitutionally mandated, federally enforced, and state-protected slavery. Congressional and state legislative enactments that established blacks as an inferior class and state and federal court rulings that legitimized and reaffirmed the government's racist agenda are well known. But is any level of government more to blame than the others? Are the framers or the courts more at fault for providing the grounds upon which legislatures and courts could justify perpetuating slavery? Are they at fault for lacking the moral courage to strike down laws repugnant to the natural law? Should the courts actually be commended for upholding the meaning of the Constitution, or be criticized for failing to uphold the natural law? There are multiple layers of complexity behind these questions.

THE DEBATE OVER THE CONSTITUTION

The Constitutional Convention encompassed some of the "most brilliant displays of learning in political theory ever shown in a deliberative assembly."[1] The delegates were neither bound by tradition, nor compelled to answer to any leaders outside of themselves. They were free to design the best form of government from scratch at a time when common familiarity with political philosophy had reached its peak. The delegates discussed the broadest and most profound range of issues regarding man's relationship with government. These debates—in June 1789—solidified the reputations of these men as national heroes, champions of limited government, and an example for freedom lovers throughout the world.

However, their reputations are not uniformly held in such high regard. Justice Thurgood Marshall once wrote: "I do not find the wisdom, foresight, and sense of justice exhibited by the Framers particularly profound. To the contrary, the government they devised was defective from the start, requiring several amendments, a civil war, and momentous social transformation to attain the system of constitutional government and its respect for the individual freedoms and human rights we hold as fundamental today."[2] Further, in 1843, after the whole of James Madison's papers were released following his death, William Lloyd Garrison, the prominent abolitionist and editor of *The Liberator*, called the Constitution a "covenant with death and an agreement with hell" and proposed that the Northern states secede from the union.[3] These beliefs are by no means unique to Marshall and Garrison.

In a very real sense, Justice Marshall was right. The vast tragedy that followed the birth of the Constitution is inexcusable in a country that indoctrinated such revolutionary principles and individual freedoms. The wide range of opinions of the framers reflects the contradiction of their ultimate product. Simply stated, none of the protections articulated in the Constitution applied to blacks. Yet slaves were not excluded from the Constitution altogether, although the words *slave* and *Negro* were. Instead, their existence as slaves was implicitly recognized in three distinct constitutional provisions: The Fugitive Slave Clause, the Importation Clause, and the infamous Three-Fifths Clause.

Article I, Section 9, Clause 1 prohibited Congress from outlawing the "importation of such Persons as any of the States now existing shall think proper" until 1808. This provided an almost twenty-year constitutional mandate to continue the international slave trade and the importation of new slaves. Article IV, Section 2, Clause 3 required states to return any "person held to Service or Labour in one State" who had escaped into their jurisdiction.[4] The courts would interpret this clause as providing slaveholders with a right to their slave property that no free state could qualify or control.

Third, and perhaps most odious, Article I, Section 2, Clause 3 required apportionment of seats in the House of Representatives on the basis of the "whole number of free Persons" in each state, minus the number of "Indians not taxed," plus "three fifths of all other Persons"—the last obviously referring to slaves. This clause has come to be known as the Three-Fifths Compromise. Taken as a whole, these provisions provided the federal justification necessary to perpetuate slavery and government-sponsored racism in its most extreme incarnation.

PHILADELPHIA, 1789

James Madison's Virginia delegation was first to arrive in Philadelphia in May 1789 for the Constitutional Convention. Obtaining a head start, the delegation quickly put together and proposed what would become the Virginia Plan. The plan called for a government divided into three coequal branches: executive, legislative, and judicial. The legislative branch would contain two houses; the lower house would be elected by the people and the smaller upper house would be chosen by the elected representatives of the states. However, under this plan, the number of each state's allotted representatives would be based on its population and would thus favor the larger states. In response, William Paterson proposed the New Jersey Plan, which gave each state one vote, regardless of size or population. Both plans faced an equal amount of opposition, and the two camps could not move forward without a compromise.

The Connecticut Compromise (dubbed the Great Compromise) provided just that. It called for Congress to consist of a House of Representatives and a Senate. Representatives in the House would be allotted based on population, while each State would have two senators. This satisfied both sides, as large States would have the advantage in the House and all states would be on equal footing in the Senate. While the plan resolved the initial big state/small state conflict, a key question remained: what—or who—does a state's *population* consist of?

One of the Convention's defining characteristics was the collegial manner in which the framers debated, discussed, and compromised. They understood that the states were barely held together by the Articles of Confederation and knew that establishing a stronger central government was their goal. Sensitivities were kept firmly in mind at every turn in order to avoid potential state secession. This was especially true for the issue of slavery, at least in the beginning. While the Convention grappled with issues of lesser importance, the fundamental question of who would control the government—the Southern slaveholding states or the Northern states where slavery was now of minimal importance—remained on the back burner. But this issue, when it arose, ignited the tension that had been kept carefully at bay.

As James Madison would make clear, the debate stemmed from the conflicting interests of the Northern and Southern states, the result of the differences inherent in two different climates, economies, cultures, and ways of life. The North was blossoming into a predominantly urban economy, fueled by finance and emerging industry, whereas the South was a largely agrarian economy fueled by slaveholding farmers and plantation owners. These differences generated the competition for power and led to state sovereignty becoming a paramount concern in the constitutional scheme.

Slaves represented approximately 40 percent of the Southern population in 1789. Because apportionment was the vehicle through which interests would be represented in the new government, the more representatives apportioned to a State, the more powerful that State would become—and the number of allotted representatives was determined by population. Thus, Southern interests would be significantly threatened if slaves were not fully counted. Conversely, the North did not want the slaves counted at all in order to curtail Southern influence.

The result was the Three-Fifths Compromise. Widely considered to be the chief pro-slavery clause in the Constitution, it epitomized the racism of the document—as it reduced each slave to three-fifths of a person, a reflection of the inferior, subhuman class blacks would come to represent in the coming decades.[5] Inherent in this compromise is a bitter irony, as it was the Southern slaveholding states that wanted slaves counted as full persons while the North and its abolitionists wanted slaves to remain uncounted; the slaves themselves, of course, had no say whatsoever in their constitutional standing.

The Southern delegates were ready to accept a relatively powerful central government as long as that government kept its hands off slavery. But the issue of slavery was in many ways an irreconcilable difference between the North and South. Northerners wanted to eliminate it from the Constitution, while most Southerners wanted to preserve it, namely through keeping the power to regulate or proscribe the institution from the new federal government. Because the framers could not reach a national consensus over such a polarizing issue, they instead sought to prevent friction over the issue between the states.[6] Thus it happened that the Constitution contained no power bestowed upon the federal government to abolish slavery and no explicit provision that would prevent the government from doing so, but three textual recognitions of it.

The issue of apportionment highlighted some inherent contradictions. If apportionment was based on free population alone, as the Northerners wanted, this would have left an implicit recognition of slavery in the Constitution. If the slaves were counted as whole persons, political power would be even more concentrated in the South and would thus further strengthen the slaveholders.[7] Considering how entrenched slavery was in the South by this time, the Northern delegates had virtually no chance at achieving a national government without making significant concessions to the South. While the tragedies that came out of the Three-Fifths Compromise might seem glaringly evident today, representative government might never have been achieved in America without that damnable compromise.

Nonetheless, the compromise had the effect of giving slavery a constitutional seal of approval. The three-fifths number agreed upon was hardly arbitrary, as it was an estimation of the slaves' wealth-producing capacity compared with that of free men.[8] But it had far-reaching political consequences as well. In 1793, slave states would have been apportioned 33 seats in the House of Representatives had the seats been assigned based on the free population only. Instead, they were apportioned 47. In 1812, they had 76 seats instead of 59, and in 1833, they had 98 seats instead of 73. Southerners dominated the presidency, the speakership of the House, and the Supreme Court for decades. Presidents Washington, Jefferson, Madison, Monroe, Jackson, Van Buren, Harrison, Tyler, Polk, Taylor, and Andrew Johnson were all Southern slaveholders. Jefferson, Madison, Jackson, and Polk actually brought their slaves with them to the White House. The White House itself was constructed by slave labor.

The compromise was driven by sheer practicality. It was an example of sacrificing ethical and moral standards in order to forge a new national government. These sacrifices were quite clear to the founders. John Dickinson wrote in his notes on July 9th 1789: "Acting before the World, What will be said of this new principle of founding a Right to govern Freemen on a power derived from Slaves . . . themselves incapable of governing yet giving to others what they have not. The omitting the Word will be regarded as an Endeavor to conceal a principle of which we are ashamed."[9] Dickinson hit the nail on the head. Slaves would be used to empower those who held them in bondage and ensure the perpetuation of their own servitude.

Yet historians over the decades have argued that the founders had little choice in the matter. Both Southern and Northern delegates alike were ashamed of slavery during the Convention and often took pains to dance around the issue in their debates. If both sides had held to their guns, a national government might never have been formed—and if a national government had never been formed, the South would have been free to perpetuate slavery without serious domestic governmental opposition. By coming together and recognizing such an abhorrent institution, the framers perhaps set in motion a chain of events that would eventually lead to the end of slavery, albeit, because of Lincoln, at the expense of hundreds of thousands of innocent American lives.

WHAT IS THE PROPER ROLE OF THE COURTS?

Throughout the nineteenth century, American courts would repeatedly put the judicial stamp of approval on the institution of slavery.

Facially, these cases place the judiciary in the realm of fault for perpetuating the horrors that the Constitutional Convention mandated. However, despite slavery's patent incompatibility with natural law, is it the role of the courts to sidestep the positive law of the land when natural law is violated? My own view, shared by some giants throughout history (and rejected by others), is an unequivocal: YES.

In 1788, Pennsylvania amended one of its statutes, making it a crime forcibly to remove fugitive blacks from that State and return them to the South to be reenslaved. The original law granted slaves their freedom if they remained in Pennsylvania for six months. Clever slaveholders who sought to bring their slaves with them on extended trips to Pennsylvania would take advantage of the inherent loophole in this law, rotating their slaves in and out of Pennsylvania in order to avoid coming within the statute. Perhaps the most famous of these clever slaveholders was the father of our country himself, President George Washington. During his presidency, when the seat of the federal government was in Philadelphia, Washington and his wife Martha would keep their slaves within the state's borders just under six months before sending them home and replacing them with new ones, thereby avoiding mandatory emancipation.

After the law was amended, Margaret Morgan, a former slave, moved to Pennsylvania from Maryland without any freedom papers granted by her master John Ashmore. Ashmore's heirs eventually decided to reclaim her and hired the slave-catcher Edward Prigg to seize her from Pennsylvania. Prigg abducted Morgan and her children from Pennsylvania in 1837 and took them all back to Maryland to be sold as slaves. All of Morgan's children were subsequently sold, including one who had been born free in Pennsylvania. However, Prigg was arrested, charged, and convicted for violating the Pennsylvania statute. He eventually appealed to the U.S. Supreme Court, claiming that the Pennsylvania law was unconstitutional in the face of both Article IV, Section 2 of the Constitution (permitting and requiring the return of fugitive slaves) and the Fugitive Slave Act of 1793, which essentially gave teeth to the Fugitive Slave Clause by making it a federal crime to assist fugitive slaves.

In 1842, the Court sided with Prigg and reversed his conviction. Justice Story concluded that Article IV, Section 2 "contemplates the existence of a positive unqualified right on the part of the owner of the slave, which no [free] state law or regulation can in any way qualify, regulate, control, or restrain."[10] Furthermore, the Court held the Constitution implicitly vested Congress with the power to assist private slave owners in securing the return of escaped slaves, that Congress had exercised that power by enacting the Fugitive Slave Act, that this national power was exclusive and thus any State laws regulating the means by which slaves were to be returned to the owners were unconstitutional.[11] With the judiciary validating the federal legislation, the federal government (in addition to the framers themselves) had now stamped its seal of approval on the institution of slavery. Federal judges appointed by every president from George Washington to Andrew Johnson enforced this dreadful law.

Several other cases helped define the status of slaves and the nature of the institution as a whole. In 1837, three slaves belonging to Christopher Graham boarded a steamboat in Louisville, Kentucky, bound for Cincinnati, Ohio. Upon their arrival in Cincinnati, the slaves managed to escape further north into Canada. Graham brought suit against the owners and master of the boat, seeking to recover the value of the lost slaves. In response, the defendants claimed that the slaves were in fact free when they were given passage on the steamboat, as they had been sent to Ohio previously by Graham to perform as musicians. Echoing a popular theory among abolitionists at the time, the defendants claimed that once slaves were brought into free territory, they acquired their unconditional freedom.

However, in 1851, the Court disagreed. In an opinion by Chief Justice Roger B. Taney, the Court held in *Strader v. Graham* that the status of slaves who went from Kentucky to Ohio was determined by Kentucky law, and not Ohio law.[12] In an eerie foreshadowing of the *Dred Scott* decision six years later, Taney explained that every state had an "undoubted right" to determine the status and social conditions of persons domiciled within its borders so long as the classifications were consistent with the Constitution. As the coming chapter will demonstrate, the logical next step would be to strip blacks of their citizenship altogether.

Chief Justice Taney, however, did not always rule against slaves. In the *Amistad* case, the Court freed a group of Africans in 1841 who were seized as slaves and rebelled aboard a slave trip. Because the slave trade had been constitutionally outlawed in 1808 pursuant to the Importation Clause, the Court found that the Africans had been illegally seized and their status as slaves could not be justified by the plain text of the Constitution.

But absent plain violations of the ban on the international slave trade, American courts would not only uphold slavery but routinely color the law with language that more disturbingly limited the status of slaves. In *Bailey v. Poindexter*, for example, the Virginia Supreme Court in 1858 refused to allow Poindexter to give his slaves an option for freedom upon his death. Poindexter instructed his executor to offer his slaves the option of returning to Liberia or being sold as slaves for the benefit of Poindexter's heirs. In rejecting this provision of the will, the court held "the legal status of a slave is that of a personal chattel; that he is mere property; that he can do no legal civil act, can make no contract; and all this for the purpose of showing that he cannot make himself free by his own choice; that he can have no effectual will on the subject, and cannot be invested with any power of emancipating himself."[13]

How can these cases be reconciled? One of them restored to slaves their natural freedom while the others reaffirmed the slaves' abhorrent, unnatural legal status. Did the courts simply follow the letter of the law? If so, should they be to blame for perpetuating what the law requires?

A famous New Jersey Supreme Court case provides some interesting insight. In 1804, the State of New Jersey enacted a law that declared "every child born of a slave, after the fourth of July of that year, should be free, but remain the servant of the owner of the mother until he or she should arrive at a specified age."[14] The act was intended to abolish slavery gradually in New Jersey. However, in 1844 the state adopted a new constitution that contained a provision declaring that "all men are by nature free and independent, and have certain natural and unalienable rights, among which are those of enjoying and defending life and liberty, acquiring, possessing and protecting property, and of pursuing and obtaining safety and happiness."

Abolitionists brought suit claiming that this provision of the new New Jersey Constitution prohibited slavery in the State irrespective of the 1804 act. Justice James S. Nevius, writing for New Jersey's highest court in 1845, disagreed. In *State v. Post*, he found that if the State had wanted to abolish something as paramount as slavery, it would have done so explicitly and not through some "doubtful construction of an indefinite abstract political proposition."[15] Further, he noted that American slavery as a whole had existed alongside the similarly constructed Declaration of

Independence and that this was demonstrative that those general declarations in favor of liberty were not incompatible with the provisions that recognized slavery.

According to Justice Nevius, there was a distinction between freedom in the state of nature and freedom in a society; the latter was subject to the involuntary surrender of certain rights for the better protection of others via the social contract. While Nevius openly sympathized with the slaves and respected the arguments made by their counsel, he noted that "much of the argument seemed rather addressed to the feelings than to the legal intelligence of the court."[16]

Justice Nevius' reasoning is rooted in positivism. The theory's fundamental premise is that there is a difference between what the law is and what the law *should be*, and that a responsible jurist should adhere to the current law and refrain from casting value judgments that are best reserved to the people through the exercise of their voting rights and the democratic process. This dilemma has confounded the legal world for millennia. Should societal change be effectuated by an unelected judiciary or through the democratic processes embedded in our constitutional system? Should it perturb us when change is spurred by appointed judges, even if we find the change liberating? Or should it bother us when judges do not use their power to strike down laws that are consistent with positive law but inconsistent with natural law?

Interestingly enough, the Massachusetts Supreme Court reached the opposite conclusion of the New Jersey court in *Commonwealth v. Ames* in 1859. The language of the Massachusetts Constitution contained virtually the same language as the New Jersey Constitution. Chief Justice Lemuel Shaw found that language to be enough to hold slavery illegal in Massachusetts, noting that "slavery is contrary to natural right, to the principles of justice and humanity, and repugnant to the constitution."[17] To a legal positivist like Justice Nevius, natural law principles should never influence judges, even if the outcome restricts human liberty and freedom. As Nevius argued in *State v. Post*, "judges must be more than men, if they can always escape the influence of a strong popular opinion of society upon great questions of state policy and human benevolence, which have been long agitated and much discussed."[18]

As the Nevius opinion makes clear, positivism does not align itself easily with the ideas of natural law. In fact, it often runs contrary to them. Those who endorse the separation thesis argue that the validity of a law does not rely upon its consistency with principles of natural law. Under positivism, if a law is enacted by a legitimate government pursuant to its proper legislative processes, then the law is valid irrespective of what morality or justice dictate.

Yet in many cases laws are, in fact, reflective of natural law and morality. For instance, laws against murder or seizure of private property by the government take into account our natural right to live peacefully and to use independently and enjoy privately the things that we possess. Thus, these laws are justified by both positive and natural law.

But where positivism is limited to laws passed by governments, natural law is not. Natural law knows only one authority: Our own human nature that is created by God. Therefore natural law allows judges to strike down properly passed laws that infringe on our freedom of speech, worship, or assembly even if the Constitution did not protect these freedoms. The great individual liberties guaranteed by the Constitution reflect natural God-given rights that no government can properly restrict, absent a violation of natural law itself.

In *Calder v. Bull*, a 1798 U.S. Supreme Court case, Justices Samuel Chase and James Iredell famously debated the tension between positivism and natural law. While the two justices agreed that an order of the Connecticut legislature for a new trial in a will contest was not an *ex post facto* law, they disagreed on the appropriate role of the natural law in the Court's decision-making process. According to Justice Chase, "an act of the legislature (for I cannot call it a law), contrary to the great first principles in the social compact, cannot be considered a rightful exercise of legislative authority. A law that punishes a citizen for an innocent [action]; a law that destroys or impairs the lawful private contracts of citizens; a law that makes a man a judge in his own cause; or a law that takes property from A and gives it to B: it is against all reason and justice, for a people to entrust a legislature with such powers; and therefore, it cannot be presumed that they have done it."[19]

Justice Iredell disagreed, writing, "if any act of congress, or of the legislature of a state, violates those constitutional provisions, it is unquestionably void. [If], on the other hand, the legislature of the Union, or the legislature of any member of the Union, shall pass a law, within the general scope of their constitutional power, the Court cannot pronounce it to be void, merely because it is, in their judgment, contrary to the principles of natural justice. The ideas of natural justice are regulated by no fixed standard: the ablest and the purest men have differed upon the subject."[20]

This is perhaps one of the earliest American examples of the debate not only between natural law theorists and positivists, but between the schools of judicial restraint and judicial activism. Where a judge stands on this often determines the outcome of the case over which he or she presides.

So who was right? Was Chief Justice Shaw right to bring in natural law, or was Justice Nevius right for sticking to explicit positive law? Was Justice Chase correct for not considering an act in violation of natural law a proper law, or was Justice Iredell correct for relying solely on what positive law dictates?

Answering these questions requires us to assign ranks of value to both the substantive change we seek and the means through which the change occurs. As a more contemporary example, do we value the right of a baby in a womb to live more than we do the individual states' rights to permit a mother and her physician to decide the issue for themselves? Similarly, although slavery is always wrong, were certain nineteenth century judges wrong for interpreting the law for what it actually was when presented with questions of slavery's legality? Can't a judge be repulsed by slavery yet feel duty bound to uphold it in the face of laws that clearly protect it? Can't a judge be pro-abortion and anti–*Roe v. Wade* at the same time? Judges have faced these questions in various areas of the law and have often reached seemingly inconsistent results.

This dilemma inevitably forced judges to uphold slavery in the face of their repulsion by it. In other words, under positivism, laws can be unjust and constitutional at the same time; and under the natural law, laws can be just and unconstitutional at the same time. Many judges to this day seek to check their own power through dispassionate adjudication of the law. Justice Nevius' reasoning in *State v. Post* typifies judicial analysis of slavery before the Civil War, as most judges personally opposed to slavery usually ruled against abolitionists.

Essentially, the fundamental question is where do laws come from? Do they come from the government, or do they come from our God-created human nature? The appropriate answer is both. For instance, some conduct criminalized by the government is *malum prohibitum*, or wrong because the government says so. Examples of these may include various drug or motor vehicle laws. Conversely, laws that prohibit behaviors that are wrong in and of themselves, like murder, rape, or theft, for example, are *malum in se*. That is, they are wrong because nature and God say so.

As already discussed, this differentiation extends to rights as well. Throughout human history and up through the present day, governments have confused which rights are ours by nature and which are given to us by the government. Because our right against involuntary servitude is one that stems from our natural rights as humans, no government by legislation, custom, or order (that is, without due process) can ever strip us of this right. Yet as the preceding chapters have demonstrated, most governments throughout human history have done just that. Likewise, our most pressing social issues today stem from whether or not the particular rights in question—such as the right to life, the right to marriage, and the right to keep and bear arms—stem from the government or from our nature as free human beings given to us by our Creator.

My view on this is no secret; it is rooted in an unmistakable deference to liberty. When society forms, its people already possess freedoms and liberties integral to our nature. This state is nonnegotiable. No social compact can involve stripping people of these God-given rights.

The idea of national security provides an appropriate point of reference from which to measure the extent to which our natural liberty is superior to anything the government may want or may do. Nowadays especially, we often hear discourse about striking an appropriate balance between liberty and security. Yet—through my experiences as a lawyer, a constitutional law professor, a New Jersey Superior Court judge, a public commentator, and an author—I am utterly convinced that the relationship in America between liberty and security should not be about balance, but about *bias* in favor of liberty. Government is essentially the negation of liberty. By its very nature, government removes natural rights in one way or another. Hence every benefit of the doubt should be given to liberty. Whenever liberty and security clash, liberty should be in the favored position, the default position, the presumed position. While security needs affirmative justification (the government must justify publicly, explain truthfully, and convince constitutionally whenever it seeks to keep us safe by impairing our natural rights), the exercise of natural rights requires no excuse, affirmative explanation, or justification. Liberty is natural. Security is artificial.

Whatever any government does (unless it is preserving freedom by enforcing the natural law) should be suspect. Think about it: Government either compels behavior or forbids behavior. Some behavior should be compelled (driving safely, for example) and some behavior should be forbidden (violating another's right to life, liberty, and property, for example). Whatever else the government does, no matter what it claims the goal is and no matter the stated justification, because it curtails human freedom it should be suspect and presumed to be unlawful and unconstitutional. If these libertarian principles had been accepted throughout history, then slavery—government-sponsored destruction of natural rights—and all the evils it has spawned would never have existed here. And had our European cousins truly believed in the natural law, then the Inquisition and all its terrors, the Holocaust and all its horrors, both world wars, and the Communist destruction of life, liberty, and property would never have taken root.

Individual ideology notwithstanding, the American judiciary would remain at the forefront of the race issue throughout the nineteenth century. The courts' decisions would not be consistent. They would at times follow positivism and stick to the letter of the law and other times follow the natural law and free the oppressed. They would both take the lead in spurring change in American race relations and also hinder it. They would necessarily hand down some of the most heroic and some of the most infamous decisions in American history. But the one case that would come to epitomize America's ideological bipolarity and the federal government's racist agenda was just right around the corner.

4

Dred Scott and the Missouri Compromise

In 1820, Thomas Jefferson, the now-retired president, wrote an ominous letter to John Holmes, a U.S. senator from Maine, concerning the prevalent issue in American politics at the time. "This momentous question," he wrote, "like a fire bell in the night, awakened and filled me with terror. I considered it at once as the knell of the Union. It is hushed indeed for the moment. But this is a reprieve only, not a final sentence. A geographical line, coinciding with a marked principle, moral and political, once conceived and held up to the angry passions of men, will never be obliterated; and every new irritation will mark it deeper and deeper."[1]

Jefferson was alluding to Congress's ongoing efforts to implement and pass what would become known as the Missouri Compromise, an agreement between the North and South to regulate slavery in the former Louisiana Territory (including the proposed State of Missouri). But Jefferson was also predicting and anticipating the compromise's tragic repercussions. History would undoubtedly vindicate this great visionary and show that this was not a compromise but a temporary and ineffective solution that continued to fester and exacerbate sectionalism in the United

States as the nineteenth century progressed. America was essentially procrastinating.

The sectionalist tensions would come to a climax in the aftermath of the Supreme Court's most infamous decision, *Dred Scott v. Sandford.* Taken together, the Missouri Compromise and the *Dred Scott* case represent an unsuccessful effort first to compromise on slavery through legislation, and then to settle the issue permanently through the judiciary. These efforts were based on the flawed assumption that slavery could be resolved through either route; stated differently, that positivist laws which violate the natural law could long survive among a free people. We know that they cannot.

THE EXPANDING UNION

The political discourse in the early nineteenth century centered not only on slavery itself, but on its proliferation. America as a country was expanding; land to the west was vast and represented a seemingly infinite opportunity for Americans. The Northwest Ordinance, which was the major piece of territorial legislation passed under the Articles of Confederation, provided for the formation of new states as the country spread westward. The Ordinance also prevented existing states from extending their borders endlessly into the territories to the west and, as well, prohibited slavery from being established in any of the new states created from the territory.

In his inaugural address in March 1817, President James Monroe discussed what he perceived to be the threats facing the young nation. In addition to threats from abroad, Monroe voiced his concern over the problematic consequences of unchecked expansion, particularly upon national unity. To offset these effects, President Monroe planned to pursue a network of roads and canals that would "shorten distances . . . and bind the Union more closely together."[2]

Yet America's biggest problem—slavery—went unmentioned in Monroe's address. As a slaveholder himself, President Monroe was quite familiar with the institution. Interestingly enough, Monroe had come to view slavery as not only morally wrong, but as a major obstacle to national development and the biggest threat to the country's unity (and thus the safety of its citizens).[3] While slavery had expanded exponentially along with the country in the nearly three decades since the ratification of the Constitution, there had been a growing awareness of its evil. It was becoming more and more a threat to American society, even from the perspective of slaveholders.

This blatant contradiction operating within America's moral fabric created a natural tendency to acknowledge slavery's evil. As Thomas Jefferson, the most famous of slaveholders (because he was otherwise utterly devoted to the natural law), recognized as much when he said: "There must doubtless be an unhappy influence on the manners of the people, produced by the existence of slavery among us. The whole commerce between master and slaves is a perpetual exercise of the most boisterous passions; the most unremitting despotism on the one part, and degrading submissions on the other. The man must be a prodigy who can retain his morals and manners undepraved by such circumstances."[4] More ominously, Jefferson once wrote, "I tremble for my country when I reflect that God is just, that His justice cannot sleep forever."[5] We know that is true.

As it turned out, American unity, as fragile as it always had been, was on the brink of complete collapse, and more than just roads and canals were needed to save it. Slavery, an issue too sensitive to be discussed in President Monroe's address, was what really made unchecked expansion a threat to national unity. America's expansion naturally became the basis for a new quarrel between slaveholders and abolitionists: Whether newly admitted territories should be slave states or free states. While the quarrel may have seemed new, it was nonetheless an extension of the Constitutional Convention debates. At stake was control of Congress and the extent to which slavery would be permitted in the country.

Although the country was founded with thirteen states, it was able to maintain the balance of free states and slave states as it expanded. In 1817, there were twenty-two states in the Union, eleven slave states and eleven free states. While more representatives were allotted to the slave states because of the three-fifths compromise, each state had two senators. The equal balance gave both sides an equal opportunity to strike down any threatening legislation. Consequently, the debate over Missouri's fate as a free state or slave state would implicate the merits of the debate over American slavery in its entirety, and the admission of the Missouri territory as a State would reveal just how a divided America was plunging the country into its greatest crisis since the Revolution.[6]

THE ROAD TO COMPROMISE

Nine months after President Monroe's inauguration, the Fifteenth Congress assembled in Washington, D.C. In March 1818, a man named John Scott submitted an application for statehood on behalf of the Missouri Territory. By April, a bill was sent to the House that sought to authorize Missouri to draft a state constitution and assemble a state government.[7] The bill contained no provisions addressing slavery explicitly, which essentially meant that slavery would be permitted in that State. Silence was deemed to be consent.

The bill would remain idle in Congress until the following session. In April 1819, Representative James Tallmadge of New York proposed an amendment to the bill which explicitly addressed the slavery question, albeit to one end of the two extreme views. Tallmadge's amendment called for a provision against the further introduction of slaves in that territory and another for the gradual emancipation of slaves already there.[8] The bill barely passed in the House, with the voting reflecting America's sectionalism.

The Senate, however, passed the bill without the Tallmadge provisions. Upon return to the House for approval, the representatives struggled to reach a consensus on the Senate's version. After much debate, the House agreed to disagree and the bill was officially dead. As it turned out, the House refused to accept Missouri as a State without a slavery restriction, and the Senate refused to accept it with such a restriction.[9] These two extremes represented America's lack of a unified voice and symbolized the extent of the nation's polarity on the issue of slavery—and the time was more than forty years before the Civil War began.

When the Sixteenth Congress met in December 1819, the debate over Missouri had by then turned into a national drama. States had passed individual resolutions favoring or disfavoring restrictions, pamphlets were published and distributed, and the debate seemed to involve almost everyone. Once again, Scott submitted a bill on behalf of Missouri, and Representative John W. Taylor of New York offered another amendment that Missouri be admitted only upon the prerequisite that slavery would not exist within its borders.[10]

As the debate raged yet again in the House, the Senate passed its own proposal that Maine be admitted as a free state so long as Missouri was admitted without restriction.[11] Up until that point, the admission of Maine was an independent issue. Now, the admission of Maine as a free State rested upon Missouri remaining open to slavery. Shortly thereafter, the Senate attached the key additional amendment that proved to embody the compromise: It proposed that slavery would be forever prohibited in all of the territory obtained through the Louisiana Purchase north of parallel 36°30' north.

The United States had purchased the vast Louisiana territory from France in 1803. The treaty with France provided that "all inhabitants shall be incorporated in the United States . . . according to the principles of the federal constitution, to the enjoyment of all the rights, advantages, and immunities of citizens of the United States; and in the meantime they shall be maintained and protected in the free enjoyment of their liberty, property, and the religion which they profess."[12] While this would mean something totally different today, in 1803 Southerners argued that this provision guaranteed slaveholders in that territory property rights over their slaves and established the newly acquired territory as friendly to slavery. From the pro-slavery perspective, this treaty offered a strong argument for allowing slavery in the newly acquired lands.

Nevertheless, the House refused to accept the Senate's manipulation and consolidation of the two independent bills for Maine and Missouri statehood. After debate on both sides, the Senate submitted a final proposal. It called for the following: Maine was to be addressed independently and admitted as a state without condition; all conditions on Missouri's statehood would be removed, insofar as those conditions affected Missouri itself; and the provision outlawing slavery in the rest of the Louisiana territory would be adopted.

The Maine and Missouri bills passed independently. In what became known as the Missouri Compromise of 1820, the bills echoed the approach taken by the framers decades before. It permitted slavery in Missouri but forever prohibited slavery in that vast portion of the Louisiana territory, a region encompassing modern-day Kansas, Nebraska, Oklahoma, Iowa, North Dakota, South Dakota, Montana, and parts of Wyoming, Colorado, Texas, Minnesota, and New Mexico. While a new saga later emerged concerning the ratification of Missouri's constitution, Missouri was eventually admitted into the Union as a slave state.

It is important to note that the extremists on both sides were equally unsatisfied and, in fact, had little to do with the bills being passed. The compromise was the product of the moderates in both factions and did nothing to extinguish the tensions between slavery expansionists and abolitionists. Had the hardliners been smaller in number, perhaps this would have proven to be insignificant. But they weren't, and the inevitable showdown was simply postponed for another generation.

Nevertheless, Congress effectively repealed the Missouri Compromise when it passed the Kansas-Nebraska Act in 1854. In addition to creating the territories of Kansas and Nebraska, the Act essentially instituted popular sovereignty with regard to slavery in all the open territories.

THE STORY OF DRED SCOTT

The division of the country into free states and slave states created a contradiction with regard to the status of blacks in American society. In large part, whether or not blacks were free or slaves depended upon the State in which they resided. As a result, abolitionists were quick to advocate the position that slaves would be permanently freed when taken to a free state. This position, however, was difficult to reconcile with the right to "property," upon which slaveholders and slavery defenders justified their possession of slaves, even when taking them to a free State. It was upon this theory that Dred Scott brought his claim to freedom to the United States Supreme Court. In a case that attracted worldwide attention, the United States would reveal the darkest element of its society.

Dred Scott was born enslaved to Peter Blow, the owner of an 860-acre farm in Virginia.[13] During his early years, Scott moved with Blow from Virginia to Alabama, and from Alabama to St. Louis, Missouri. There, Scott worked in Blow's boardinghouse until he was sold to Dr. John Emerson in 1833.

Emerson was a Pennsylvanian, and was an aspiring army medical officer. However, obtaining a position in the Army was no easy task, as the demand was low and appointments were made in proportion to a state's representation in Congress.[14] In 1833, Emerson was appointed assistant surgeon general of the U.S. Army as a Pennsylvania appointment. His duties required him and his slaves to report to Rock Island, Illinois.[15]

Emerson did not enjoy his stay at Rock Island, as made evident by his numerous requests for transfers. His goal was to be transferred back to Missouri, yet all of his transfer requests were rejected. When the Army itself vacated Rock Island two years after his arrival, Emerson got his wish. However, his transfer took him not to Missouri, but to what is modern-day St. Paul, Minnesota, part of the territory acquired by the Louisiana Purchase and a free territory pursuant to the Missouri Compromise.[16]

Upon his arrival with his master in Minnesota, Dred Scott met Harriet Robinson, a slave owned by the local Indian agent, Major Lawrence Taliaferro. By 1837, Scott and Robinson were married in a ceremony presided over by Taliaferro himself, who was also a justice of the peace. Soon after, Taliaferro either gave or sold Robinson to Emerson. After Emerson was given a transfer to Fort Jessup, Louisiana, he decided to hire out Scott and Robinson and return for them when the time was appropriate.[17]

Emerson was married to a woman named Eliza Sandford within two months of his arrival at Fort Jessup. After his marriage, Emerson sent for Scott and Robinson, who joined the newlyweds in Louisiana. Once again growing discontent with his location, Emerson requested a transfer back to Fort Snelling, Minnesota. En route, Robinson gave birth to a baby girl; all evidence suggests she was born north of the Missouri boundary and thus in free territory.[18]

After a year and a half in Fort Snelling, Emerson was transferred to Florida to lend his services in the Seminole War. However, his wife and the Scotts went to St. Louis to stay with Mrs. Emerson's father, Alexander Sandford. After his service in Florida, Emerson and his wife moved to Iowa, where Dr. Emerson died in 1843. When the Emersons moved to Iowa, the Scotts were hired out to Capt. Henry Bainbridge; in 1846, Mrs. Emerson hired them out to Samuel Russel.[19]

After attempting to purchase their freedom from Mrs. Emerson for $300, Dred Scott and Harriet Robinson Scott commenced independent legal actions against Irene Emerson in Missouri state court, seeking their legal freedom. In order for the Scotts to prevail, they had to show that they had become free while in Illinois or the Wisconsin territory and that they remained free when they were brought back to Missouri. At trial, Dred Scott lost because he could not actually prove that he was owned by Mrs. Emerson. He appealed all the way to the Missouri Supreme Court, which ruled that Scott's case should be retried.

After a second trial, the St. Louis Circuit Court declared Scott and his family free in 1850. But Irene Emerson was concerned about losing such valuable property, so she appealed to the Missouri Supreme Court, and in 1852, the Supreme Court reversed the lower court's decision, sending Dred Scott back to slavery. At this point, Irene Emerson turned the case over to her brother, John Sandford, who thereafter acted on her behalf. John Sandford, who undoubtedly thought he was just doing a favor for his sister, would thus unwittingly become the defendant in one of the most infamous litigations in American history.

Scott decided to try his luck in the federal court system and filed suit in Missouri's federal circuit court. After that court agreed with the Missouri Supreme Court's ruling, Dred Scott's last hope was an appeal to the United States Supreme Court.

THE SUPREME COURT RULES

The Court's composition in 1857 was hardly sympathetic to slaves. Of the nine justices, seven had been appointed by Southern presidents, and five were from slaveholding families themselves. Chief Justice Taney, the man who would author the Dred Scott opinion, was himself once a slaveholder and a staunch supporter of slavery and defender of the South from what he saw as Northern aggression. It is no surprise, then, that one of the Supreme Court's most infamous decisions came down through an opinion by Roger Brooke Taney.

The Court's holding in *Dred Scott v. Sandford* was that blacks were not considered (and were not intended to be considered) citizens under the Constitution. They could not claim any of the rights and privileges the Constitution guaranteed and secured to citizens of the United States. According to Chief Justice Taney, "it [was] too plain for argument, that they [blacks] had never been regarded as a part of the people or citizens of the State, nor supposed to possess any political rights which the dominant race might not withhold or grant at their pleasure."[20] Thus, because Dred Scott was not a citizen, he could not sue in the federal courts and diversity jurisdiction—which allows federal courts to hear cases between *citizens* of different states—was inappropriate.

Chief Justice Taney explained the justification for his ruling as follows: "We have the language of the Declaration of Independence and of the Articles of Confederation, in addition to the plain words of the Constitution itself; we have the legislation of the different states, before, about the time, and since, the Constitution was adopted; we have the legislation of Congress, from the time of its adoption to a recent period; and we have the constant and uniform action of the Executive Department, all concurring together, and leading to the same result. And if anything in relation to the construction of the Constitution can be regarded as settled, it is that which we now give to the word 'citizen' and the word 'people.'"[21]

It is difficult to overstate the magnitude of this insult to blacks. This component of the decision placed racism explicitly into the American Constitution. For decades, the Constitution's slavery provisions permitted local governments to enact laws that perpetuated slavery and indoctrinated racism. Up to this point, however, this racism was prevalent primarily in the South and was not rooted, at least not so explicitly, in constitutionally and federally mandated law. While it was arguably present in between the lines of the Constitution's text, such an enunciation by the nation's highest court—that humiliated blacks and seemingly permanently placed them outside of American society and outside the protection of the law—was utterly shocking.

It seems peculiar that the chief justice justified the court's decision on the independent laws passed by the states. American sectionalism was no secret to anyone. Why paint the entire country with the laws of the Southern states? By that logic, Chief Justice Taney could have easily applied the Northern laws to the South. True, the Constitution did contain provisions that protected slavery, but they were not so explicit as to strip citizenship from all blacks.

As Justice Benjamin R. Curtis's dissent made clear, if jurisdiction (the legal power of the court to hear the case before it) was inappropriate, the Court should have ended its inquiry right then and there. After all, Justice Curtis argued, jurisdiction is the first issue to be considered and if the Court cannot hear the case, then it should not reach its merits. However, Chief Justice Taney did not stop there. "An act of Congress which deprives a citizen of the United States of his liberty or property, merely because he came himself or brought his property into a particular Territory of the United States, and who had committed no offence against the laws, could hardly be dignified with the name of due process of law."[22] Blacks were not persons.

According to the chief justice, the right of slaveholders to their slave property was expressly affirmed in the Constitution. Citing the twenty-year guarantee of the slave trade and the Fugitive Slave Clause, the Court concluded that the Missouri Compromise was unconstitutional because it prohibited a citizen from holding and owning property that was expressly guaranteed in the Constitution.

Justices Curtis and McLean vehemently criticized the Court's decision to strike down the Missouri Compromise as unconstitutional. Aside from the aforementioned jurisdictional grounds, the dissenters noted that none of the framers objected to the antislavery provisions of the Northwest Ordinance, which had been passed by Congress under the Articles of Confederation. Furthermore, they found it impossible to read the Constitution in such a way as to strip citizenship from all blacks.

The effect of this part of the decision was to nullify the key amendment to the bill of 1820 that allowed the Missouri Compromise to be passed. Rather than upholding the immunity to slavery bestowed upon that territory by an act of Congress, the Court held that the federal government had no power to prohibit slavery in *any* part of the United States. According to the

Court in *Dred Scott v. Sandford*, slavery as a legal institution was now completely beyond the reach of any branch of the federal government.

THE DRED SCOTT LEGACY

The *Dred Scott* case is widely considered to be one of the greatest disasters in Supreme Court history because it defined blacks as non-persons. It would be followed by similar disasters in which Japanese-Americans (in *U.S. v. Korematsu* [1943]) and babies in the womb (in *Roe v. Wade* [1973]) would also be held by the Court to be non-persons. The case constitutionalized the status of blacks in the United States and made black freedom and equality essentially unobtainable. Yet the reasons for its particular infamy are numerous.

First, many feel that the court unnecessarily reached out to decide the merits of a case in which it had no jurisdiction. Chief Justice Taney could simply have stated that Dred Scott was not a citizen under Missouri Law and stopped short of discussing the citizenship of blacks from a greater constitutional perspective.

A second point of view is that Chief Justice Taney's opinion was rooted in racism. This is true. American slavery was a racist institution, and the Court upholding it was necessarily an extension of that racism. However, Chief Justice Taney did not flat-out declare that blacks were inferior or unqualified for freedom by some absurd or backward theory. Rather, he justified his opinion on originalist grounds; that is, he based his opinion on what a strict interpretation of the Constitution, the supreme law of the land, would entail. As he expressly stated in his opinion: "It is not the province of the Court to decide upon the justice or injustice, the policy or impolicy, of these laws . . . the duty of the court is, to interpret the instrument they have framed, with the best lights we can obtain on the subject, and to administer it as we find it, according to its true intent and meaning when it was adopted."[23]

Here Chief Justice Taney reveals his adherence to the ideas of legal positivism. He is justifying his opinion on a dispassionate adjudication of the merits of the case. But to say that the Constitution's slavery provisions stripped all blacks of citizenship is absurd. The Three-Fifths Clause, the Importation Clause, and the Fugitive Slave Clause simply cannot be read to remove citizenship from *all* blacks. At the time of the founding, ten of the thirteen states allowed free blacks to vote, as Justices Curtis and McLean pointed out in dissent. While five of those ten states had either limited or completely withheld the right, assigning such meaning to the Constitution's text requires more than dispassionate adjudication; it represents an aggressive form of judicial activism to carve new meaning into the text of the Constitution. The logical conclusion of the *Dred Scott* decision is that the states were empowered to enslave *free* blacks.

A third critique of the decision is predicated on the possibility the justices thought (wrongly) they could settle a divisive issue by taking it out of politics. There is evidence suggesting that President Buchanan influenced the Court by communicating his desire to use the judiciary to reach a national consensus on slavery. In seeking a clear majority vote, Buchanan wrote to Justice John Catron, persuading him to join the majority to give an impression of unity. Catron did exactly that, creating the illusion of a seven-to-two decision. But rather than settling the issue, the seemingly one-sided decision pushed abolitionists and slaveholders deeper into their respective corners and exacerbated existing sectionalism. Abolitionists grew more and more radical as a result and concluded that only the destruction of the Union could end slavery. The violent reaction in the decision's aftermath helped ignite the Civil War.

A fourth point is that the Court was actually right to impose a solution to slavery, but it simply chose the wrong side. However, the Court had little, if any, positive law on which to justify striking down slavery, given the explicit slavery provisions in the Constitution. The Court would have had to base its holding wholly on natural law and thereby circumvent the supreme law of the land. A natural law theorist would argue that this is exactly what the Court should have done, consistent with the philosophy of St. Thomas Aquinas discussed in chapter 2. An unjust law carries with it a duty of disobedience, and the Court of last resort had a duty to recognize it.

THE POLITICAL REACTION

The reaction to the Court's ruling was vehement and plunged the country into crisis. Abolitionists saw the decision as a judicial endorsement of slavery and a fatal wound to the integrity of the nation's highest court. Because Justice Curtis released his dissent for publication to a Boston newspaper before Chief Justice Taney released his opinion, the abolitionists obtained an enormous advantage in the propaganda war that ensued.[24]

Many did not see the *Dred Scott* decision as the end of the Court's participation in the slavery debate. There was a widely held belief that Chief Justice Taney was prepared to take slavery to its next logical step: The States had no authority whatsoever to prohibit the practice within their respective borders. This fear was clearly predominant in the North, where abolitionists, at the very least, insisted that slavery be confined to its then-current borders.

As expected, Southern slaveholders hailed the Court for upholding the rule of law and protecting the South from the abolitionist radicals. Even some Northern Democrats supported the holding. The *Illinois State Register* wrote that "the people who revered the Constitution and the laws . . . will hail the decision with satisfaction."[25] But the Democrats were nonetheless split. Northern Democrats were content with the idea of "popular sovereignty" that the aforementioned Kansas-Nebraska Act embodied. On the other hand, Southern Democrats vehemently endorsed the nonintervention theory that would have allowed slavery in all of the territories. But the Republicans were unified in their disgust for Chief Justice Taney's opinion. Their unification helped them seize the momentum created by the decision's backlash and take control of the White House in 1860.

In the end, it is somewhat ironic that the Missouri Compromise would be struck down as unconstitutional in a case brought to the Supreme Court by a Missouri slave. After the decision, Peter Blow's sons, who had helped Scott pay for his legal fees over the years, purchased him and set him free. Dred Scott died nine months later from tuberculosis. Harriet Robinson Scott outlived her husband by eighteen years and died in 1876. The legacy of what the Supreme Court did to their humanity haunts America even today.

The *Dred Scott* holding was overruled by the adoption of the Thirteenth Amendment, enacted and ratified in 1865, and by the *Slaughter-House Cases*, decided in 1873. There, the Court held the Reconstruction Amendments, which are discussed in the preceding chapters, superseded the Taney Court's ruling. But in essence, Chief Justice Taney's despicable opinion was not overruled and continues to exist in the soul of American society. That blacks continue to be regarded as second-class citizens is difficult to dispute. That racial stereotypes stemming from government-sponsored ideas of black inferiority continue to prevail across our nation is crystal clear. That the *Dred Scott* case is a reflection of government-endorsed racism that no constitutional amendment or court ruling can possibly undo is evident every day.

History shows that American sectionalism in the nineteenth century was too acute to extinguish through compromise or judicial intervention. The extent to which the presence of slavery affected society combined with the passions that the issue exposed in Americans made conflict inevitable. But in the end, it was the federal government that ignited and brought these tensions to their tragic apex. And it would be the federal government that would pay for its frightful Constitution with nearly seven hundred thousand American lives. But it was all Americans, white and black, who would suffer Dred Scott's revenge—even up to the present generation.

5

The Civil War

One of the greatest misconceptions of American history is that the Civil War was fought over slavery. Those who subscribe to this belief see President Abraham Lincoln as the benevolent leader who made unimaginable sacrifices in human blood to wipe out America's greatest sin. While the human sacrifice is indisputable and the sin was monumental, the war's purpose was not to free blacks from the shackles of bondage. Rather, the Civil War was fought with one purpose in mind: To preserve the Union at *all costs*. And, to put it in Lincoln's terms, with no ifs, ands, or buts. You'd better agree with the president, or else.

THE SETTING

The North and South were divided both morally and economically. As the previous chapters have chronicled, the debate over slavery had firmly gripped the country in the decades preceding the Lincoln presidency. Since the country's founding, the states and the federal government kept deeply rooted passions concerning slavery and abolition at bay by constantly compromising. The balance of free states and slave states was maintained as slavery expanded. States were given autonomy to deal with the issue of slavery as they saw fit, so long as they did not interfere with another's property rights. But the *Dred Scott* case placed the federal government firmly on the side of the slaveholders, redefining the slavery provisions in the Constitution in a way that created a seemingly insurmountable obstacle to obtaining the human moral equality for which so many Americans yearned.

In addition to the country's division over slavery, there was the concern over which economy the federal government favored—the South's agrarian economy or the North's commercial interests. Interestingly enough, the *Dred Scott* decision did not accurately reflect to which side of the debate the federal government was committed. Northern states had gained control of the federal government as the 1850s drew to a close, and the South found itself on the defensive. Its agricultural economy, sustained by slave labor, was attacked on both moral and economic grounds.

A QUESTIONABLE STANCE

Abraham Lincoln emerged as a candidate for the presidency at a time when national anticipation was at its peak. How would a new president balance the interests of the North and South? In the wake of *Dred Scott,* would he steer the country toward democracy or slaveocracy? Adding to the uncertainty were Lincoln's own unclear and often contradictory statements over slavery itself.

Lincoln never argued that slavery was unjust. Rather, he asserted that it threatened to weaken the Union and its democratic values. During the Lincoln-Douglas debates of 1858, Lincoln stated: "A house divided against itself cannot stand. I believe this government cannot endure, permanently, half slave and half free. I do not expect the Union to be dissolved—I do not expect the house to fall—but I do expect it will cease to be divided."[1] A skilled politician, Lincoln appealed to the antislavery interests of Northern abolitionists as well as moderates in border slave states who were opposed to racial equality.

But the common tale that Lincoln was a sympathetic and heroic defender of black freedom is simply a myth. As Union armies met the forces of the Confederacy on the battlefield, he openly argued, "What I do about slavery, and the colored race, I do because I believe it helps to save the Union; and what I forbear, I forbear because I do not believe it would help to save the Union. I shall do less whenever I shall believe what I am doing hurts the cause, and I shall do more whenever I shall believe doing more will help the cause."[2]

It is important to analyze the magnitude of what Lincoln says here. He admits that the emancipation of blacks will only happen because it is of assistance to the Union; slaves are only pawns in the game of politics and warfare he is playing. Lincoln places the freedom of blacks on a low priority compared to his desire to unify the nation, and his words here seem more becoming of a Confederate Army officer than the so-called Great Emancipator. Yet it is the latter title that we've all been taught to attribute to Abraham Lincoln. In my opinion, such a title is the least deserved sobriquet accorded any president.

Lincoln's rhetoric notwithstanding, Southerners were uncertain about his commitment to protecting their slavery interests. His consistent manipulation of the issue of slavery along the lines of Union preservation earned him the fraudulent title of a political moderate in the North, but Southerners were still adamant about having a Southerner as president.

LINCOLN IGNITES WAR

Despite Southern opposition, Lincoln was nonetheless elected as the sixteenth president of the United States in 1860. Far from overwhelming support, he received only 39 percent of the popular vote, and his name was stricken from the ballot in Alabama, Arkansas, Florida, Georgia, Louisiana, Mississippi, North Carolina, Tennessee, and Texas. In South Carolina the legislature chose not to have candidates for president on the ballot, in apparent anticipation of secession. Only 1.1 percent of white voters supported Lincoln in Virginia. These were the same states that would secede from the Union the following year.[3]

The Southern states were increasingly discontented as their interests were of secondhand concern to the federal government. Without political influence in Congress, the Southern legislatures still retained the right to nullification and secession. Nullification was the legal theory by which states could declare federal laws unconstitutional, while secession was the right claimed by states to separate from the Union. As soon as Lincoln became president, states' rights disappeared in the shadow of national power when he declared secession to be illegal. During his first inaugural address, Lincoln associated secession with anarchy as he stated,

> Plainly the central idea of secession is the essence of anarchy. . . . In 1787, one of the declared objects for ordaining and establishing the Constitution was to form a more perfect Union. . . . It follows from these views that no State upon its own mere motion can lawfully get out of the Union; that resol[ution]s and ordinances to that effect are legally void.

However, Lincoln chose to ignore the historical underpinnings of the American political system; the right of secession followed from the American Revolution as the colonists separated from the British Empire and declared their independence. President Lincoln also made the faulty assumption that the Union takes precedence over the states, as the goal was "to form a more perfect Union." He failed to recognize that states are free and independent, and combined they form the Union. As Ronald Reagan would say in his first inaugural address over a century later, "the federal government did not create the states; the states created the federal government." This subtle distinction is an important aspect of State sovereignty. The United States was founded on the ideals that federal power could be challenged by the states. Lincoln overlooked the fact that the states had formed a voluntary agreement and did not have the ability to surrender their sovereignty forever to a centralized power.

Nullification was also a fundamental state right to prevent federal domination. States enjoyed the right to use nullification as a protective measure against unconstitutional federal laws by making them ineffective against their citizens. Nullification had become a states' rights tradition, and both the North and the South exercised it prior to 1861. The most famous examples of this in the North centered around Northern states' personal liberty laws, a series of laws that were passed in response to the Fugitive Slave Act. Even though the U.S. Supreme Court found these laws, and thus nullification, unconstitutional—in the 1842 case *Prigg v. Pennsylvania*—Northern states, *yes, Northern states*, continued to enact laws that criminalized the return of fugitive slaves in direct defiance of federal law. Lincoln's attempt to trample the states' sovereignty, even the rights of those opposed to slavery, only heightened the conflict between the advocates of a supreme, unchecked federal government and the advocates of a modest central government, tempered by nullification.

South Carolina started the trend of secession in December 1860. Concerned with preserving the Union at all costs, Lincoln was determined to use military force to bring the rebel states into line. But he did not want to be portrayed as an aggressor and needed the South somehow to ignite the conflict. This would make the Southerners look like the aggressors and would give the impression that Lincoln simply had no choice but to declare war as a defense against aggression.

The solution devised by Lincoln triggered a war that would kill seven hundred thousand Americans. Advised by his top military commanders that an incoming ship would be considered a threat to Confederates and would prompt an attack, Lincoln deliberately sent a ship of food provisions as well as additional armed soldiers to Fort Sumter, South Carolina. The Confederates fell for the ploy and fired the first shot. Lincoln responded by sending armed warships and deployed a total of seventy-five thousand troops to invade all of the Southern states.[4]

His plan, however, did not go unnoticed. Northern newspapers were quick to inform the public that Lincoln had instigated the Fort Sumter incident. *The Jersey City American Standard* wrote, "there is a madness and ruthlessness" in Lincoln "which is astounding . . . this unarmed vessel . . . is a mere decoy to draw the first fire from the people of the South, which act by the pre-determination of the government is to be the pretext for letting loose the horrors of war." The *Providence Daily Post* also wrote, "Mr. Lincoln saw an opportunity to inaugurate civil war without appearing in the character of an aggressor." These headlines and stories were replicated by other newspapers in the North. Lincoln's plan to bring the country into a war was no longer a hidden political strategy.[5]

A substantial number of free blacks from the North offered to serve in the Union army, but their attempts were met with federal opposition. Freedom and equality were not intertwined in the North, and blacks were constantly reminded of this disparity. Requests by blacks made to the War Department went unheard, often for political reasons. President Lincoln was ultimately concerned with the border slave states possibly abandoning the Union if blacks' status were elevated to that of a soldier in the Union army.[6]

Lincoln's position on slavery was made even more evident in the first few weeks of war. The fighting immediately prompted Virginia, North Carolina, Tennessee, and Arkansas to secede from the Union. In a clear display of Lincoln's priorities, the President *proposed to permit the continuation of slavery* in Missouri, Kentucky, Maryland, and Delaware so long as those states remained in the Union. To save the Union from further division, Lincoln *was willing to continue the subjugation of blacks.*

In the end, this proposal worked, as those States chose not to secede. However, many citizens from those border states still joined the Confederacy. Both Kentucky and Missouri had two state governments, one supporting the Confederacy and the other supporting the Union.[7]

By May 1861, a total of eleven Southern states had seceded from the Union and established their own nation, the Confederate States of America. The Confederacy was comprised of South Carolina, Mississippi, Florida, Alabama, Georgia, Louisiana, Texas, Virginia, Arkansas, North Carolina, and Tennessee. The Confederacy's Constitution contained provisions that expressly protected the institution of slavery, limited the power of the new central government, and clearly reflected state sovereignty. Lincoln refused to recognize the Confederacy, declared secession to be a violation of the Constitution, and effectively declared war on the people of the Southern states that refused to recognize his presidency.[8]

WHY WAR?

Lincoln can clearly be accused of changing his public opinion to suit political expediency. A generation earlier, in a speech to Congress in January 1848, the young Illinois congressman and future president had said,

Any people anywhere, being inclined and having the power, have the right to rise up and shake off the existing government, and form a new one that suits them better. This is a most valuable, a most sacred right—a right which we hope and believe is to liberate the world. Nor is this right confined to cases in which the whole people of an existing government may choose to exercise it. Any portion of such people, that can, may revolutionize, and make their own of so much of the territory as they inhabit.[9]

Notwithstanding what he had said as a congressman, Lincoln as president declared war on the states that seceded from the Union (even though, under the Constitution, only Congress may declare war) because he feared two events might occur if the seceding states were permitted to leave. In an era of no federal income tax, the government was largely funded by user fees and tariffs. (Lincoln and the Radical Republicans had enacted an income tax, but it was declared unconstitutional—the Constitution at the time expressly forbade it—after the war ended.)

First, Lincoln feared that the loss of revenues from tariffs collected at southern ports (including major ports such as Newport News, Virginia; Savannah, Georgia; Tampa, Florida; Mobile, Alabama; New Orleans, Louisiana; and Houston, Texas) would starve the federal budget. He also feared that if he raised tariffs on goods coming into Northern ports to compensate for the lost revenue from Southern ports, his days in the White House would be numbered.

His fears were realistic. By the time of Lincoln's inauguration in March 1861, many Republicans, prodded by northern newspapers and business leaders, had come to the conclusion that somehow either the federal government needed to continue collecting revenues from the southern ports in the now-seceded states, or all the ships from Europe and South America that were entering those ports needed to be diverted to the North so that Lincoln's government could collect the tariffs.

Lincoln's answer was war. War of Americans against Americans. War waged against citizens and slaves whose state legislatures had enacted resolutions that Lincoln had argued were well within their power to enact. War more deadly to more American citizens than all wars combined in which Americans have fought.

THE ALLEGED PROMISE OF FREEDOM

As the war progressed, the government took explicit steps to frustrate the slaveholders' interests. First, in 1862, Congress implemented an article of war that prevented the Union army from returning fugitive slaves to their masters. A few months later, Congress enacted the Second Confiscation Act to free the slaves living in Union-occupied territory. As a result, thousands of blacks fled to Union lines as the army advanced farther into the South.

But Lincoln's true colors were displayed after General David Hunter declared that slaves in Georgia, Florida, and South Carolina were to be freed under General Order Number 11. Fearing for his reputation among Northern and Southern Democrats in favor of both slavery and the Union, Lincoln immediately rescinded General Hunter's order. Furthermore, he attempted to reduce the effect of emancipation under the Confiscation Act and General Hunter's decree by allowing slave masters to claim compensation from the federal government for slaves freed by the Union army. It is clear, at the very least, Lincoln never publicly recognized the moral depravity of slavery, and yet he favored a gradual process of emancipation.[10] Why didn't he just buy the slaves and then set them free?

But for many slaves, the momentum they needed was finally theirs. The fulfillment of freedom, enforced by the occupation of Union forces, gave former slaves the confidence to defy masters, demand wages, refuse to work, and abandon plantations. Taking advantage of the destructive forces of war, they began to exercise limited freedoms. As a Northern reporter wrote in 1862, "slavery is forever destroyed and worthless, no matter what Mr. Lincoln or anyone else may say on the subject."[11]

Lincoln's Emancipation Proclamation extended no freedoms to slaves. While the Proclamation is often considered a symbolic document that brought freedom to thousands of blacks and confirmed the gradual end of more than 250 years of slavery in the United States, it was issued explicitly as a war measure to promise freedom to slaves in Confederate states, weaken Southern strength, and incite internal disorder.[12] In the Proclamation itself, Lincoln revealed the underlying rationale for the gesture, stating that he sincerely believed it to be "an act of justice, warranted by the Constitution *upon military necessity.*"[13]

The Proclamation was issued in two parts. The first part, issued on September 22nd 1862, promised all slaves would be freed on January 1st 1863, in areas still fighting against the Union; thus the Emancipation Proclamation itself permitted slavery to remain in those states that rejoined the Union. The second part, issued on January 1st 1863, proclaimed that slavery was abolished in the ten states listed in the document (Texas, Arkansas, Louisiana, Mississippi, Alabama, Georgia, Florida, South Carolina, North Carolina, and Virginia). Since the Proclamation only applied to Confederate states that were still fighting against the Union, slavery still existed for over eight hundred thousand blacks living in the border states of Kentucky, Missouri, Maryland, and Delaware, as well as in conquered regions of Virginia, Louisiana, and Tennessee.

That the document did not apply to the North, the border states, any area of the South already under Union control, or the city of New Orleans and the six parishes contiguous to it was a shrewd calculation on Lincoln's part designed to garner support among recently conquered areas now behind the front lines.[14] That Lincoln was willing to trade the slavery of some blacks for the nominal freedom of others showed that Lincoln internally harbored racist views akin to that of slave owners.

Lincoln knew that ending slavery was an instrumental war measure that could weaken the Confederate military position. In October 1863, a friend and fellow Illinois attorney, Leonard Swett, told Lincoln that he believed the end result of the war would be the extermination of slavery. Swett told Lincoln that though it would be an unpopular position, if he failed to take it, his rivals would.[15] Lincoln agreed. But his Emancipation Proclamation, which purported to end slavery, was largely a symbolic gesture. Since it applied only to those states still under control of the Confederacy (and therefore could not be enforced), it was propaganda designed to undermine the institution of Southern slavery and not a pledge that the president would or even could free every slave in one grand gesture.

As historian Allan Nevins succinctly noted, "The popular picture of Lincoln using a stroke of the pen to lift the shackles from the limbs of four million slaves is ludicrously false."[16] President Lincoln's own Secretary of State, William H. Seward, interpreted the document by commenting, "We show our own sympathy with slavery by emancipating slaves where we cannot reach them and holding them in bondage where we can set them free."[17]

The president attempted to minimize the implications of his Emancipation Proclamation when he quickly lost political support. Northern whites did not support wartime emancipation, and many of the Union soldiers showed their disgust by resigning from the

Army. *If the slaves were freed, what were the Union soldiers fighting for?* At least two hundred thousand federal soldiers deserted the Army, one hundred twenty thousand young men evaded Lincoln's draft, and ninety thousand relocated west. Northern whites believed that the Proclamation altered the war's purpose from saving the Union to ending slavery.

Slavery was a cause that Northern whites were unwilling to lose their lives for. As one Massachusetts sergeant put it, "if anyone thinks that this army is fighting to free the Negro . . . they are terribly mistaken."[18] As a result, Lincoln sought to distance himself from the belief that he was sympathetic to slaves. In a letter to the *New York Tribune,* he expressed his true sentiment:

> My paramount objective in this struggle is to save the Union, and is not either to save or destroy slavery. If I could save the Union without freeing any slave, I would do it, and if I could save it by freeing all the slaves, I would do it; and if I could save it by freeing some and leaving others alone, I would also do that. What I do about slavery and the colored race, I do because I believe it helps to save the union.[19]

This was a significant departure from Lincoln's earlier insinuation that he did not have the constitutional authority to interfere with slavery. Now he claimed it was a "military necessity" to violate the Constitution in order to save the Union. Further, the Proclamation had no legal justification, as Lincoln did not have the power to force states to comply with it, given their disassociation with the Union.[20]

As a war measure and as an instrument that would end the institution of slavery, the Emancipation Proclamation was a failure. Freedom could be promised but not guaranteed to black Americans—because at the time freedom was not a consideration for Abraham Lincoln. The good that came from the Proclamation was only that it sparked hope among slaves and encouraged them to rebel against their enslavement, backed by the destructive force of war. This deprived the South of necessary resources and weakened its military position, as it now faced not only the Union army but internal conflicts between master and slave.

How can this be justified? Did Lincoln's shrewd calculations regarding freeing the slaves really make him worthy of the title Great Emancipator? Shouldn't this title be given to one who unconditionally returned to blacks in the United States their natural freedom based on the inherent immorality of slavery and without regard to politics, military necessity, or inner racial prejudice? If it is the traits of a hero and a moral authority that we look for in Lincoln, then we clearly should keep looking.

While emancipation provided a military benefit to the Union, it also created a new class of blacks who were free—but nonetheless homeless, destitute, and repressed by the government that freed them; this in the midst of war. Blacks were unprepared to support themselves after generations of bondage. Newly acquired freedom did little to quell discriminatory tendencies by white people and local governments. Society would continue to subject blacks to unfavorable laws, thereby eliminating any prospect for economic advancement.

The lack of a coherent government policy providing the relief that freed blacks required caused thousands to suffer. Lincoln's administration was committed to expanding the federal government with his wartime powers. This led to increased spending on the war effort as well as government programs and agencies that continue to be in existence today.

Yet the government failed to provide federal relief for freed slaves.[21] Instead, private philanthropic organizations from the North supplied food and clothing to the former slaves and established schools and an education system. While helpful to some, it did not solve the problem. In the South, many Union officers even encouraged blacks to rescind their freedom and continue to work on the plantations.[22] That these blacks willingly chose to live in bondage demonstrates how limited they considered the freedom offered by the Union to be.

The Union government also directly caused starvation and death by herding blacks into "contraband camps."[23] General Benjamin F. Butler, commander of Fort Monroe, Virginia, and a war Democrat at the time, devised a plan in 1861 whereby fugitive slaves were considered contraband of war. This was in accordance with the Confiscation Act of 1861, which allowed the Union to seize any Confederate property, including slaves. Lincoln and the Republican Congress had no use for the Fifth Amendment to the Constitution, which (among other things) expressly forbids government confiscation of property unless for a public use and unless with just compensation. The purpose of General Butler's plan was to prevent blacks from congregating on abandoned lands that the Union army was looking to seize. The conditions in the camps, as expected, were deplorable. The living quarters were overcrowded. Inmates lacked basic necessities and were supplied with meager food rations. Outbreaks of disease were frequent and often led to death.[24] And they were not free to leave. Shamefully, President Lincoln was well aware of these conditions. As it was reported to him by the Western Sanitary Commission:

> [W]e can easily account for the fact that sickness and death prevail to a fearful extent. No language can describe the

suffering, destitution and neglect which prevail in some of their "camps." The sick and dying are left uncared for, in many instances, and the dead unburied. It would seem, now, that one-half are doomed to die in the process of freeing the rest.[25]

In 1862, General Butler was sent to capture New Orleans. After the campaign, he initiated a policy that required blacks to continue working on plantations for those slaveholders who were loyal to the Union. In exchange, the slaves received marginal wages, food, and medical care. While General Butler described the plan as a transition to a free labor economy, this was essentially a perpetuation of federal government–endorsed slavery; Lincoln's federal government and Lincoln's slavery.

General Butler's successor, General Nathaniel Banks, extended the program throughout Louisiana. Eventually, this system of forced free labor spread throughout the South and lasted until the end of the Civil War. Blacks were still treated like property, now by the army that liberated them. Their emancipation would not be legally realized until the passage of the Thirteenth Amendment.[26] It would not be politically recognized for at least another one hundred years.

BLACKS ON THE FRONT LINES

While Lincoln originally claimed that he did not have constitutional authority to grant freedom to slaves that were not within Union control, he quickly used emancipation to the Union's advantage. To offset declining Union manpower, slaves were allowed to enlist in the Union army.[27] By the end of the war, a total of 186,000 blacks enlisted as the United States Colored Troops, every one of them segregated from white troops.

The government maintained separate commands for black soldiers and white soldiers. Exploitation proved unavoidable; while blacks were ordered to fight in the war, navigate the Southern countryside, and serve as spies, the Lincoln administration paid black soldiers less than half of what white soldiers received. After many protests, the War Department avoided internal conflict by providing blacks with equal wages to whites in 1865, nearly at war's end.[28]

But black enlistment sparked controversy across the North and South. Many felt that it represented unwanted progress toward racial equality and a potential threat to whites. While there was a large-scale abolitionist movement in the North, not all Northerners were sympathetic to the plight of blacks. Newspapers spurred these hostile views and influenced public opinion with inflammatory statements that the nation was involved in a civil war to help the cause of free blacks *over* the needs of poor whites. The newspapers also reported allegations of blacks raping white women so as to portray abolitionists as encouraging the mixing of races. It is doubtless that these reports helped to arouse white hostility against blacks in the North.

Meanwhile, the Confederacy treated black Union troops as if they were rebellious slaves. Many black troops were captured and sold back into slavery or executed. The Confederacy was hesitant to enlist black troops of its own to support its war effort. Eventually military necessity forced the Confederates to revise this policy in order to check the Union's superiority in strength on the battlefield.[29]

Lincoln's wartime policies alienated white Northerners and created a hostile social environment for freed blacks. By March 1863, Congress passed the Conscription Act to draft all able men between the ages of twenty and forty-five. Those who could afford to pay a three hundred–dollar fine or enlist a replacement were exempt from the draft. Northern whites resented the draft, as it only applied to white men, and they felt that blacks would take over their jobs while they fought in the war. Those unable to afford the fee for not going to war were often immigrants and other working-class whites; the antiwar press blasted the draft law as targeting these poor whites and sending them to fight in the federal government's war against slavery.[30]

The first draft lottery for New York City was held on July 11th 1863, and within twenty-four hours, angry white mobs had begun rioting. At first the rioters focused on government buildings, but the mob soon turned against blacks, attacking black people on the streets, looting and torching an orphanage for black children, and destroying tenements and entertainment venues that catered to black workers.[31] While Lincoln sent troops to suppress the riots, this only intensified the conflict and led to even more casualties. This scene of federal troops being sent in to protect blacks from hostile whites would be reenacted one hundred years later, when President John F. Kennedy sent federal agents and the National Guard to confront Governor George Wallace of Alabama, who was personally blocking the entrance of black students to the University of Alabama. Both instances underscored the federal government's inability to reach out to both sides of the racial divide without falling back on the use of authoritarian measures, military force, violence, death, and extrajudicial punishment.

Northerners were also affected by Lincoln's excessive wartime spending on the military. Even though expressly prohibited by the Constitution, Congress instituted the first federal income tax to help fund the war. The tax against individuals was progressive and obligatory for all annual incomes over $600 and was enforced by the Bureau of Internal Revenue. This tax greatly affected Northern merchants and industrial laborers, who had to shoulder the burden of paying this tax in addition to a host of other increased taxes, including real estate, excise, sales, and license taxes. Lincoln's policies have had lasting repercussions, as he established dangerous precedents on the role of the executive and the expansive powers of the federal government in wartime.[32]

The Conscription Act was a failed measure, and Lincoln was forced to pursue an alternative path to increase army strength. He resorted to paying as much as $1,000 to convince men to enlist, since many Northern whites were unwilling to continue to fight in a war that was believed to be for the benefit of Southern blacks and at the expense of whites.[33] This decline in morale among white support for the Union created more of a need for black troops to fight on the front lines for the sake of their own freedom.[34] Black soldiers played an important role in the Union's victory over the Confederacy. Their freedom would be secured by the Thirteenth Amendment in 1865, but slavery and discrimination simply took new forms under the law.

LINCOLN'S PLAN FOR RECONSTRUCTION

Nearly a year after issuing the second part of the Emancipation Proclamation, Lincoln developed a plan for reconstruction of the Union. In his Proclamation of Amnesty, delivered on December 8th 1863, he articulated a plan that was nothing more than a series of concessions to the Confederacy. His lenient policy included full pardons and immediate restoration of rights upon swearing an oath of loyalty and vowing to abolish slavery.

Lincoln's vision for reconstruction was for the South to transition quickly back into the Union. But the notion of equality for blacks stuck in the craw of many whites and would hinder the process of establishing loyal governments, further alienating the South. Under Lincoln's plan, a State could be reintegrated to the

Union when just 10 percent of its voters had taken an oath of allegiance to the United States, pledging also to support emancipation. Therefore, a vast majority of the voters were excluded from the process of deciding the terms by which they would be governed. (High-ranking Confederate civil and military officers were not given the privilege of receiving pardons and rights at all.)

Congressman Thaddeus Stevens, a Republican from Pennsylvania and a leader of the House, argued that "when the doctrine that the quality and not the number of voters is to decide the right to govern, then we no longer have a republic, but the worst form of despotism."[35] Lincoln's plan also allowed the South to maintain discriminatory practices against blacks within the state constitutions as long as slavery itself was abolished. Lincoln noted that these measures could be "consistent . . . with their present condition as a laboring, landless, and homeless class."[36] Once a new state constitution acceptable to the Republicans was adopted, the South would also regain representation in Congress.

Lincoln was reluctant and unwilling to secure rights for blacks beyond emancipation. Never a supporter of complete suffrage for blacks, he suggested giving the vote to a select group of freedmen, including "the very intelligent, and especially those who have fought gallantly in our ranks."[37] He even attempted negotiations with Liberia, Haiti, and Panama to deport masses of freed blacks out of the country.[38]

While Lincoln promised an end to slavery, he did not authorize equal rights for blacks. In response, Congress challenged Lincoln's plan for Reconstruction by presenting an alternative bill. The Wade-Davis Bill of 1864 included equal rights for freedmen and required a majority of voters (who were, of course, exclusively white and male) to make an oath of allegiance to the nation before a new state government and state constitution could be created. It was a clear message by Congress that the president had overextended his executive power and that political reconciliation of the former Confederate states should be under the supervision of Congress.

Astoundingly, Lincoln vetoed the alternate bill. This action initiated a series of presidential Reconstruction failures and the start of a decade-long process of federal intervention to reintegrate the South, restore the Union, and ensure equality of rights to freed blacks. While blacks enjoyed momentary freedoms during the war and the emancipation that followed, future generations of blacks were to suffer the consequences. The South adamantly fought against Reconstruction and made sure that blacks would not be able to rise out of the legal entrapments and hostilities that were to develop from the war's aftermath. Race relations took a violent and repressive turn.

It is vital for a country's citizenry to have an accurate representation of its own history. Enshrining Lincoln as the Great Emancipator obscures a more complicated and less pleasant truth: Lincoln had the same racist tendencies as other whites in those days and cared solely about preserving the Union, not freeing the slaves. Slaves were freed in the South only when it was clear that a proclamation of freedom would aid the Union psychologically, economically, and militarily in its victory over the Confederate South.

Perhaps more interesting is the fact that across the world and in the Northern states of the United States, slavery was ended peacefully. Most Americans have only heard of how slavery was ended in the Confederacy and are unaware of how it was ended peacefully in the Northern states and in the rest of the Western Hemisphere during the nineteenth century. Abolitionists around the world combined religion, politics, public education campaigns, and the legal system to put an end to slavery. There were no wars of emancipation anywhere else but in Lincoln's America.

What if America had followed the example of the rest of the

world and ended slavery peacefully? What if we had celebrated the natural rights philosophy that man's rights to life and liberty are given by our Creator and not by the government?

Because we did not, the achievement of any semblance of equality was delayed indefinitely. Because of the violent way in which slavery was ended in the South, blacks in the former Confederacy would be victim to a vengeful white majority for the next several generations. The death and destruction caused by the Civil War only intensified the determination of former slaveholders and their allies to suppress black Americans.

The idea that the federal government would protect its black citizens was an illusion. They were a minority, and a minority has no safe harbor in a democracy that does not recognize, respect, and enforce natural rights. These troubling times for black Americans were but a presage of the evils that would afflict blacks under Jim Crow and official federal discrimination in the decades to come.

6

Abraham Lincoln and Human Freedom

Engaged in a fierce political battle for the presidency, a relatively unknown and untested politician said:

> I will say then that I am not, nor ever have been, in favor of bringing about in any way the social and political equality of the white and black races—that I am not, nor ever have been, in favor of making voters or jurors of Negroes, nor of qualifying them to hold office, nor to intermarry with white people; and I will say in addition to this that there is a physical difference between the white and black races which I believe forever forbid the two races living together on terms of social and political equality. And in as much as they cannot so live, while they do remain together there must be the position of superior and inferior, and *I as much as any other man am in favor of having the superior position assigned to the white race.*

These were Lincoln's words from his fourth debate with Stephen A. Douglas in Charleston, Illinois on September 18th 1858.

As we have seen, these were not the words of George Wallace, America's symbol for bigotry during its ugly segregation period, nor the words of David Duke, one-time Louisiana State representative and former Grand Wizard of the Ku Klux Klan. Oddly enough, they were the racist, ugly, un-American words of the so-called Great Emancipator. Lincoln has long been regarded as a champion for freedom and equal rights for blacks, but his esteemed legacy is a pretense based on myth, lies, deception, and incomplete historical accounts. Aside from a history of misleading facts, Lincoln's actions and words reveal his mainstream racist values. He actively counteracted proposals to achieve equality for blacks; in many political debates and speeches, he argued both sides of the slavery issue, and often chose to defend openly the institution of slavery, limiting his discontent only to the effect its expansion would have on the Union. A look into Lincoln's two-faced approach will reveal his inconsistencies and true aversion to social equality and freedom.

RACIST ROOTS

Abraham Lincoln first began supporting slavery in public during his time as a lawyer in Illinois. He was known to be a skilled litigator and practiced law for twenty-three years, from 1837 to 1860. Not once did he ever defend a slave, but he did represent a slave owner. In 1847, Robert Matson, a wealthy farmer who owned land in Kentucky (a slave state) and Illinois (a free state), brought his slaves from the former to the latter to be seasonal workers each spring. Controversy arose when Matson's mistress in Illinois threatened to sell the slaves. The slaves managed to escape from the plantation, but were apprehended soon after and confined to a county jail.

Matson claimed the slaves as his property and brought a lawsuit for their return. Lincoln argued on his behalf. His argument claimed that the slaves rightfully belonged to Matson because, though they temporarily worked in Illinois, they primarily resided in the slave State of Kentucky. The Illinois Supreme Court disagreed and Lincoln lost his first battle regarding the issue of slavery. Historians who present an idealized version of Lincoln's legacy emphasize that the Matson case does not suggest that he harbored pro-slavery sentiments; rather it exemplifies his unwavering commitment to the law. However, the case was the beginning of Lincoln's habit of arguing both sides of the issue.[1] To make matters worse, where Lincoln failed to uphold the institution of slavery, the federal government stepped in.

By enacting the Fugitive Slave Act of 1850, the federal government limited the court's power to emancipate slaves. The act declared that all runaway slaves were to be brought back to their masters. It also denied slaves any legal protection. They could not be represented in court, like the Matson slaves, nor were they entitled to a trial or hearing. Local authorities were also given financial incentives to enforce the law, receiving $10 for each slave's return to his or her master. Ten dollars in the nineteenth century was enough for any man to go above and beyond to ensure the institution of slavery remained intact. Further, local authorities who did not abide by the law would face $1,000 fines. On these terms, authorities aggressively captured suspected runaways. As a result, many free black Americans were arrested and sold back into slavery. Not having the right to defend themselves against the allegations, these free blacks had no other choice but to deal with injustice.[2]

Abraham Lincoln adhered to the common perception that the Constitution of the United States protected slave owners. He publicly announced it in the 1854 speech that launched his senatorial campaign in Illinois.

When the [slave owners] remind us of their constitutional rights, I acknowledge them . . . and I would give them any legislation for the reclaiming of their fugitives, which should not, in its stringency, be more likely to carry a free man into slavery, than our ordinary criminal laws are to hang an innocent one.[3]

The injustices of the Fugitive Slave Act were well known, but ignored. The United States Supreme Court upheld it and it had Lincoln's full support.

Lincoln's swift rise in the political arena gave him a national audience. Without clearly defining his position on slavery, he was able to attract wide support. Proving to be a shrewd and calculating politician, Lincoln cleverly used narrow arguments that were filled with misleading distinctions and blatant contradictions. His debates with Stephen A. Douglas for the U.S. Senate seat focused on the *expansion* of slavery as a danger to the Union, but never mentioned any opposition to the *existence* of slavery: "I have no purpose, directly or indirectly to interfere with the institution of slavery in the States where it exists. I believe I have no lawful right to do so, and I have no inclination to do so."[4] He reinforced this promise in his first inaugural address, when he repeated this very same line to the nation and reassured the nation that "those who nominated and elected me did so with full knowledge that I had made this and many similar declarations and had never recanted them."[5] In reality, Abraham Lincoln's ambiguous view on slavery was best deciphered by biographer Robert W. Johannsen when he described it as "opposition to slavery in principle, toleration of its practice, and a vigorous hostility toward the abolition movement."[6]

LINCOLN'S FIRST THIRTEENTH AMENDMENT

Lincoln strategically used the United States Constitution as a tool to resist interference with the institution of slavery. Before he was elected president, he proposed an amendment which stated in part:

> No Amendment shall be made to the Constitution which will authorize or give Congress the power to abolish or interfere, within any State, with the domestic institutions thereof, including that of persons held to labor or service by the laws of the State.[7]

The reference to domestic institutions served as a euphemism for slavery. After Lincoln was inaugurated, he instructed his Secretary of State, William H. Seward, to usher the proposed amendment through Congress. The amendment passed both the House and the Senate, but failed to gain momentum toward state ratification.

Even Lincoln's opposition to the expansion of slavery is clearly racist in origin, as it guaranteed that new territories in the West would be used exclusively by whites. His position symbolized a compromise between the small contingency of northern abolitionists, who hoped that preventing the spread of slavery would eventually lead to its demise, and white settlers, who wanted the West all to themselves. Horace Greeley, editor of the *New York Tribune* and an avid abolitionist, explained this reasoning, "All the unoccupied territory . . . shall be preserved for the benefit of the white Caucasian race—a thing which cannot be except by the exclusion of slavery."[8] The justification to end slavery in America's new territories was not based on any moral duty to uphold the natural law or need to right inherent wrongs; it came from a desire to keep blacks out of the West. The future president said as much when, in 1857, he explained why he opposed the Kansas-Nebraska Act, which would have admitted Kansas into the Union as a slave state:

> There is a natural disgust in the minds of nearly all white people to the idea of indiscriminate amalgamation of the white and black races. . . . A separation of the races is the only perfect preventive of amalgamation, but as an immediate separation is impossible, the next best thing is to keep them apart where they are not already together. If white and black people never get together in Kansas, they will never mix blood in Kansas.[9]

The concern for congressional balance of power was another key argument against the expansion of slavery. As a Republican, Lincoln wanted to ensure that Northern Republican interests were at the forefront of government policy and represented a majority in Congress. This goal could not be achieved if Southern Democrats outnumbered Republicans in Congress. According to the Three-Fifths Compromise, every five slaves were to be counted only as three persons. As a result, Democrats wielded greater political power, given their additional seats in the House of Representatives, which are calculated according to the population. As long as the Democrats controlled Congress, slavery would continue to persist without federal government interference. By keeping blacks out of the West, Lincoln kept congressional seats away from Democrats.

In reality, the Great Emancipator sought to alleviate the racial problems that plagued our country by sending the black population to settlements in either Africa or Central America. Deportation was his answer:

Racial separation must be effected by colonization of the country's blacks to foreign land. The enterprise is a difficult one, but where there is a will there is a way. . . . Let us be brought to believe it is morally right and, at the same time, favorable to, or, at least, not against, our interests, to transfer the African to his native clime, and we shall find a way to do it, however great the task may be.[10]

This statement suggests President Lincoln's willingness to rid himself and his country of its blacks, regardless of their natural rights and regardless of whether or not it was in the country's best interest. To accomplish this, he had to affirm the humanity of blacks. Only by acknowledging the fact that blacks were entitled to their natural rights would public sentiment for colonization strengthen. By crushing all sympathy for them, hatred and disgust would reign and colonization would fail. Lincoln argued that by denying the black person's humanity, supporters of slavery were laying the groundwork for "the indefinite outspreading of his bondage." The Republican program of restricting slavery to where it presently existed, he said, had the long-range benefit of denying to slaveholders an opportunity to sell their slaves in new slave territories and thus encouraged the support of gradual resettlement of blacks outside of America.

"WE SHOULD BE SEPARATED"

Colonization has always been associated with emancipation. The American Colonization Society was created in 1816 with a mission to formulate a program of black resettlement to reduce the escalating black population. The organization was able to attract each living former U.S. president, several Supreme Court justices, and many prominent politicians, including Abraham Lincoln. Because of its members, the society was able to garner federal support for its goal. In 1819, Congress approved spending $100,000 in federal funds to purchase the country known as Liberia on the west coast of Africa. Three years later, the Colonization Society began freeing slaves so they could ship them to Liberia. In short, the federal government raided Africa, robbed her of her sons and daughters, dragged them to a foreign land, denied them humanity by chaining, working, beating, brutalizing, and murdering them, then sought to send them back where they were found, as if nothing at all had happened.

As president, Abraham Lincoln attempted to implement this policy, first in May 1861, just two months into his presidency. He contemplated transporting black Americans to Panama to establish a colony that would mine the abundance of coal there for the Chiriqui Improvement Company. The plan, known as the Chiriqui Project, would have allowed the federal government to acquire discounted coal that could have been used to fuel the transcontinental railroad. It was American slavery outside of America. Lincoln ordered a secret investigation to determine if the project could be successful. The first opportunity to test the Chiriqui Project came in 1862, when Congress ended slavery in the District of Columbia and appropriated $600,000 toward the president's plan. During this time, Lincoln had already entered negotiations for colonization in Africa, Haiti, and Central America.

In order for his plan to be a success, Lincoln also needed to gain support among the free blacks. Lincoln wanted them to embrace the idea of their own deportation! To effect this, Lincoln invited five leaders in the black community to the White House to discuss the possibility of resettlement. It was the first time a black delegation ever received an invitation to the White House to discuss matters of public policy. In spite of, or maybe because of, this fact, the president made no effort to engage in conversation with his visitors, who were bluntly informed that they were there only to listen. Lincoln did not mince words:

> You and we are different races. We have between us a broader difference than exists between almost any other two races. Whether it is right or wrong I need not discuss, but this physical difference is a great disadvantage to us both, as I think your race suffers very greatly, many of them, by living among us, while ours suffers from your presence. In a word, we suffer on each side. If this is admitted, it affords a reason at least why we should be separated.[11]

Lincoln went on to tell his guests that their people would never find equality in his country, that their best bet would be to leave the continent and go where they would be treated the best. His plea was hardly persuasive. Free blacks who were sent to Liberia as part of Lincoln's test run had died shortly thereafter. Coal mines didn't provide the healthiest environments, and malaria often occurred in epidemic proportions. Still, Lincoln continued to promote colonization, despite the lack of support by the black community. His chief emigration officer, James Mitchell, placed advertisements in Northern newspapers calling for correspondence with free blacks favorable to Central American, Liberian, or Haitian emigration. Mitchell also sent a memo to black ministers in which he accused black Americans of being "half responsible" for the Civil War. He claimed that only a black exodus from America could avoid more bloodshed.[12]

Despite these efforts, black Americans were unwilling to accept deportation, and the colonization effort was further disrupted in 1862 when Central American countries learned of the idea and vehemently opposed the plan. They denounced the idea as a U.S. invasion of their territory and a brazen attempt to pass off its race problems to Central America.

President Lincoln made one last effort for black resettlement when he tried to deport black Americans to the island of Ile a Vache, off the coast of Haiti. He handed over $250,000 in federal funds to a profiteering businessman, Bernard Kock, who agreed to settle five thousand blacks on the island and provide them with housing, food, hospitals, churches, schools, and employment. Fraught with disorganization and corruption, this project also failed. Haiti's government was opposed to it, and several of the first black settlers died of starvation and disease. As a result, Lincoln was forced to transport the survivors off the island and back to the United States. He would have to find some other way to deal with the mounting racial hostility in his country.

LINCOLN'S SECOND THIRTEENTH AMENDMENT

Much of President Lincoln's actions regarding emancipation were dictated by timing. He understood the limits of the Emancipation Proclamation. "Mr. Lincoln believed that as soon as the war was over, the proclamation would become void," wrote Lincoln biographer Ida M. Tarbell. "Voters would have to then decide what slaves it freed—whether only those who had under it made an effort for their freedom and had come into the Union lines or all of those in the States and parts of States in rebellion at the time it was issued."[13] Only a constitutional amendment would provide certainty that slavery was prohibited across the United States. Not surprisingly, President Lincoln had little to do with its formation.

A bill to support an amendment to abolish slavery throughout the United States was first introduced by Representative James

Mitchell Ashley of Ohio on December 14th 1863. A similar proposal soon followed from Representative James Falconer Wilson of Iowa. Both these proposals preceded Lincoln's Emancipation Proclamation. Eventually Congress took notice. Senator John Brooks Henderson of Missouri submitted a joint resolution for a constitutional amendment abolishing slavery on January 11th 1864. Though the abolition of slavery had been primarily associated with Republicans, Henderson was a War Democrat. In February of the same year, the emphatic Massachusetts Senator Charles Sumner submitted an amendment to abolish slavery and guarantee equality: "Everywhere within the limits of the United States and of each State or Territory thereof, all persons are equal before the law, so that no person can hold another as slave."[14] As the number of proposals and the extent of their scope began to grow, on February 10th 1864, the Chairman of the Senate Judiciary Committee, Senator Lyman Trumbull of Illinois, presented the Senate with an amendment proposal combining the drafts. Numbered as Article XIII of the Amendments to the United States Constitution, it read:

> Section 1. Neither slavery nor involuntary servitude, except as punishment for crime whereof the party shall have been duly convicted, shall exist within the United States, or any place subject to their jurisdiction.

> Section 2. Congress shall have the power to enforce this article by appropriate legislation.[15]

Radical Republicans—northern Republican officeholders who advocated harsh penalties against the former Confederacy—had hoped to abolish slavery with simple congressional action and were not happy with Trumbull, but they lined up behind his amendment.

Still, the amendment was evidently thought to be in an experimental stage, for more than six weeks elapsed before the Senate took it up for action again. On March 28th 1864, Chairman Trumbull formally opened debate on the amendment in an elaborate speech. Debate continued until April 8th Speeches that attracted the most attention were those given by senators representing slave states: Senator Reverdy Johnson of Maryland and Missouri's Senator John Henderson. Senator Sumner pleaded earnestly for his phrase "all persons are equal before the law," copied from the Constitution of revolutionary France. But Senator Jacob M. Howard of Michigan, one of the soundest lawyers and clearest thinkers of the Senate, pointed out how far blacks really were from being equal before the law.[16]

The resolution passed the Senate easily on April 8th by a vote of thirty-eight to six. The battle in the House of Representatives in the spring of 1864 was much more difficult. Though President Lincoln let it be known that he favored the amendment when it entered the House, there was such formidable party strength arrayed against it that failure was a foregone conclusion. The party classification of the House stood at one hundred two Republicans, seventy-five Democrats, and nine votes from the border states. This left little chance of obtaining the required two-thirds vote in favor of the measure.[17] Nevertheless, there was still enough Republican strength to secure its discussion. Congressman Thaddeus Stevens, one of President Lincoln's strongest critics, proved to be one of the strongest supporters of the Thirteenth Amendment:

Those who believe that a righteous Providence punishes nations for national sins believe that this terrible plague is brought upon us as a punishment for our oppression of a harmless race of men inflicted without cause and without excuse for ages. I accept this belief; for I remember that an ancient despot, not so cruel as this Republic, held a people in bondage—a bondage much lighter than American slavery; that the Lord ordered him to liberate them. He refused. His whole people were punished. Plague after plague was sent upon the land until the seventh slew the firstborn of every household; nor did they cease until the tyrant "let the people go." We have suffered more than all the plagues of Egypt; more than the first-born of every household has been taken. We still harden our hearts and refuse to let the people go. The scourge still continues, nor do I expect it to cease until we obey the high behest of the Father of men.[18]

The Amendment failed by just one vote. However, it wouldn't fail twice.

In order to amend the Constitution, the proposed amendment must first be approved by two-thirds of each house of Congress and then needs to be approved by three-fourths of the states. Here, the issue was so close that only one state more was necessary. Thus the State of Nevada was organized and admitted into the Union to answer that purpose.

Another sign of encouragement followed when the State of Maryland, by popular vote, amended its constitution and abolished slavery. By this point the people had already spoken. All Abraham Lincoln had to do was give Congress a second chance. After his reelection, in his last message to Congress in December 1864, he did just that:

I venture to recommend the reconsideration and passage of the measure [Thirteenth Amendment] at the present session . . . an intervening election shows, almost certainly, that the next Congress will pass the measure if this does not . . . It is not claimed that the election has imposed a duty on members to change their views or their votes, any further than, as an additional element to be considered, their judgment may be affected by it. It is the voice of the people now, for the first time, heard upon the question. In a great national crisis, like ours, unanimity of action among those seeking a common end is very desirable—almost indispensable. And yet no approach to such unanimity is attainable, unless some deference shall be paid to the will of the majority, simply because it is the will of the majority. In this case the common end is the maintenance of the Union."[19]

Despite the numerous voices across the nation and in Congress that spoke to the equality of men and the institution of slavery as an absolute evil, the only goal for Abraham Lincoln was the "maintenance of the Union." On January 31st 1865, the House of Representatives passed the Thirteenth Amendment to the United States Constitution by a vote of 119 to 56. President Abraham Lincoln signed the Joint Resolution on February 1st 1865, and submitted the proposed amendment to the states for ratification. Secretary of State William H. Seward issued a statement verifying ratification on December 18th 1865.

Abraham Lincoln was politically manipulative and truly Machiavellian. He and his cabinet believed that they could "ride into power on the two horses of Liberty and Slavery."[20] Because of the crippling attitudes that conquered the time, attitudes that were unfortunately fostered by our forefathers, they were able to do just that. The eminent black activist Frederick Douglass best illustrated Abraham Lincoln's character:

In his interest, in his association, in his habits of thought, and in his prejudices, he was a white man. He was preeminently the white man's President, entirely devoted to the welfare of the white man. He was ready and willing at any time during the first years of his administration to deny, postpone, and sacrifice the rights of humanity in the colored people, to promote the welfare of the white people of this country.[21]

It's safe to say Lincoln wasn't the first, and certainly not the last, president to put the interests of whites in front of those of blacks.

Anyone who attempts to deviate from the common perception of Abraham Lincoln is subjected to ridicule. It is considered blasphemous to be anti-Lincoln. Lincoln has been portrayed as a saint. His defenders are so sanctimonious that they consider themselves to be self-appointed "Gatekeepers of the Truth."[22] They do whatever is necessary to keep unflattering information about Lincoln from the public discourse. As a rule, they ignore the unpleasant facts about Lincoln, like his support of a constitutional amendment prohibiting the federal government from ever interfering with Southern slavery, his repeated attempts to deport the entire black community, and his constant white supremacist rhetoric. There have been heated debates over the legacies of every other American president, but no such debate is politically acceptable regarding Lincoln.

This is yet another reason why legitimate discussions about race are taboo in our culture. Only by facing the truth, accepting the flaws of our forefathers, and learning from our past can we achieve cross-racial, cross-historical, and cross-cultural understanding. And only with this understanding can we move forward together and foster the environment that is so essential to the American way, an environment where one can earnestly say with a straight face that all men are created equal. And facing the truth about race necessarily begins with facing the truth about Abraham Lincoln.

7

Reconstruction: Military Rule in the Post–Civil War South

The military rule of the former Confederacy during Reconstruction transformed Southern society. If the South felt humiliated by its defeat in the Civil War, the period of Reconstruction proved to be even more demoralizing and painful. In just over a decade, a hostile occupying power wiped away economic and social institutions that had persevered for 250 years. Reconstruction was to leave bitter and lasting memories for Southerners, and, as soon as federal troops departed, this bitterness led them to react by creating the racist laws of the Jim Crow system.

But if white Southerners saw their world turned upside down, blacks in the former Confederacy hardly saw their lives improve after Emancipation. Although blacks could no longer be held in bondage, they were marginalized by discriminatory laws that were embedded in state constitutions and supported by the federal government. Four million blacks suddenly found themselves free in name but struggling to merge with a society where their rights were consistently restricted to ensure their status as a laboring class. Even constitutional guarantees in the form of the Thirteenth, Fourteenth, and Fifteenth Amendments did not have any practical influence on giving blacks equal treatment before the law. The Southern states quickly enacted laws and codes to circumvent the new amendments to the Constitution, and the federal government overlooked these legal digressions to avoid aggravating the tenuous postwar relationship with the South. Throughout the era of Reconstruction, equality did not follow freedom for blacks, as governments at all levels sought to widen the distinction between the races and erect racial barriers. Reconstruction was intended to be a period of reformation, but federal mandates provoked white resentment and created a lasting legacy of hatred against blacks that would endure to the twenty-first century.

The end of the Civil War marked the complete destruction of Confederate authority and exposed the vulnerability of the South. Plantations lay neglected, battlefields were abandoned, and there was an overwhelming sense of defeat that weakened Southern morale. The war had drained the South of all its resources, and transformation of Southern society was the only hope for economic recovery. While Southern cities lay in ruin, wartime industrialization and free market commerce had led to rapid growth and prosperity in the North. The Southern states were denied political representation in the federal government and actually lost their sovereignty. The North radically reorganized the economies and the political structure of the South. However, these policies excluded federal assistance for blacks, who were left defenseless and economically debilitated by slavery and therefore unprepared to enter society as freedmen without necessary changes to federal and state institutions.[1]

Restoring order to the South and reuniting the nation was the government's primary concern. The solution was for the Union army to maintain control of the civil and military affairs of the

South. This was the first time in U.S. history when the army played such a substantial role in political, judicial, and police functions. The South was under martial law; the Constitution was exiled. Such intrusion and denial of self-governance led to widespread resentment of the new order by white Southerners. Strict regulations were imposed, and citizens were required to declare ironclad oaths of allegiance and loyalty to the Union before being allowed simple freedoms like mailing a letter or allowing children to play in the streets.[2] Daily activities became luxuries, as occupation forces could prohibit any action they deemed contrary to the interests of or disloyal to the Union. The very soldiers who were stationed to promote peace contradicted this objective by inciting violence and instability.[3]

Military forces often protected blacks from violent riots and other instances of mistreatment and abuse by Southern whites.[4] This interference with daily life led to conflicts between the occupation forces and civilians who were unwilling to have the federal government restructure their way of life through military rule.[5]

THE FAILED ATTEMPTS OF
PRESIDENTIAL RECONSTRUCTION

After the surrender of the Confederate army at Appomattox Court House, Virginia, the Union army remained in the Southern states without formal directions from either Congress or the president. President Lincoln's premature Reconstruction policy had already faltered in a few states, as it extended pardons and restored power to the former Confederate leaders and plantation aristocracy who had revolted against the Union. These policies put the president in direct conflict with Congress, which was unwilling to recognize disloyal Southern governments run by the same pre-war political leaders.

However, Lincoln was assassinated just nine days after the South's surrender, so Reconstruction efforts were temporarily halted. Vice President Andrew Johnson assumed the presidency, and he quickly implemented a forgiving Reconstruction policy that was influenced in part by his racial attitudes, his Southern roots, his belief in a limited federal government, narrow interpretation of the Constitution, and agreement with Lincoln's sympathetic approach to the South. The military was to have limited interference with the governance of the states and would use its authority as a last resort, and only to preserve public peace. Johnson's policy appealed to the South because it gave the promise of self-government while denying any civil rights to the freedmen.[6]

Congress treated the former Confederacy like conquered territory, forcing the formerly rebellious States to ratify the Thirteenth Amendment as a condition for returning to the Union. With little alternative, seven of the eleven former Confederate states satisfied this condition, and by the end of 1865, the Thirteenth Amendment was incorporated into the Constitution. Once freedom was legally granted to the slaves, the South felt the true economic impact of losing the Civil War when the labor base for the plantation system disappeared. This force-feeding of an amendment was the first of many instances when the people in the South were made aware that failure to accept certain policies of the Republican-dominated Congress would result in prolonged interferences with basic freedoms, their own natural rights, principles of democracy, state rights, and further rejection of political representation in Congress.[7]

The abolition of slavery under the Thirteenth Amendment led to great uncertainty and instability for the freedmen, who were exercising basic rights for the first time. The unresolved issue was how to integrate and accept the freedmen into a society founded on racial divisions. The Freedmen's Bureau, originally created by the Lincoln administration in 1863 after the Emancipation Proclamation, was extended as a temporary government program to help emancipated slaves adjust to their new freedom. In creating the bureau, the federal government aimed to encourage economic and political stability for the freedmen by providing medical supplies, building schools, managing abandoned property, and approving labor contracts between freedmen and employers. The Freedmen's Bureau was highly disliked by whites, since federal assistance was looked upon as preferential treatment for blacks. Even free blacks worried about the Bureau's aims; Frederick Douglass speculated that government assistance may "serve to keep up the very prejudices, which it is so desirable to banish" if blacks were given special treatment.[8]

President Andrew Johnson, who owned eight slaves before the war, supported emancipation but argued against equality for the freedmen.[9] Johnson's racist attitudes were well known by his contemporaries and even the American public. In 1867 Johnson delivered his annual message to Congress in which he stated that blacks had

> less capacity for government than any other race of people. No independent government of any form has ever been successful in their hands. On the contrary, wherever they have been left to their own devices they have shown a constant tendency to relapse into barbarism.[10]

This inflammatory statement is surely one of the most ignorant, racist statements ever made by an American president on public record. It is also wrong. A revolt by slaves in Haiti that was led by Toussaint L'Ouverture, a former slave himself, resulted in complete emancipation of all slaves and the 1804 declaration of the first black-ruled nation in the Western Hemisphere. And Johnson also ignored the many African countries such as Egypt, Carthage, Morocco, Ethiopia, Sudan, and the kingdoms of West Africa that had created advanced and independent civilizations, many lasting for hundreds of years. He probably never read *Othello*.

Johnson favored quick restoration of the economy and political structure of the South, and black rights and racial equality had no place in this goal. Johnson contemplated a policy of black emigration to other countries and maintained that black suffrage and equal rights were within the control of the states, not the federal government. It was this uncompromising racial attitude, rooted in prejudice and hatred, which shaped Andrew Johnson's Reconstruction policy.[11]

President Johnson's Reconstruction plan was executed through two proclamations. The first, on May 29th 1865, was issued just forty-five days after taking office and fifty-four days after the end of the Civil War. It extended amnesty and pardons for former Confederates who expressed loyalty to the Union and supported emancipation of the slaves. Johnson believed that the states did not forfeit their right to self-governance by seceding from the Union, and this was reflected in his extremely conciliatory attitude toward the leaders of the Confederacy.[12] Johnson excluded Confederate leaders and the economic elite who had taxable property that exceeded $20,000 in value, but they were allowed to request presidential pardons on an individual basis.[13] But even these prominent rebels and Southern leaders were eventually cleared by the president. By the end of Johnson's presidency in 1868, he abandoned this policy and issued a universal pardon of all former Confederate leaders, including those who were indicted for treason or any other felony. It was Johnson's belief that these leaders were necessary to maintain white influence and political leadership in the South.[14]

President Johnson appointed provisional governors to each of the eleven Southern states to carry out executive Reconstruction measures and to secure Southern political support for the president. (He had no authority to do this. The Constitution guarantees and requires a republican form of government in all states, meaning that the governor and the legislature must be popularly elected.) To achieve this goal, the governors were given the power to appoint state and local officials across the South. The former Southern ruling class was restored to power as state governors allowed former Confederate leaders to take control of local offices to influence the public into accepting Reconstruction policies.[15] In effect, these measures undermined the basic idea of Reconstruction by allowing the leaders of antebellum Southern society to return to power post-war.

The federally appointed State governors did very little to aid the cause of blacks, instead preferring to court the good favor of whites by reassuring them that emancipation would not change the social status of blacks. Whites were assured that blacks would remain subordinate, and equality and the right to vote would not accompany their freedom.[16] In fact, in many states slavery was allowed to persist, and this blatant denial of emancipation was endorsed by some of the federally appointed State governors. Florida Governor William Martin directed freedmen to "call your old Master 'Master,'" and in Mississippi blacks were forced back to work on plantations.[17] In fact, Mississippi did not formally ratify the Thirteenth Amendment until 1995.

A subversive form of slavery was reintroduced in the South and mandated by state laws, as a system of labor was required for plantations to resume operations. What developed from these state laws was the system of sharecropping. Since former Confederate leaders had control of political affairs across the Southern states, laws were implemented to enforce plantation labor agreements by fining or punishing blacks who were unemployed. In certain states like South

Carolina, blacks were fined if they attempted to pursue occupations other than farmer or servant.[18] Freedmen were ultimately forced into labor agreements with planters in which they farmed the land in exchange for giving a portion of their profits to the landowner. These contracts were based on good faith, and white employers often betrayed the terms of the agreements. The system was marred by discriminatory practices, as unfair rates led to mounting debts and some freedmen were auctioned off as servants to satisfy these debts. Once again, black workers made significant contributions to the revitalization of the South's economy, and the South's recovery from its losses was at the expense of black labor.[19]

Southern states further circumvented the Reconstruction plans of President Johnson by enacting a number of laws and penalties to reinstate slavery and plantation discipline. The first of these were referred to as "black codes." Really just slave codes with a different name, the black codes hindered black freedom by denying the blacks the right to vote, the right to serve on a jury unless a black person was on trial, and the right to relocate around the country unless employed.[20] The Southern states also established labor regulations and biased criminal laws against blacks, so that plantation labor contracts were their only real option for employment in the South. These regulations were enforced by both the police and the courts, since it was the state that had the power to use bodily punishment, enforce unpaid labor for public projects, and impose long prison terms.[21]

The state had replaced the master.

Blacks were subject to taxes without receiving any state benefits and were excluded from public institutions and services like public transportation, hospitals, schools, parks, and public meetings. The states insisted that it was the responsibility of the federal Freedmen's Bureau to provide public services and necessities to blacks, not the states themselves. The states that did provide services for blacks used only the revenue raised from taxes collected from blacks for those services. The state courts continued to uphold these repressive legal measures, and they were not directly challenged until the passage of the first federal Civil Rights Act in 1866, which overturned many of these state laws.[22]

Reconstruction did not rid the South of the relics of slavery and instead spawned new state regulations that were committed to enslaving blacks by the rule of law. President Johnson failed to move the Southern states to adopt the principles of free labor. The South returned to its pre-war system of forced plantation labor, instead of reshaping the economy to keep up with the North's industrial growth and the trend toward free markets and labor. For many stubborn former Confederates, losing the Civil War did not mean they needed to reject the economic and social system of the antebellum South.[23] Any federal attempt to disrupt this system was met with intense opposition from the planter class. As the need for plantation labor dissolved, white Southerners associated modernization of the South with economic independence for blacks. These unrepentant former Confederates were joined by the president in fighting to keep the planter class in power so as to avoid any possible change.[24] Discrimination against blacks only confirmed that their vindication would have to come from the federal government in the form of additional constitutional guarantees to trump state laws and practices.

CONGRESSIONAL TAKEOVER OF RECONSTRUCTION

When Congress reconvened in December 1865, the Joint Committee on Reconstruction was established and the failure of

President Johnson's Reconstruction efforts began to come to light. The Joint Committee, composed of fifteen members from the House and fifteen from the Senate, received reports and heard testimony by army officers, Southern unionists, freedmen, and Freedmen Bureau agents on the unfavorable conditions of blacks in the South. The riots of 1866 also revealed the insufficiency of presidential attempts at Reconstruction, when violence between blacks and whites erupted in the streets of Southern cities like Memphis and New Orleans. The Radical Republicans in Congress used these reports to argue that the Southern States could not manage their own affairs despite presidential Reconstruction efforts, and that federal military intervention was necessary.[25]

Congress approved the First and Second Reconstruction Acts over President Johnson's vetoes in March 1867; these prolonged military rule in the Southern states except Tennessee (the President's home state). The stated purpose of these acts was to create loyal governments and overhaul pre-war state constitutions; they were about power, not freedom or equality. The South was carved into five military districts, with military commanders overseeing the political Reconstruction process. The first district encompassed Virginia; the second district was North and South Carolina; the third district was Georgia, Alabama, and Florida; the fourth district was Mississippi and Arkansas; and the fifth district was Texas and Louisiana. Congress granted extensive powers to the military commanders, who had the right to remove civil officials from office, interfere with judicial proceedings, amend judgments, conduct military trials, and use troops to suppress any disturbances. While the military was given considerable powers under the law, it was weak in numbers, with only twenty thousand troops to police the entire South.

Military rule was intended to be a temporary measure, but the Radical Republicans in Congress used wartime expansion of federal power to reshape and strengthen the Union at the expense of states' rights.[26] The Radical Republicans came to power after the elections of 1866 and were largely concerned with preventing amnesty from being granted to Southerners who had fought for the Confederacy, barring these so-called traitors from exercising their right to vote. Did anyone in Washington pay any attention to the Constitution?

President Johnson was opposed to Congress's expansion of the federal government and believed that there was no constitutional justification or established precedent to violate state sovereignty. Johnson argued that every U.S. citizen should have the right to "be left to the free exercise of his own judgment when he is engaged in the work of forming the fundamental law under which he is to live." He also argued that the Reconstruction Acts constituted a "stride toward centralization, and the concentration of all legislative powers in the national Government."[27] He agreed with the Southern states that the Union was composed by agreement of the states, not dominated by a federal power.

However, Senator Charles Sumner, a Radical Republican from Massachusetts and a Senate leader, and Congressman Thaddeus Stevens, a Radical Republican from Pennsylvania and a leader in the House, teamed up to form a coalition to direct congressional policy to increase federal power to reconstruct the South and focus on civil rights for blacks. Both of these Northerners had already become well known in the South as virulent opponents of the Confederacy, who often launched into personal attacks on Southern politicians. Before the war, Sumner had so cruelly mocked a Southern senator as to provoke a beating with a cane by the senator's relative on the floor of the Senate.

Like many of his fellow Radical Republicans, Congressman Stevens described the South as a fallen foe when he said, "We are making a nation. . . . The vanquished Southern states had sacrificed their constitutional standing and could be treated by Congress as conquered provinces."[28] Other members of Congress looked to the Constitution for justification of federal power over states that had ceased to provide republican governments. Senator Sumner made the following statement on Congressional power, revealing some belated constitutional qualms: "There is no other clause which gives to Congress such supreme power over the states."[29] Meanwhile the Democrats in Congress recognized that military rule symbolized "the death-knell of civil liberty."[30]

Congress passed the Civil Rights Act of 1866 over President Johnson's veto, to ensure equality for the freedmen. The bill declared that all citizens were to have equal rights regardless of race, and no state could deprive any citizen of these rights. It was the first legislative measure to define citizen rights and gave the federal government the right to interfere against discriminatory state laws. Congress feared that the Civil Rights Act was susceptible to a constantly changing political environment that could be overturned by presidential veto, congressional repeal, or judicial review. To safeguard these rights, a constitutional amendment was needed. The Joint Committee on Reconstruction proposed the Fourteenth Amendment. It was designed to embody the rights outlined in the Civil Rights Acts of 1866.[31]

Like the Thirteenth Amendment, Congress promised readmission for the Southern states if they ratified the proposed Fourteenth Amendment. While an express provision for readmission died in both houses of Congress, it was still used to entice the Southern states to adopt the amendment. Tennessee was used as an example when the state's senators and congressmen were allowed to regain their seats in Congress after the state ratified the amendment. The South had little choice but to comply with the demands of Congress. With the Southern members of Congress locked out and

President Johnson, the South's primary ally, weakened by impeachment trials, the South was left politically powerless to counter Congress's Reconstruction amendments. In fewer than two years, the Southern states ratified the Fourteenth Amendment, allowing it to be adopted into the Constitution in 1868.[32]

After the passage of the Fourteenth Amendment, one final element of citizenship for blacks remained to be addressed from the federal perspective. Congressional Republicans saw the right to vote as a political freedom that would allow blacks to secure economic independence. If blacks were given the right to vote, they would be responsible for their future success without having to rely on the government. A Congressional Act of March 2nd 1867, granted blacks the first opportunity to vote when Congress dictated that male citizens twenty-one years and older, regardless of race or color, could participate in writing new constitutions while former Confederates were barred from the process. The aim was to transfer political power away from the former Confederates and rebels associated with secession, as well as the wealthy planters who had maintained political dominion throughout the antebellum period and during Johnson's post-war provisional governments. Only three groups qualified as delegates under the Act: Blacks whose loyalty was evident by their participation in the war, northerners who migrated to the South seeking business opportunities (commonly referred to as carpetbaggers), and white Southerners who had submitted to the oath of allegiance (but were considered traitors by Confederate Southerners and were accordingly referred to as scalawags).

In most states, blacks represented only a small minority among the three groups, and there were only a few black leaders with educational training who were influential in shaping the new constitutions.[33] Overall, Southern whites were not eager to have blacks and

Northerners reconstruct their state constitutions. An anonymous Louisiana legislator writing in The New Orleans *Crescent* on January 13th 1869, referred to the new state constitutions as the "work of the lowest and most corrupt body of men ever assembled in the South. It was the work of ignorant negroes cooperating with a gang of white adventurers, strangers to our interests and sentiments." This statement echoed the public sentiment of many Southern whites, who resented the fact that blacks were politically endowed with voting rights while many whites had been stripped of their own.[34]

The Fifteenth Amendment made voting rights permanent for black males a year after the franchise was extended to them in the Southern state conventions. Congress passed the proposed amendment on February 26th 1869, and it was ratified days before Ulysses S. Grant took office as president on March 4th of the same year. The leading Union general during the war, President Grant was considered a Radical Republican. After years of conflicts between Congress and President Johnson over the best course of action for the South, Congress saw Grant as a likely supporter of Radical Reconstruction.[35]

COUNTER-RECONSTRUCTION MOVEMENT

Southern resentment at the domination and control by the North only increased as the Radical Republicans reformed Southern politics, restructured the economy, and attempted to confer equal rights on blacks. In reaction to Congress's enforcement of the Fourteenth and Fifteenth Amendments, organizations of white militants began to flourish to counteract Reconstruction. White militant organizations were created immediately after the Civil War, but their influence increased during Radical Reconstruction and white supremacist ideology became the reigning policy of the South.

These groups believed that violence against blacks and white sympathizers would deter any progress toward equal rights for blacks. White supremacist ideals calmed the fears of white Southerners who believed that Congress was trying to rob them of their elevated social, economic, and political standing by conferring equal rights on blacks. Organizations such as the White League, the Red Shirts, and the Ku Klux Klan used violence to intimidate blacks from holding political office or voting for anyone supporting congressional Reconstruction. These groups effectively destroyed the weak political and economic stability that Congress was trying to build in the South.[36]

Washington recognized that counter-Reconstruction by white militant organizations would reverse Reconstruction efforts, raising fears that the South would once again succumb to white rebellion against the federal government. President Grant recognized that blacks were driven away from the polls by threats of violence, undermining the aims of the Fifteenth Amendment. In a message to Congress in December 1870, Grant acknowledged, "the free exercise of the elective franchise has by violence and intimidation been denied to citizens in several of the states lately in rebellion."[37] He sought to conserve black voting rights by forcing the South to comply with congressional demands, such as supervised elections and criminal laws that made interference with elections punishable by fines or imprisonment. Grant also threatened to suspend *habeas corpus* (as Lincoln had done) and used martial law to combat the growing power of white supremacist organizations.[38] These measures were met with bitter opposition and only increased backlash among white Southerners. White Southerners were now emboldened to rid the South of federal interference. Congressional Reconstruction was heading toward collapse, as Southerners refused to pay taxes to fund the ever-expanding government and continued their campaign of violence. Slowly, Democrats were growing in strength against the Republicans in local and state Southern governments.[39]

Southern whites persisted in keeping black males away from the polls. Each state created a system of laws and conditions that effectively disenfranchised blacks without violating the terms of the Fifteenth Amendment, which prevents federal and state governments from restricting the right to vote on account of race, color, or prior condition as a slave. These rules included poll taxes, voter registration waiting periods, and intricate ballot and voting rules that excluded the poor and illiterate. Since these measures also disenfranchised poor whites, complex loopholes were created to prevent their exclusion and ensure a majority of white voters. Exceptions to the rules barring citizens from voting included subjective and biased "good character" clauses or an understanding of the state constitution as a substitute for literacy tests. There were also "fighting grandfather" clauses for those who had a grandfather who had voted or fought for the Confederacy during the Civil War. Despite these measures, the loopholes failed to enfranchise poor white voters, who were unwilling or hesitant to exercise their voting rights.[40] These deceptive tactics were widely practiced across the South and largely went uncontested. Southern efforts to restrict the vote were so coordinated that "[e]ach state became in effect a laboratory for testing one device or another. Indeed, the cross-fertilization and coordination between the movements to restrict the suffrage in the Southern states amounted to a public conspiracy."[41]

Southern methods of disenfranchisement continued to gain strength and momentum through the late 1890s and considerably weakened voter turnout. In Mississippi, black voter turnout had dropped to 17 percent by 1900 after the state adopted both a $2.00 poll tax and a literacy test at the constitutional convention in

1890. Black voter turnout in South Carolina also fell from 83.7 percent in 1880 to 18 percent in 1900. Florida, Tennessee, and Arkansas had similar results.[42] These statistics show that the voting regulations created by white Southerners completely marginalized the political power of blacks by denying them their constitutional right to vote under the Fifteenth Amendment. It would not be until the passage of the Voting Rights Act of 1965, one hundred years after the Civil War, that Southern blacks would see their constitutional right to vote guaranteed.

REDEMPTION AS A RETURN TO THE STATUS QUO

The political climate that had kept Southern power at bay began to change in 1870, as conservative Southern Democrats began to trump Radical Republican control of Congress. After meeting congressional measures, eight Southern states were readmitted into the Union by 1875, leaving Florida, South Carolina, and Louisiana under military rule. Once they returned to power, conservative Southern Democrats stripped each state of all Reconstruction measures enacted over the years. The defeat of radical rule was in part due to the decline of any federal interest in reforming the South. Many of the most passionate leaders for Reconstruction had either died or left office. The North was now eager to mend political relations with the South and renew business relations.

In a further blow to Radical Reconstruction, federal troops were completely removed from the South by 1877. The results of the presidential election of 1876 between Republican Rutherford B. Hayes and Democrat Samuel J. Tilden left neither with a majority in the Electoral College. The Constitution states that if no presidential candidate receives a majority in the Electoral College, then the president-elect will be selected by a vote of the members of the House of Representatives, with each state casting a single vote. Southern Democrats in the House of Representatives struck an informal deal with the Republicans to support Hayes if all federal troops were removed from the South. The Republicans agreed to the deal, sealing a formal end to the Reconstruction era.

Reconstruction was ultimately a failure. The efforts by the federal government to impose conditions upon the South to gain readmission to the Union and the continued efforts by Radical Republicans to force change on an unwilling South did more harm than good. These demands only inflamed the sense of shame that many white Southerners had felt at the loss of the Civil War. The Reconstruction amendments and preferential government programs for freedmen only added to the sense among whites in the South that the Union was making them pay for their defeat.

In the end, the South was able to return to its pre-war ways of trampling the rights of blacks, but with an intensified sense of blacks as having caused the federal government to intervene in Southern affairs. Were it not for the federal government seeking to protect and elevate blacks, the reasoning went, the Southern states would have been free to return to the way things were before the war. Although designed to bring social equality and civil rights, the Reconstruction amendments sparked bitterness and rage as whites conspired to disenfranchise and demoralize blacks. In effect, blacks came to personify federal interventionism and interference in the minds of white Southerners. This is not to say that racism did not also play a role, but the white supremacist movement gained much of its traction with white Southerners by tapping into a widespread feeling of humiliation and defeat. Reconstruction spawned a bitterness that would reverberate well into the twentieth century.

8

Jim Crow

We often hear that everyone is entitled to his own opinion. Imagine a world in which a select group of people is able to codify its opinion into law and decide on its own, without trial, whether or not someone else violated that law. These people then violently torture and murder their targets while having complete support from the community, the police, and the government. This was America during Jim Crow.

A dark era in American history, Jim Crow dates from the late 1890s (when Southern states began to reinforce, in law and state constitutional provisions, the subordinate position of blacks in society) to 1964, when the Civil Rights Act and, a year later, the Voting Rights Act finally began to chip away at it. After almost two hundred years of the devastation that was American slavery, there followed almost a hundred years of sickening white supremacy aimed at crushing the spirit of black Americans everywhere.

FOREFATHERS OF JIM CROW:
THE UNITED STATES SUPREME COURT

Jim Crow laws separated blacks from whites in all public accommodations, forbade the commingling of the two races, and prevented blacks from exercising the right to vote. The term *Jim Crow* origi-nated in a song performed by Daddy Rice, a white minstrel show entertainer in the 1830s. Rice covered his face with charcoal paste or burnt cork to resemble a black man and then sang and danced in caricature of a black buffoon whom Rice called Jim Crow.[1] The Jim Crow character was one of many that stereotyped black Americans as inferior and subordinate to whites. The phrase became shorthand for the continued lawful degradation of blacks.

This racial ostracism extended to churches, schools, housing, jobs, all forms of public transportation, sports, recreation, hospitals, orphanages, prisons, funeral homes, morgues, and even cemeteries. In Alabama, it was a crime for blacks and whites to play cards at the same table or walk down the same sidewalks. Blacks and whites who worked in the same factories were required to look out different windows (with the window reserved for blacks rarely having a decent view). As witnesses in court, blacks and whites had to swear on dif-ferent Bibles. In every state in the South, this system of legalized seg-regation was fully in place by 1910.[2]

During the period of Reconstruction, blacks were accepted on trains and streetcars, at the polls, in the courts and legislatures, and in the police service. Studies throughout the South indicated that at no time was it the general demand of the whites in the Reconstruction-era South that blacks be disenfranchised and white supremacy be made the law of the land. Blacks and whites in the South went to the same restaurants and both were served at the same tables. In fact, it would be no surprise for white and black people to engage in conversation for no other purpose than to pass the time. T. McCants Stewart, corresponding editor of the *New York Freeman* once acknowledged, "I think the whites of the South are really less afraid to have contact with colored people than the whites of the North."[3]

The reality is Jim Crow laws gained significant momentum from decisions and laws of the federal government. The United States Supreme Court fathered Jim Crow by ruling unconstitutional the Civil Rights Act of 1875. The act stated in part, "All persons within the jurisdiction of the United States shall be entitled to the full and equal enjoyment of the accommodations, advantages, facilities, and privileges of inns, public conveyances on land or water, theaters, and other places of public amusement; subject only to the conditions and limitations established by law, and applicable alike to citizens of every race and color, regardless of any previous condition of servitude."[4] The Court reviewed five separate cases—referred to collectively as the *Civil Rights Cases*—in 1883, all involving discrimination across the nation. In declaring the act unconstitutional, Justice Joseph Bradley held that the Fourteenth Amendment, which states that "no state shall deprive any person of life, liberty, or property, without due process of law; nor deny to any person within its jurisdiction the equal protection of the laws,"[5] did not protect black people from discrimination by private businesses and individuals in their private capacity, but only from discrimination by the government or individuals in their official governmental capacity. Ignoring the argument that public services were operated under state permission and were sometimes owned by the states, thus subject to public control, and that private racial segregation had the force of state law behind it, he went on to declare that it was time for blacks to assume "the rank of a mere citizen" and stop being the "special favorite of the laws."[6]

Making sure to treat black people as mere citizens, organized bands of white vigilantes terrorized blacks who tried to vote, associate with whites, or consciously or unconsciously defied the "color line" inherited from the slave era. Waves of violence and vigilante terrorism swept across the South during the 1860s and

1870s. In each Southern state, blacks found themselves exercising limited suffrage due to their votes being manipulated by white landlords and merchant suppliers, stolen by fraud at the ballot boxes, or otherwise compromised at every turn. In Mississippi, the method of controlling black votes and regulating blacks' economic and public lives through full-scale and openly brutal violence was known as the Mississippi Plan of 1875—mobs of whites openly killed hundreds of black voters in a bloody rampage that recognized no boundaries. Riots erupted as white people attacked campaign rallies, killing schoolteachers, church leaders, and Republican Party organizers. President Ulysses S. Grant refused to send in troops.[7]

As if the Mississippi Plan weren't enough, in the 1890s the Second Mississippi Plan came about as the State began formally and legally to segregate and to disfranchise blacks by changing its state constitution and passing supportive legislation. Other Southern states soon followed suit.

Prior to the flood of segregation and political disfranchisement statutes that emerged in the late 1890s, Southern whites took legal steps to subordinate blacks in every other aspect of life as well. Between 1870 and 1884, eleven Southern states banned interracial marriages. According to the historian William Cohen, these bans were the "ultimate segregation laws," in that they clearly spelled out the idea that whites were superior to blacks and that any mixing of the two threatened white status and the purity of the white race.[8] School segregation laws were also enacted in nearly every Southern state prior to 1888.

The South's embrace of extreme racism was due to a number of factors: The horrific violence of the Civil War; the destruction by the Union Army of private property in the South; the abandonment of the basic rules of war by General William Sherman in North

Carolina, South Carolina, and Georgia; the abandonment of the rule of law by Lincoln's troops and the federal government during Reconstruction; and the attitude that blacks were utterly inferior to whites, to name a few. All of this, and the decades of hell that followed, might have been avoided had the federal government immediately freed the slaves rather than kill their masters in the Civil War.

After the horrendous bloodshed that came with the Civil War, the North ended up conceding that it could not prevent the South from keeping blacks in a position of inferiority. Northern retreat on race allowed Southern Redeemers—those Southern politicians who opposed Reconstruction and civil rights for blacks—to break their pledge to protect the constitutional rights of black individuals. As the South continued to veer toward extremism, Northern opinion shifted further and further away from shielding blacks from oppression.[9]

The failure of liberal politicians in the North and South to resist Jim Crow was due in part to political factors. Reconciliation with the South was of paramount importance, and since race relations was the source of sectional strife, liberals joined in defending the Southern view of race in its less extreme forms. It was quite common in the newspapers of the time to find Northern liberals and former abolitionists supporting white supremacy by bemoaning the innate inferiority of black human beings and their hopeless unfitness for full participation in "the white man's civilization."[10] Such expression added to the reconciliation of the North and South but did so at the expense of blacks. Just as blacks gained their emancipation and new rights through a falling-out between white men, they now lost those rights through a reconciliation of white men.

America desperately needed to transcend the racism that had clutched its soul and reaffirm the belief in liberty and equality on which our nation was founded. Only by upholding the natural law and the Fourteenth Amendment principles of a color-blind government could this be accomplished.

SEPARATE BUT EQUAL

In 1896, the Supreme Court of the United States had its opportunity, its second chance. Unfortunately, instead of bravely taking a stand against segregation, eight of the Court's nine justices refused to rule against Jim Crow. The Supreme Court's decision in *Plessy v. Ferguson* was to serve as the organized legal justification for racial segregation for the next fifty years. As part of its attempts to reverse the gains made by blacks during Reconstruction, the State of Louisiana passed the Separate Car Act, a law which required railroads to provide separate accommodations for whites and blacks. The Citizen's Committee to Test the Separate Car Act, a coalition of both white and black citizens of New Orleans, drafted a man named Homer Plessy to challenge the law directly. Because Plessy was one-eighth black and could "pass" as white, the Citizen's Committee hoped to expose the racial prejudice that was at the core of the law.

On June 7th 1892, Homer Plessy boarded a whites-only car of the East Louisiana Railroad. When he refused to leave the car when asked to do so by whites, he was arrested and jailed. In *Homer Adolph Plessy v. The State of Louisiana,* Judge John Howard Ferguson ruled that Louisiana could regulate railroad companies so long as they operated in state boundaries. Plessy took it to the Supreme Court of Louisiana, where he again found an unreceptive ear. Plessy appealed to the United States Supreme Court in 1896.

In that decision, the Supreme Court of the United States decided, seven to one (one justice did not participate), that the Louisiana law was constitutional, enshrining the separate-but-equal doctrine that would be used to defend Jim Crow laws from judicial scrutiny until the second half of the twentieth century. The challenge to the law argued that it denied equal protection under the law guaranteed under the Fourteenth Amendment and violated the Thirteenth Amendment's prohibition of slavery by continuing its central features.

The majority opinion, delivered by Justice Henry Billings Brown, attacked the Thirteenth Amendment claim by distinguishing between political and social equality. He reasoned that blacks and whites were politically equal, in that they had the same legal rights, but socially unequal because blacks were not as socially advanced as whites:

> Legislation is powerless to eradicate racial instincts or to abolish distinctions based on physical differences, and the attempt to do so can only result in accentuating the differences of the present situation. If the civil and political rights of both races be equal, one cannot be inferior to the other civilly or politically. If one race be inferior to the other socially, the Constitution of the United States cannot put them on the same plane.[11]

The majority rejected the Fourteenth Amendment's spirit by claiming that both races were treated equally under the law, since whites were forbidden to sit in railroad cars designated for blacks the same way blacks were forbidden to sit in railroad cars designated for whites. The Court went on to say that enforced separation does not "stamp" blacks with a badge of inferiority unless the "colored race chooses to put that construction on it."[12]

In a phrase that would become the legal underpinning for Jim Crow laws for the next sixty years, the Court ruled that the

Constitution permitted the states to allow separate accommodations and facilities for each race, but they must be equal. Indeed, "separate but equal" facilitated, encouraged, and protected Jim Crow laws for the next three generations. Exercising common sense and thinking years ahead of his time, Justice John Marshall Harlan,[13] in the lone dissenting opinion, noted that while the law may appear to treat blacks and whites equally, "every one knows that the statute in question had its origin in the purpose, not so much to exclude white persons from railroad cars occupied by blacks, as to exclude colored people from coaches occupied by or assigned to white persons."[14]

In *Plessy*, not only did the Supreme Court deny that state-enforced separation discriminated against black people, it also implied that racial segregation was in the nature of things.[15] By sanctioning such laws, the Court stimulated brutal aggression against the rights of black citizens.

With the Supreme Court—the last lawful protector of blacks' rights—giving a green light, Jim Crow laws were rapidly expanded across the South and into many Northern states as well. The right of black Americans to vote came under heavy attack. And while the Fifteenth Amendment prohibited denying the right to vote on the grounds of "race, color, or previous condition of servitude," the men who framed the new state constitutions freely admitted that their suffrage provisions were designated to eliminate black voters. "Discrimination! Why, that is precisely what we propose," admitted Carter Glass of Virginia. "Doesn't it let the white man vote," asked E. B. Kruttschnitt of Louisiana, "and doesn't it stop the Negro from voting, and isn't that what we came here for?" The South's new qualifications for voting—literacy tests, residency requirements, property qualifications, poll taxes, and tests of how well a prospective voter "understood" the Constitution—never mentioned race. Since they did not discriminate "on their face," with its decision in *Williams v. Mississippi* in 1898, the Supreme Court accepted them.[16]

PERFECTLY NORMAL HUMAN BEINGS

These new restrictions on black voting were accompanied by inhumane acts of violence and a wave of vicious lynchings that gripped the South for decades. Between 1882 and 1901, nearly two thousand black men and boys were lynched in the United States, and by 1932 close to four thousand black Americans had been killed in this appalling manner.[17] Blacks had suffered death at the hands of white vigilantes since the earliest days of slavery, but that periodic violence was nothing like the spectacle associated with public lynching. Human beings were hung, burned, beaten, mutilated, dismembered, dragged behind wagons, urinated and defecated upon, raped, maimed, and murdered. Witnesses often included the entire white community, and, in many cases, the victim's body was cut up and pieces were handed out as souvenirs. *Time* magazine noted that even the Nazis "did not stoop to selling souvenirs of Auschwitz."[18]

The local police, governments of each Southern state, and every American president from Ulysses S. Grant to Harry S Truman allowed this to take place. When railroad companies sold tickets to attend lynchings, when white families brought their children so they could witness the torture and death of blacks, when newspapers carried advance notice of when lynchings would take place, when whites proudly posed for pictures of themselves with the burned, broken bodies of lynched black men and women swinging from trees and then allowed the images to be reproduced on pictures and postcards, *and when no level of American government interfered*, it was clear America had lost its way.

Blacks were lynched for being economically successful, being more than minimally educated (they were "too uppity"), failing to step aside for a white man's car, being politically active, staring whites in the eye, and even for protesting against lynchings. Many victims were innocent bystanders guilty of only being in the wrong place at the wrong time. The men and women who committed these crimes were not crazed or uncontrolled barbarians; rather, they were educated merchants, laborers, machine operators, teachers, physicians, lawyers, policemen, and students; they were family men and women who came to believe that keeping black people "in their place" involved nothing less than pest control.[19] They were perfectly normal human beings who knew very well what they were doing.

On August 28th 1955, in Money, Mississippi, apparently normal human beings snatched fourteen-year-old Emmett Till from his home. They crushed his skull, gouged out his eyeballs, shot him in the head, then tied a fan around his neck and dumped him in the Tallahatchie River. His crime in their warped minds was saying "Bye baby" to a white girl after his friends bet him he wouldn't talk to her. Three days later, Emmett Till's shattered body was recovered, the corpse unrecognizable. His mother could only identify his body because of an initialed ring he wore. Officials supported the accused murderers and, after a four-day trial, on September 23rd barely a month after the crime, in Greenwood, Mississippi, they were found not guilty. The defense attorney told the jurors in his closing statement, "Your fathers will turn over in their graves if [Milam and Bryant are found guilty] and I'm sure that every last Anglo-Saxon one of you has the courage to free these men in the face of that pressure."[20] Jury deliberations took only sixty-seven minutes; one juror shared his priorities: "If we hadn't stopped to drink pop, it wouldn't have taken that long."[21]

Normal human beings, in the early morning of Sunday, September 15th 1963, planted nineteen sticks of dynamite outside the basement of the Sixteenth Street Baptist Church in Birmingham, Alabama. At about 10:22 A.M., when twenty-six children were walking into the basement assembly for closing prayers after a sermon entitled, "The Love That Forgives," the bombs exploded.[22] Four little girls, Addie Mae Collins (age 14), Denise McNair (11), Carole Robertson (14), and Cynthia Wesley (14) were blown to pieces. The perpetrators were not all arrested until forty-five years after the bombing.

These young people were not just the victims of rampaging white mobs, they were also victims of racist state and local governments that magnified the prejudices of their white citizens for political gain, and a racially indifferent and sometimes even hostile federal government. Despite decades of lobbying by various civil rights organizations, Congress refused to pass a federal antilynching law. In 1921, the United States House of Representatives and Senate debated the Dryer Bill. The bill provided for fines and imprisonment for persons convicted of lynching and for penalties against states, counties, and cities that failed to use reasonable efforts to protect citizens from lynch mobs. The bill was killed by filibustering Southerners who claimed it was an unconstitutional infringement on states' rights (though when local agencies could not handle interstate crimes like bank robbery or auto theft, Congress passed federal anti–bank robbery laws and the Justice Department enforced them without any outcry about states' rights, constitutional violations, or limits on federal power).

Regardless, two federal statutes, enacted right after the Civil War and aimed specifically at punishing racial attacks against blacks, gave the Justice Department the power to prosecute public officials and law enforcement officers who committed or conspired with others to commit acts of racial violence, which was often the case. Federal officials also could have prosecuted many of the lynch murders under the Lindbergh Act, passed in 1934, which made the interstate transport of kidnapped victims a federal offense, which was also often the case.[23] However, because they were afraid to offend the politically powerful South, presidents and attorneys general refused to prosecute racial murders; the FBI rarely investigated and even more rarely made arrests. As a result, from 1889 to 1923, there were anywhere from fifty to one hundred lynchings annually across the South; still, less than 1 percent of lynch murderers was tried in state courts, and none were tried in federal court.

Lynching was justified by framing blacks as subhuman brutes. As whites deprived blacks of every inalienable right, their view of blacks became increasingly vicious. The brute caricature portrayed black men as innately savage, animalistic, destructive, and criminal. Popular media depicted them as hideous, terrifying predators who targeted helpless victims, usually white women. The writer Charles H. Smith claimed, "a bad Negro is the most horrible creature upon earth, the most brutal and merciless."[24] George T. Winston, another opinionated writer, declared:

When a knock is heard on the door [a White woman] shutters [sic] with nameless horror. The black brute is lurking in the dark, a monstrous beast, crazed with lust. His ferocity is almost demoniacal. A mad bull or tiger could scarcely be more brutal. A whole community is frenzied with horror, with the blind and furious rage for vengeance.[25]

At the turn of the twentieth century, much of the anti-black propaganda that found its way into the scientific journals, local newspapers, and best-selling novels of the time focused on the stereotype of the black rapist. The claim that black men were raping white women in epidemic numbers became the public rationalization for the lynching of blacks. In 1900, Charles Carroll's *The Negro Beast* reasoned that blacks had been the "tempters of Eve."[26] Thomas Dixon's 1902 novel *The Leopard's Spots* reasoned that "emancipation had transformed blacks from a chattel to be bought and sold into a beast to be feared and guarded."[27] Dr. William Howard, writing in the *Journal of Medicine* in 1903, claimed that "the black birthright was sexual madness and excess."[28] In 1905, Thomas Dixon published *The Clansman*, in which he described blacks as "half child, half animal, the sport of impulse, whim, and conceit . . . a being who, left to his will, roams at night and sleeps in the day, whose speech knows no word of love, whose passions, once aroused, are the fury of the tiger."[29] *The Clansman* includes a detailed account of the rape of a young white virgin by a black man that reads, "A single tiger springs, and the black claws of the beast sank into the soft white throat."[30]

This brutish image bore no relationship to reality. In fact, most of the white women who were raped during the Jim Crow era were raped by white men[31]; but since the mob that made the accusation of rape was secure from any real investigation or legal retribution, black men were easy targets. Further, many states in the South had a broad definition of rape (often including consensual sexual relations between black men and white women), such as Alabama Code 4189: "If any white person and any negro, or the descendant of any negro to the third generation, inclusive, though one ancestor of each generation was a white person, intermarry or live in adultery or fornication with each other, each of them must, on conviction, be imprisoned in the penitentiary or sentenced to hard labor for the county for not less than two nor more than seven years." Another factor adding to the perception of black men as rapists was the tendency of white women—who feared being found to have consented to sex with a black man—to pretend to have been raped instead.[32]

Whites could maintain their dominance only by preventing blacks from entering the white group through marriage, and also by excluding all children born of black-white unions,[33] defined as black men and white women. White men could continue to have sexual relations with black women. They rationalized their own interracial urges by portraying black females as lewd, promiscuous, and sexually knowledgeable. At the same time, they constructed the image of white women as chaste maidens, high on a pedestal, lacking sexual passion, thus banishing the idea that white women and black men could ever engage in consensual sex.

For whites, black animalistic sexuality was a necessary myth. The white obsession with rape performed the crucial task of reinforcing white supremacy. The rape threat justified denying blacks the right to vote and excluding them from juries. It justified job discrimination, for black men could not be allowed to work alongside, let alone in authority over, white women.[34] White Southerners used their portrayal of black sexuality as a reason for strict segregation. With whites predicting such dire consequences for racial mixing, social equality would be forbidden.

SEPARATE AND [UN]EQUAL

"White" and "Colored" signs bloomed all across the South. Whites had their accommodations and blacks had theirs; white accommodations were always much more abundant and far superior. If a black woman became thirsty, she would walk over to the water fountains—one polished and new, labeled "white," the other rusty and broken-down, labeled "colored." Nine out of ten times the colored fountain would be out of service, and the black woman would remain thirsty. If a black man had been traveling for hours and wanted to stop in town to use the restroom of a diner that only served whites, the man would be forced to use the bushes. A seven-year-old black girl would have to walk two miles to the nearest school for blacks, even though there was a public school two blocks away from her home.[35]

That said, the most obvious and gross showing of racial discrimination caused by the Supreme Court's separate but [un]equal doctrine proved to be in the field of education. Black schools in the South were almost always substandard, lacking basic materials, facilities, and quality teachers. There had been a campaign to improve black education between 1917 and 1932, a massive effort on the part of black Southerners to donate money, land, building materials, and labor to the building of new schoolhouses, called the Rosenwald Fund.[36] Despite such fund-raising, one could photograph any black school and capture the dirt floors and dilapidated, unsanitary, and unsafe shacks, compare them with the new brick buildings that housed white schools, and note the huge difference. "It would be difficult for the most gifted writer to picture the actual conditions as being worse than they really are,"[37] reported Nathan C. Newbold, Director of Negro education in North Carolina. "The Negro schools of North Carolina are a disgrace,"[38] added Carl Reynolds, the state health officer. On October 8th 1946, four hundred schoolchildren in the town of Lumberton, North Carolina, walked out of their classes to protest against the conditions. For nine days they paraded down Lumberton's main street, waving signs that read "How Can I Learn When I Am Cold" and "It Rains on Me."[39]

State statistics across the South show the differences in per capita spending between schools for black and white children, as well as the disparity in salaries paid to black and white teachers during Jim Crow. In Mississippi and South Carolina, spending favored whites ten to one, in Kentucky and Virginia it favored whites three to one, with most of the Southern states falling between the two extremes.[40] White teachers in eleven former Confederate states were paid $118 a day, as opposed to black teachers who were paid $73 a day—with black teachers having more students (a teacher-student ratio of forty-seven to one for black teachers compared to twenty-eight to one for white teachers) and acting as janitor for their classrooms. The disparities were a way for white communities to guarantee that their children would be favored economically—with superior educations and job opportunities compared to blacks. Needless to say, there was a complete absence of opportunity for blacks to pursue graduate and professional training.

Black teachers were forced to bend to the ideological demands of segregation. After black disenfranchisement, triumphant white supremacists tightened their control over state-funded black colleges and pressured black educators to keep academic standards low. White support for black education was contingent upon black acquiescence to white supremacy.[41] Blacks could not demand, bargain, or negotiate. In some instances, in order to secure white support, some black women teachers even had to resort to providing sexual favors to white school board members.[42]

Boys from black schools were sent by their principals to do odd jobs at white schools in exchange for periodic donations of dog-eared books and worn-out equipment. "I was struck by the round-about fashion in which, by various subterfuges, Negro education has been improved," wrote John J. Coss, a professor of philosophy at Columbia University, when he visited Georgia in 1936. "The teachers who succeeded in influencing white leaders were almost miracles. They have come through the state of the despised, been subject to condescension, and still have kept their steady goodness without bitterness."[43]

However, as black schools in the South improved they became even more dependent upon whites, and thus increasingly trapped in their substandard role. Philanthropic money and increased state funding brought about improvements in black education, but at the cost of greater bureaucratic control by Southern whites. Black teachers were appointed by white county school superintendents who had every intention of ensuring white supremacy. They treated black principals as chauffeurs, gardeners, repairmen, and errand boys. "They asks [sic] you to do things," a black principal in Louisiana said, "and it's right that you should do it. They give you your job. The other night I was got up at two o'clock in the morning doctoring on one of the school board members' horses."[44]

School superintendents also called on black principals to act as informants as to what was going on inside the black community. Because black school principals had to act as double agents, it made it impossible to tell where their ultimate loyalty lay.[45] During the height of segregation, there was a widespread perception among blacks that their principals would sell out the black community for personal gain. Once-beloved teachers were now considered spies for white control. The position of black teachers as community leaders was therefore deeply compromised. By the 1940s, many blacks were questioning whether the campaign for better schools could ever bring about fundamental social change.

The North hardly presented a better educational climate for blacks. As discussed in Thomas J. Sugrue's history *Sweet Land of Liberty*, Northern blacks had to contend with the same substandard and segregated schools as their Southern neighbors did.[46] While much of this was *de facto* segregation based on differences in demographics across school district lines, it remained a problem until well into the twentieth century and was at the center of the busing controversies that tore apart communities in the 1970s.

QUITTING THE SOUTH

This was life for blacks in the South during the Jim Crow era, and it could never be challenged. Short of migration, black Southerners had no choice but to make the best of a dreadful situation. Economic circumstances had trapped the vast majority of blacks into having to endure the hell that was the South, but those who could leave did. They chose instead to face the obstacles of the North: Lack of skills, lack of money, absence of friends who could ease their transition, and, most importantly, employment discrimination. These obstacles were a welcomed relief compared to the oppression, lynching, segregation, disfranchisement, inadequate schools, insults, humiliation, murder, and other dangers that existed in the South. Unfortunately, things weren't much better "up North" than they were "down South." In all, roughly seven million black people quit the South during the decades between 1900 and 1970. Segregation, mortgage red-lining, and employment discrimination plagued the Northern cities that were destinations for migrating blacks.

It is not a stretch to claim that the treatment of blacks during the Jim Crow era rivaled the atrocities Nazi Germany dealt under the Hitler regime. And as in Nazi Germany, it was the government itself at every level that perpetuated years and years of toxic attitudes in this country. The government itself set the tone by affording no relief or justice for persecuted blacks.

"One nation, under God, indivisible"—the very phrase suggests a belief in a natural law that has validity everywhere. The natural law is rarely mentioned because it is universally understood that certain truths are natural and are not debatable. Among these truths is the fact that skin color is irrelevant to natural rights and personal dignity. Unfortunately, American government at every level denied this truth for far too long. Because of the government's failure to prevent the horrors of Jim Crow, we are still paying the price.

9

———

The Federal Government
Orchestrates Racism

Prior to World War I, the country was starkly segregated. An ambivalent federal government fostered a national attitude of hate and a feeling that black Americans were not, and could never be, equal to their white counterparts. And the president furthered this attitude.

Still, when the United States found itself intertwined in World War I—the war fought to "make the world safe for democracy," according to President Woodrow Wilson—blacks wanted to fight. It would be fair to say that, at that time, black soldiers belonged to no country. Yet, they saw World War I as an opportunity to show their patriotism and bravery for a country in which they so fervently sought inclusion. Despite the soldiers' eagerness, racism in the army and in the administration of President Wilson prevented this opportunity from being realized. Black men were not allowed to volunteer as white men were able to do, and most of the branches of military service were closed to them. However, with the formation of the selective draft (vehemently opposed by the South), over seven hundred thousand black soldiers were able to serve during World War I.

The military considered blacks to be savage beasts, fit to

endure the animalistic rigors of slavery, but unfit for combat, despite a commendable record in the Civil War and in the Spanish American War. Consequently, they were confined to support groups. Support group duties consisted of cleaning white soldiers' rooms, serving them food as mess attendants, and preparing their uniforms. (Just imagine American soldiers today expecting other American soldiers to clean their rooms or iron their shirts, simply because they were a different race!)

President Wilson, in his book *A History of the American People*, wrote that after the Civil War, "congressional leaders were determined to put the white South under the heel of the black South and white men were roused by the mere instinct of self-preservation." [1] Wilson, who was born and raised in segregated Virginia and spent his formative years as a professor and later president of the then all-white Princeton University, seemed to share that sentiment. He felt strongly that blacks should not hold high positions of authority in the army. When the war broke out, Colonel Charles Young, the highest-ranking black officer in the country, was ordered to retire for "high blood pressure." In 1917, when an all-black National Guard regiment formed after several hundred men attended the officers' training camp for blacks at Fort Des Moines, Iowa, President Wilson purposely had all field-grade officers in the regiment sent home and replaced by white officers.

As the war escalated, black soldiers were soon needed for combat. Still, the commander-in-chief would not let the necessity of troops succumb to the desire to keep the races segregated. The first two all-black regiments, the Ninety-Second and the Ninety-Third, had to be separated from each white regiment. The Ninety-Third was placed under the direct control of the French Army, but not without notice. In a memo to the French, the U.S. Army chief of staff warned, "Although a citizen of the United States, the black man is regarded by the white American as an inferior being with whom relations of business or service only are possible. . . . We must not eat with them, must not shake hands with them, seek to talk to them or to meet with them outside the requirements of military service. We must not commend too highly the black American troops, particularly in the presence of white Americans."[2]

There also seemed to be another fear. Brigadier General James B. Irwin issued an order forbidding black soldiers from speaking with French women. Soldiers who disobeyed the order were swiftly arrested. The general noted, "White Americans become very incensed at any particular expression of intimacy between white women and black men."[3] Why should that be, so long as the intimacy was voluntary? Why should the federal government care about personal intimacy? How could someone sworn to uphold freedom of speech authorize the arrest of a colleague for merely exercising that freedom?

France was smart enough to dismiss the warning. The same soldiers who were relegated to support groups by their United States commanding officers were now inducted into the French Army's cavalry, infantry, field and coast artillery, radio, medical corps, ambulance and hospital corps, sanitary and ammunition trains, stevedore regiments, labor battalions, depot brigades, and engineer corps.[4] They were properly trained for combat by the French, using French equipment. Their service elicited overwhelming gratitude from the French government, which awarded the French Legion of Honor to 171 black American soldiers. Colonel James Moss, the white commanding officer of the 367th all-black infantry regiment, which saved a white regiment from defeat in France, wrote,

If properly trained and instructed, the colored man makes as good a soldier the world has ever seen . . . he is amenable to discipline, he takes pride in his uniform; he has faith and confidence in his leader, he possesses physical courage— all of which are valuable military assets. Make the colored man feel you have faith in him. Be strict with him but treat him fairly and justly making him realize that in your dealings with him he will always be given a square deal . . . In other words, treat and handle the colored man as you would any other human being out of whom you would make a soldier, and you will have as good a soldier as history has ever known.[5]

Not only were the French and black American soldiers able to work together on the battlefield, they were able to bond off it as well. Black regiments in World War I were often members of bands; these bands introduced French troops to blues, jazz, and many black performance styles. The black soldiers were also able to befriend French civilians. An article in a small village newspaper in France commented on an initial fear that grew into a special bond.

They [the French] dispute among themselves; they are a little irritated [about the arrival of an all-black regiment of soldiers to their town] . . . I reassure [them]: "Two or three days from now you will be perfectly used to them." I said two or three days but from that very evening the ice is broken. Native and foreigner smile at each other, and try to understand each other. The next day we see the little children in the arms of the huge Negroes, confidently pressing their rosy cheeks to the cheeks of ebony, with their mothers looking on in approbation . . . Very quickly it is seen that they have nothing of the savage in them, but that, on the other hand, one could not find a soldier more faultless

in his bearing, and his manners more affable or more delicate . . . Now one is honored to have them at his table. He
spends hours in long talks with them.[6]

Any fear held by white American commanders that blacks and
whites would not be able to work together should have certainly
been nullified by the success of the French and African American
soldiers who worked side by side. It did not. The soldiers of the all-
black Ninety Second Division, who were stationed in the United
States, did not have nearly as good a reception from locals in
Houston as did their fellow soldiers from foreigners in Paris.

Faced with a clear disadvantage due to inferior equipment, poor
training, and blatant racism by the War Department, the army, their
fellow soldiers, and white Americans alike, black soldiers at home
were at a terrible disadvantage. At one point, a race riot erupted
between whites in Houston, Texas, and black soldiers stationed
nearby. The riot was a result of insults and abuse heaped upon the
black soldiers by the white locals.

With total disregard of the success of the Ninety-Third
Division, military authorities placed blame for the shortcomings of
the Ninety-Second on the "cowardly" behavior of the black officers.
"The Negro division seems in a fair way to be a failure," remarked
General Robert L. Bullard, commander of the Second American
Army. "They are really inferior soldiers. There is no denying it. Poor
Negroes! They are hopelessly inferior."[7]

Any success the black soldier achieved during World War I was
undermined by the federal mandate that he had to be commanded
by white officers. After the war, studies were compiled that would
assess the use of black soldiers' viability in further wars. One such
study by the Army War College "analyzed the physical, mental,
moral and physiological qualities and characteristics of the negro as

a subspecies of the human family."[8] The study reflected both the racist views of the federal government and the attitude of white military personnel toward black soldiers. It expressed a belief that "the black was immoral—his ideas with relation to honor and sex relations are not on the same plane as those of our white population."[9] How sexual relations relate to the ability to fight in war is beyond me. The study went on to add, "Petty thieving, lying and promiscuity are much more common among negroes than among whites."[10]

It was with that attitude in the War Department that black American soldiers took the battlefield again in World War II.

FIGHTING RACISM WITH A RACIST ARMY

Despite the treatment of their fathers in World War I, over 2.5 million black soldiers registered for service during the second world war. They returned to the same segregationist policies, the same piecemeal use of black troops divided among much larger white formations, and the same isolation on posts in racist Southern towns when training. In the interval between wars, black participation in the armed forces was drastically reduced. The black community knew very well that the refusal of the service branches to accept black recruits was part of a deliberate effort to prevent the exercise of rights of citizenship. Frederick Douglass, the former slave turned civil rights icon, once noted, "In the time of trouble the Negro was a citizen and in the time of peace he was an alien."[11] Records of congressional hearings concerning proposed amendments to the 1940 Selective Service Act show unmistakably that both the House of Representatives and Senate resisted full and equitable training and opportunities for blacks in the armed forces. President Roosevelt conveniently remained silent; he needed the votes of Southern white Democrats in Congress.

The U.S. policy angered civil rights and black advocacy organizations because even though Uncle Sam *needed* black soldiers to fight for freedom, blacks were still segregated because they were thought less worthy than whites. The growing voices in the black community worked for recognition commensurate with their sacrifice to the national effort. Black soldiers expected the federal government would protect them as it did all other soldiers. But they were still opposed by those who believed whites had a right to be segregated from blacks.

Refusal by the military establishment to accept full participation of black soldiers in this country's defense was matched by the military manufacturing industry's refusal to include them fully in the nation's defense plans. James H. Kindelberger, president of the North American Aviation Company and a spokesman for the aviation industry, openly said as much: "While we are in complete sympathy with the Negro, it is against company policy to employ them as aircraft workers or mechanics . . . regardless of their training. . . . There will be some jobs as janitors for Negroes."[12]

Soon after the attack on Pearl Harbor, the United States joined the war it had thus far avoided. Seeing an opportunity, the largest circulation black newspaper in the country, *The Pittsburgh Courier*, promoted what it called the Double V campaign: "Victory over our enemies on the battlefield abroad and victory over our enemies at home."[13] Its editor enthusiastically proclaimed, "We call upon the President and Congress to declare war on Japan and against racial prejudice in our country. Certainly we should be strong enough to whip both of them."[14]

The army and American society conspired to degrade blacks at every opportunity. Inevitably, struggles were most prominent in the South. A letter written in 1944 by Corporal Rupert Timmingham questioned what the black soldier was fighting for:

We could not even purchase a cup of coffee . . . Finally the lunchroom manager at a Texas railroad depot said the black GIs could go on around back to the kitchen for a sandwich and coffee. As we did, about two dozen German prisoners of war, with two American guards, came to the station. They entered the lunchroom, sat at the tables, had their meals served, talked, smoked, in fact had quite a swell time.[15]

In South Carolina, a similar event occurred: German POWs were allowed to sit on the white side of the military post exchange cafeteria, while black officers could not:

. . . and WE COULD NOT! We who were American citizens—many of us in training to go overseas to fight Germans, foreign enemies against whom we had sworn to defend our country. Six of us were combat flight instructors, veterans who had already fought Germans and had lost comrades killed by that enemy. WE WERE INSULTED AND HUMILIATED IN OUR OWN NATIVE LAND.[16]

For many years there had been a push for black men in the army air wing. The NAACP had repeatedly called for black representation across the branches in the army. President Roosevelt had told black leaders that he was sympathetic but that there appeared no evidence to warrant the creation of a black unit. Senator Harry S Truman, however, knew of such a location in Tuskegee, Alabama, where an initially self-taught black man who was a West Point graduate, General Benjamin O. Davis, Jr., was giving lessons to other blacks who were denied access to white schools. Eleanor Roosevelt herself flew in, saying to reporters upon landing that she had evidence that black people could fly and would present the case to the president. Reluctantly, the army agreed to accept the black fliers. These men, who became known as the Tuskegee Airmen, faced enormous odds in serving their country, all the while facing government-enforced segregation and institutionalized prejudice.

Top Army officials tried to justify having a segregated base for blacks by contending that the humiliation and possible maltreatment black cadets would face at unsegregated army air force schools would hinder them in developing the self-confidence and initiative necessary as pilots. However, when the construction of an airfield at the Tuskegee Institute for training the black fliers began, it was said that a number of experienced white officers and enlisted men would be needed at the base until blacks were sufficiently trained to operate the base. Separate quarters and mess halls were provided for white and black personnel.

Those who initially opposed a segregated base for blacks then realized that the army had deliberately planned such a program to marginalize the black airmen. Judge William H. Hastie, Judge of the U.S. District Court for the District of the Virgin Islands from 1937 to 1939 and a leading voice for black soldiers during World War II, protested against the segregation within the segregated training center. "I pointed out that if the white officers and enlisted men wanted such segregation they were obviously unfit to train Negroes. Moreover, the psychological effect upon Negro officers and enlisted men was bound to be catastrophic."[17]

Blacks were also falsely promised that black officers and enlisted men would replace the white personnel as quickly as possible. Plans were made for the early graduates of the school to replace the white instructors and for graduates from various officer training schools to replace their white counterparts. Yet during the entire existence of the base, very few replacements were made. Worse, most of the white officers believed they were being punished by being sent to the Tuskegee base.

Colonel Noel Parrish, who was in command of the airfield during its early days, noted that this was true for at least some of his officers. He revealed that two of his best flying instructors were sent to the segregated base as punishment for infractions at other bases.[18] Though there were numerous blacks qualified for each position, black officers for the most part were relegated to positions that gave them little chance for promotion. While black officers were denied equal opportunities for service and advancement, they witnessed swift advancement of young white officers, who were often less qualified.

The federal government never gave the Tuskegee Airmen the chance to succeed. When the first class completed primary training and arrived at the advanced flying field, they found it incomplete. Only one runway was sufficiently complete for flying. The ground school was located in a temporary wooden structure that housed offices and classrooms. There were no partitions separating the classrooms from the offices, and there were several classes held at a time. The babble of voices was accompanied by the clicking of typewriters. These handicaps made concentration difficult for cadets, but training went on.

After graduating, the Tuskegee Airmen faced more intensive and rigorous training. White soldiers were exempt from such training. Once they graduated they were gone, rushed off to England and Africa to see battle. Spann Watson, a Tuskegee graduate, commenting on the training experience, noted: "They made us fly all Christmas Day and New Year's Day. You know, even in combat they wind down for Christmas. It is an unwritten agreement by the enemy and the allies that they would respect the Lord's birthday. We knew it, and we were angry."[19] James Harvey, III, another devoted, enthusiastic Tuskegee airman, added, "The reason our training was so different and so demanding was because they wanted to wash us out."[20]

They didn't wash out. And on the morning of April 1st 1943, the Tuskegee Airmen began making preparations for their departure from Tuskegee and arrival to the theater of battle. They were the Ninety-Ninth Fighter Squadron, led by the Thirty-Third Fighter Group and its white commander, Colonel William W. Momyer. The flyers and ground crew were isolated by the racial segregation practices common at the time, leaving them with little guidance from the experienced white pilots. However, as at Tuskegee, the airmen of the Ninety-Ninth were able to overcome their handicaps. Their first combat mission was to attack the island of Pantelleria in preparation for the Allied invasion of Sicily. The Ninety-Ninth moved to Sicily while attached to the Seventy-Ninth Fighter Group, whose commander, Colonel Earl Bates, fully involved the squadron. The Ninety-Ninth later received a Distinguished Unit Citation for its performance in Sicily.[21]

However, Colonel Momyer told media sources in the United States that the Ninety-Ninth was a failure and its pilots cowardly and incompetent. As a result, a hearing was convened before the House Armed Services Committee to determine whether the Tuskegee Airmen experiment should be allowed to continue. To boost the recommendation to scrap the project, a member of the committee commissioned a "scientific" report by the University of Texas, intended to show that blacks were of low intelligence and incapable of handling air combat. Before the recommendation could be sent to President Roosevelt, the Commanding General of the U.S. Army Air Forces, General Henry H. Arnold, decided an evaluation of the unit should be undertaken to determine the true merits of the Ninety-Ninth. The results showed the squadron to be just as good, if not better, than the other American units at flying, maneuvering, and operating the Mediterranean P-40 fighter aircrafts.

Any success realized by the Tuskegee Airmen overseas made no difference back home, as they continued to face constant humiliation and indignation from soldiers and civilians alike. The airmen who didn't go overseas trained at Selfridge Field, Michigan. These highly trained military officers were treated as trainees and were denied access to the base officer's club. As hostilities grew, the group was transferred to Godman Field, Kentucky. The unfair treatment and hostility continued. The group was transferred again, this time to Freeman, Indiana, where hostilities finally reached a climax. When black officers tried to enter the Freeman Field officers' club, against direct orders for them to stay out, 103 of the black officers were arrested, charged with insubordination, and ordered to face courts-martial. The charges were later dropped, but each officer was given an administrative reprimand.[22]

At the Tuskegee airfield, personnel morale was extremely low due to racial friction in the area of the base. When Colonel Noel Parrish took over the command at Tuskegee, he immediately set out to address the problem by making the base so self-sufficient and attractive there would be little need for the airmen to venture off base. Under Colonel Parrish, Tuskegee developed into a place of excitement. Morale improved; Tuskegee became a place where young black men and women, both military and civilian, could witness the glamour of military flying and enjoy a life never before afforded to black Americans. Still, in the minds of those who had come from areas where racial distinction was less obvious and discrimination and segregation less enforced, there was a feeling that they were quarantined at Tuskegee. No amount of pleasure on the base could minimize their desire to be respected and treated as Americans. In other words, they would not be bought off.

The hostile conditions in the area of Tuskegee—and the entire South for that matter—caused many airmen to transfer to other areas of the country. Hamilton Field in San Rafael, California was one of the areas blacks considered more hospitable. There, when Tuskegee pilots arrived, they were cordially received and accepted by the white pilots. However, this quickly changed when Colonel Ralph Cousins visited the base. After observing black and white officers eating and socializing in the officers' club, Colonel Cousins ordered a separate mess hall and officers' club for black officers. Black pilots accepted the segregation because of the importance of the training they were receiving; however, they agreed after their training and subsequent transfer to challenge any further attempt to segregate them.

Their opportunity for challenge came at Selfridge, Michigan, in 1944. At the time, Selfridge Field was under the command of Colonel Robert R. Selway, a man whose attitude toward blacks mirrored that of Colonel Cousins. There was no officers' club for black officers, though one was being hastily built. Instead of waiting, Tuskegee pilots applied for membership in the established club used by white officers. Army Regulation 210-10 specifically stated that all officers' clubs should be open to all officers. With this in mind, black officers attempted to enter the officer's club, contending further that blacks were citizens of the United States and under the Constitution they were guaranteed the same rights and privileges as other Americans, that it was the responsibility of the federal government to enforce the laws that protected the rights of all citizens, certainly and, at least, on federal property.[23] They were correct: The Fourteenth Amendment was enacted so as to make all government decisions color-blind.

The pilots were refused entry, told by Colonel William L. Boyd that they were not welcome. General Frank Hunter, the commanding general of the First Air Force at the time, was informed of the confrontation. He made a special visit to Selfridge Field and called an assembly, stating, "The War Department is not ready to recognize blacks on the level of social equal[ity] to white men; it is not time for blacks to fight for equal rights or personal advantages; they should prove themselves in combat first. There will be no race problems here, for I will not tolerate any mixing of the races and anyone who protests will be classed as an agitator, sought out and dealt with accordingly."[24] He then urged Colonel Boyd to "stand firm" and commended him on his segregation stance. The hateful practices reached such proportions that many Tuskegee airmen resigned. One resignation letter spoke to the frustration many felt:

> The war aims were directed primarily at uprooting the evil of man against man. These evils were described under varied titles, Nazism, Fascism, etc. Notwithstanding, I find many of the basic evils of the two aforementioned conditions existing within the structure of our Army. Worse, there is no definite move under way for the abolition of these practices. Namely, the establishment of segregation and the accompanying evils of discrimination, which literally divides the Army into a caste system. These discriminatory practices together with the failure of the army to amply provide protection for personnel in hostile communities . . . has led men to ponder seriously the cause for which so many sacrifice so much.[25]

More than a year later, General Hunter and Colonel Selway were at it again, this time at Freedman Field, Indiana. The War Department directive of August 1944 prohibited the segregation of recreation facilities but, in practice, these orders were often disregarded. Colonel Selway again ignored Army Regulation 210-10 and found a way to circumvent the command. General Hunter and Colonel Selway devised a plan to designate one of the two clubs at Freedman Field to blacks and the other to whites. Until then, the black and white officers shared one club. General Hunter advised the Colonel to close the club and told him again to "stand firm." He further commented that he would be delighted for blacks to agitate, for he "could court martial some of them."[26]

Colonel Selway issued a directive stating his policy relative to the designation of the clubs. Days later, the black combat training squadron, Unit 477, let it be known that it would disregard his directive. Colonel Selway had the doors of the white officer's club locked and guards placed at the front door. The officers of the 477th arrived as anticipated and, on attempting to enter, were challenged. They pushed the guards aside and entered the club. After refusing to leave when ordered, thirty-six officers were placed under arrest. Thereafter, Colonel Selway, with the help of General Hunter, prepared a base regulation entitled, "Assignment of Housing, Messing, and Recreation Facilities for Officers, Flight Officers, and Warrant Officers." This regulation separated black and white soldiers from sharing any and every facility. The arrested officers of the 477th received letters of reprimand from Colonel Selway, which accused the soldiers of having a lack of appreciation for the high standard of teamwork expected from them.[27] In reply, the officers submitted the following:

> For the record, the undersigned wishes to indicate over his signature, his unshakeable belief that racial bias is Fascistic, un-American, and directly contrary to the ideals for which he is willing to fight and die . . . The undersigned does not

expect or request any preferential treatment for the tenure of his service, but asks only protection of his substantial rights as a soldier and as an individual, the same identical opportunities for service and advancement offered all other military personnel, and the extension of the identical courtesies extended all other officers of the Army.[28]

Why didn't President Roosevelt desegregate the Armed Forces? By the time World War II had reached its height, it was clear that blacks were able soldiers, black and white units could work well together, and forced segregation caused much more harm than good. Desegregation of the military did not come until 1948, when President Harry S Truman signed Executive Order 9981. Why did Roosevelt fail to do what Truman accomplished just a few years later? Pressure from Southern politicians and powerful military officers acted to block any legislation on military integration, but Franklin Delano Roosevelt was a popular, strong-willed leader who could have done what was right. As commander-in-chief and as the leader of the free world, the president of the United States has an obligation to do what might not be politically popular at the moment. President Roosevelt failed to fight for the rights of a group of men who were willing to fight and die for the liberties of their country.

Colonel Selway, General Hunter, and President Roosevelt allowed institutionalized racism in the armed forces to flourish, all the while ignoring the Tuskegee Airmen and their struggle to serve their country with dignity and respect. These leaders could bravely have let black soldiers prove themselves, but, instead, they yielded to the easy path of continued segregation and racial divisiveness. But even as the president and military leaders passively sat on their hands when it came to integration, the federal government was committing far more aggressive, and heinous, crimes against black Americans.

BAD BLOOD

For forty years between 1932 and 1972, the U.S. Public Health Service conducted a study of the effects of untreated syphilis on black men in and around Tuskegee, Alabama. The Tuskegee Syphilis Experiment is one of the most egregious examples of the federal government's treatment of innocent civilians as guinea pigs for the cause of "medical science" in American history. Government physicians located 339 black men with advanced syphilis, observing the effects of the disease as it caused painful tumors, paralysis, insanity, and blindness. The men were never told they had syphilis and were instead told they had "bad blood." As one of the government physicians involved explained, "As I see it, we have no further interest in these patients until they die."[29]

During the second world war, 250 of the men in the study registered for the draft and were ordered to get treatment for syphilis, but were then denied that treatment by the Public Health Service. Pleased at the government's success, a representative announced, "So far, we are keeping the known positive patients from getting treatment."[30] Even after Congress passed the Henderson Act of 1943, a public health law that required testing and treatment for venereal disease, the men remained in the dark as to why they continued to suffer. The experiment continued in spite of the World Health Organization's Declaration of Helsinki of 1964, which specified that informed consent was needed for experiments involving human beings. One might argue, and government officials certainly tried to argue, that the men gave consent to the study, but that consent was hardly informed since the men were deliberately told that they had the fatal and mysterious bad blood, rather than the treatable syphilis.[31]

The true nature of the experiment had to be kept from the men to ensure their cooperation and from the public to prevent its outrage. Under the guise of "free medical care" (a public relations ploy), the federal government was able to persuade the black community to support its Nazi-like experiments. At first, the men were given the proper syphilis treatment of the day, but in such small amounts that no real improvement could be made; eventually, all treatment was replaced with "pink medicine," which was nothing but aspirin.

The government doctors enticed the men to come in for the so-called treatment with letters promising a "Last Chance for Special Free Treatment." A majority of these men had never seen a physician before this. They received free physical examinations, free rides to and from the clinics, free meals, free treatment for minor ailments, and a promise that burial stipends would be paid to their survivors when they died. That autopsies would eventually be required was never revealed. As one government physician explained, "If the colored population becomes aware that accepting free hospital care means a post-mortem, every darkey will leave. . . . . "[32] The experiment's conspirators reached as high as the Surgeon General of the United States under President Eisenhower, Leroy Edgar Burney, M.D., who enticed the men to remain in the experiment by sending them letters of appreciation.

The experiment was never a complete secret. The Tuskegee Syphilis Experiment had been the subject of numerous reports in medical journals and had been openly discussed in professional conferences. More than a dozen articles appeared in some of the nation's best medical journals, describing the study to a combined readership of well over a hundred thousand physicians. Spokesmen for the Public Health Service called the study a cooperative project that involved the Alabama State Department of Health, the Tuskegee Institute, the Tuskegee Medical Society, and the Macon County Health Department.[33]

This begs the question: Why did no one stop it? There is blood on the hands of every medical professional who attended the conferences and lectures where the study was discussed and yet remained silent, knowing the government was using human beings as guinea pigs. Further, are we to believe that none of the American presidents during the study's duration, from Roosevelt to Nixon, knew about it? Surgeons general, who are appointed by presidents, were certainly aware of the grim details. Even when the media discovered the practice in 1972, no American president found it necessary to apologize for the federal government–caused disease and federal government–prevented cure until President Clinton finally did so in 1997.

Apologists for the Tuskegee Experiment argued that it was, at best, problematic whether the syphilitic subjects could have been helped by the treatment that was available when the study began in 1932. At the time, the treatment for syphilis was bismuth, neoarsphenamine, and mercury, highly toxic drugs that often produced a fatal reaction in patients. The treatment was painful and lengthy and might have caused more harm than good—or so the thinking went.[34] Discrediting the efficiency of the current treatment helped dull the dilemma of withholding treatment in the beginning, but public health officials had a great deal of difficulty explaining why penicillin—the real cure for syphilis—was denied to these black men when it was discovered in the 1940s. When John R. Heller, M.D., director of the Division of Venereal Disease of the Public Health Service between 1943 and 1948, was asked to comment on why the study was never shut down, he shocked reporters by declaring,

"There was nothing in the experiment that was unethical or unscientific."[35]

Those running the experiment never seemed to question whether withholding treatment from the Tuskegee men was ethical. Rather, they focused on the goal of the study, which was to observe the effects of syphilis as it ravaged the unwitting subjects. These doctors seemed to forget completely the Hippocratic oath, which commands that physicians "First, do no harm."

By 1972, when the media brought the experiment to the attention of the public, 128 innocent, government-trusting black men were dead, forty wives had been infected, and nineteen children had been born with congenital syphilis; all of it facilitated by the federal government. It took forty years before someone involved in the study took a hard and honest look at the end results, reporting that "nothing learned will prevent, find, or cure a single case of infectious syphilis or bring us closer to our basic mission of controlling venereal disease in the United States."[36] The harsh reality is that government officials, physicians, and staff used black Americans as lab rats in order to satisfy their own pseudoscientific curiosity about how long syphilis takes to kill someone. *The Philadelphia Inquirer* wrote, "Not since the Nuremberg trials of Nazi scientists had the American people been confronted with a medical *cause célèbre* that captured so many headlines and sparked so much discussion. For many it was a shocking revelation of the potential for scientific abuse in their own country. That it happened in this country in our time makes the tragedy more poignant."[37] Instead of protecting its citizens from such experiments, the government was conducting them.

Perhaps the question lingers: Why would the Tuskegee men cooperate with a study that gave them so little in return for the frightening risks to which it exposed them? *The Los Angeles Times* blamed poverty, charging that "for such inducements [free transportation, hot lunches, and burial stipends] to be attractive their lives must have been savagely harsh."[38] But it may have been more than poverty or ignorance that explains their involvement. For the first time in their lives, these men may have felt they were a part of something important, that they could be of service to the government, all the while being treated with supposed care and respect. It is one of this nation's great tragedies that these men sacrificed themselves so needlessly while federal officials and medical professionals stood by, penicillin at the ready.

Knowing this, perhaps it is not so shocking that many who listened to a Chicago preacher in the first decade of the twenty-first century could stand up and cheer when he claimed that the government created HIV to kill black people. Of course, Rev. Jeremiah Wright's claim is pure demagoguery, but the Tuskegee Experiment must have seemed equally far-fetched to the first people who learned of it. Who would imagine that the federal government, all the way up to the Surgeon General of the United States, deliberately allowed a group of American citizens to die from a terrible disease for the sake of an ill-conceived experiment? Like so many other harsh historical truths, the Tuskegee Experiment only deepened the mistrust that many Americans, blacks and whites, have toward the federal government.

10

Black Education in the South
and the End of Jim Crow After
Brown v. Board of Education

On May 17th 1954, the United States Supreme Court lobbed a cannonball against the wall of government-sponsored segregation that was the Jim Crow system. Ruling in *Brown v. Board of Education* that "in the field of public education the doctrine of separate but equal has no place. Separate education facilities are inherently unequal," the Court found that state-owned segregated schools were unconstitutional. The decision electrified many Americans, who saw it as hope that the days of segregation were coming to an end. Civil rights activists, both black and white, relied on the *Brown* decision to integrate public spaces from movie theaters to railcars to restaurants. But the victory in the Supreme Court also proved to be bittersweet. More than two decades were to pass before every segregated public school district in the nation was integrated, and white opposition to *Brown* was so ferocious than many supporters of desegregation were left wondering if the decision had been the right one.

Brown, like so many other cases in the fight against segregation, began with a group of people who stood up to Jim Crow laws that forced blacks into positions of submission, inferiority, and shame.

Ten-year-old Linda Brown had to walk through a busy rail yard to a bus stop for the mile-long ride to her segregated school because she was barred from enrolling at the all-white school only seven blocks from her home.

In what came to be known as *Brown v. Board of Education*, Linda's parents joined twelve other parents in an attempt to reverse the state-owned school's policy of racial segregation. Surprisingly, this struggle was not taking place in Mississippi or another part of the Deep South but in Kansas, a state that had never joined the Confederacy and had only briefly flirted with slavery. Like other states outside the South, Kansas had a number of segregation laws, proving that even in places where slavery had never taken root, local governments continued to endorse segregation and racist official policies. Jim Crow had spread its poisonous seeds far beyond the former Confederacy; the civil rights movement would have to dig deep to wipe out every last remnant of government-sponsored servitude.

Thurgood Marshall, the NAACP's chief litigator in the 1940s and 1950s, argued the case on behalf of the parents. Marshall was one of the most skillful and tenacious lawyers of his day and had successfully argued many cases before the Supreme Court. He had experienced the effects of segregation firsthand as a student at an all-black school in Baltimore without a library, cafeteria, or gym, and which was so overcrowded that students only attended class for a few hours each day.[1] Marshall felt the effects of Jim Crow even more bitterly when he was turned down for admission by the University of Maryland Law School due to his race. Studying instead at Howard University Law School under Charles Houston, the school's legendary dean who sought to educate a new generation of civil rights activists, Marshall learned the usefulness of using the law to challenge segregation. Only three years after receiving his law degree, Marshall won his first big civil rights case. His opponents?

The segregationists at the University of Maryland who had only recently rejected his application. Maryland's highest court agreed that the alternatives the University of Maryland offered to black students were not equal to the facilities given to whites.

Despite his previous successes, Marshall was up against a formidable obstacle in the *Brown* case. The lower court had already ruled for the school district, deciding that the Supreme Court's 1896 decision in *Plessy v. Ferguson* made separate but equal schools legal. Recall that in *Plessy*, the Supreme Court had upheld a Louisiana law that required separate but equal facilities for blacks on state-owned railroads; states from Georgia to North Dakota had then relied upon *Plessy* in creating Jim Crow laws that regulated how blacks lived in almost every aspect of life controlled by state or local government. Overturning a widely despised Supreme Court decision is always a challenge, but Marshall and the NAACP would need to convince the Court to take a stance against a system that formed one of the pillars of mid-twentieth-century Southern society.

Despite these handicaps, the opponents of Jim Crow had great hope that *Brown* would be the case that finally put an end to state-commanded segregation. In 1950, the Supreme Court had agreed with Thurgood Marshall's arguments in two cases involving separate but unequal educational facilities for blacks. In *Sweatt v. Painter*, a black man had challenged the admissions policy of the University of Texas School of Law. At the time of the lawsuit, no law school for blacks existed in the entire state of Texas, but the trial court allowed the school to delay the case while it created a sham law school that would meet the *Plessy* separate but equal standard. Reversing this decision, the Supreme Court found that this shoddy, quickly thrown together school was hardly equal to the facilities enjoyed by white students.

In *McLaurin v. Oklahoma State Regents*, the Supreme Court

considered the equally reprehensible behavior of the University of Oklahoma toward a graduate student. The student had already successfully sued the University into admitting him, but the school did its best to degrade and humiliate him, including assigning him segregated desks in the library and cafeteria and forcing him to sit in a different room from his white classmates during lectures, watching class and trying to participate through an open door. As with *Sweatt*, the Court declared that a public school could not treat black students as inferior, but it did not overturn *Plessy* completely. The Court stated that the school's treatment of the student was a violation of his constitutional rights to equal protection but did not issue any injunctive relief, only ruling "on the assumption that the law having been declared, the State will comply." Many thought these victories were as far as blacks would get in the Supreme Court and that they should continue to work toward creating equal opportunities within the Jim Crow system.

Despite opposition from many civil rights supporters, Thurgood Marshall saw the success in these early cases as evidence that the Supreme Court might be prepared to listen to a direct assault on *Plessy*.[2] He was taking a great risk. A reversal of *Plessy* would affirm that a truly color-blind government and society were possible; but a failure in the Supreme Court was likely to set back the course of civil rights for decades.[3]

WHEN DELAY IS NO LONGER POSSIBLE

Marshall and the NAACP did not want to wait and lose another generation of black children to the low standards and deliberate racism of the Jim Crow school system. The simple fact is that the supposedly separate but equal schools for blacks in many states were quite separate but not at all equal to their counterparts for white students. In the early twentieth century, very few public schools existed for blacks in the South. Whites routinely acted to weaken black schools, including withholding public funds, cutting the number of school days, and even closing black schools entirely. Almost no new schools for blacks were constructed with public funds during this time, as whites grabbed tax dollars for all-white schools.[4]

Whites were much more likely than blacks to be enrolled in public schools across the South. In many of the states with the highest percentage of blacks (such as Alabama, Georgia, Louisiana, Mississippi, and South Carolina), the percentage of blacks enrolled in public high schools was often as low as 10 percent of those of school age.[5] Overcrowding forced the black schools that did exist to run double sessions, leaving students to wander the streets the rest of the day.[6] Blacks in the South were paying taxes for white schools while their children were left with primitive facilities, often little more than windowless shacks lacking blackboards, textbooks, and desks.[7]

By crippling black education, white supremacists in much of the country aimed to keep blacks in a position of intellectual inferiority. They feared that if blacks gained better access to schools, they would snatch up jobs from whites and move beyond the low-level laboring jobs they traditionally held.[8] In both poorer rural areas and in Southern cities that were rapidly losing their industrial economic base, whites were hardly eager to see blacks compete with them for jobs.

The other great fear of white racists was that integration in the schools would lead to a mingling of the races in the bedroom. As one Alabama state senator put it, school integration would "open the doors of our white women to black men."[9] White Southerners feared that a mixing of the races would threaten white dominance, so Jim Crow laws were crafted to prevent any African blood from diluting the white race. Sometimes these laws seemed absurd in their attempts to close every possible loophole for whites and blacks to marry, such as a Mississippi statute that stated, "The marriage of a white person with a negro or mulatto or person who shall have one-eighth or more of negro blood, shall be unlawful and void," or a Florida law prohibiting "all marriages between a white person and a negro, or between a white person and a person of negro descent to the fourth generation."[10] For this reason, even in states such as New Mexico where schools were not completely segregated, black children were kept in separate classrooms and not permitted near the white students.[11] Allowing blacks into all-white schools, parents reasoned, would surely lead to the terrifying result of biracial grandchildren.

Despite these immense hurdles, Southern blacks fought desperately to secure a quality education for their children. A major campaign was started by black communities in the 1910s and 1920s to construct schools in the South. The schools were known as Rosenwald schools, because they were partly paid for with donations from Julius Rosenwald, one of the founders of Sears, Roebuck and Company. Rosenwald had made his first contribution to constructing schools for impoverished blacks when he gave Booker T. Washington $25,000 to create industrial training schools similar to Washington's famous Tuskegee Institute.[12] Rosenwald inspired blacks to get involved in filling the education gap left by white public officials with a matching funds program. In total, black families, many of them extremely poor, raised over $4.7 million for school construction from 1914 to 1932, all of which was matched by Rosenwald's fund.[13] It was an incredible financial sacrifice, as many of them went without basic necessities in order to donate money.

The push for desegregation in the schools spurred those in charge of some school boards to increase spending for black schools. Between 1950 and 1954, many black schools were improved, with the hope of undercutting the argument that the segregated school systems led to unequal facilities for blacks and whites.[14] By adhering to the separate-but-equal doctrine established in *Plessy*, and by belatedly boosting "equal," some states aimed to shield their system from federal judicial intervention.

Marshall and the NAACP responded to this strategy by arguing that segregated schools have a negative effect on black pupils, no matter how equal the facilities. Arguing before the federal district court in Kansas, the NAACP's lawyers did not aim to tug at heartstrings by mentioning Linda Brown's long walk to school or that the all-black schools were of a lower quality than the white schools. Instead, they argued that a government-sponsored system of segregated schools had the effect of making the minority children feel inferior to whites. The district court judge, Walter Huxman, agreed with this argument, stating, "Segregation of white and colored children in schools has a detrimental effect upon the colored children. The impact is greater when it has the sanction of law; for the policy of separating the races is usually interpreted as denoting the inferiority of the Negro group."[15] Although Judge Huxman had no choice but to uphold the segregated school system as constitutional under *Plessy*, the court's focus on the psychological impact of state-sponsored segregation was clearly intended as a message to Thurgood Marshall that this case should go to the Supreme Court and, as well, a message to the Supreme Court that it was time for it to rule on the separate-but-equal system once and for all.

In 1952, the Supreme Court agreed to hear *Brown* and four similar cases that had been fought in the federal district courts. Relying on the strategy that had swayed Judge Huxman in Kansas,

Marshall presented a wide range of data from researchers and psychologists indicating segregation harmed blacks by instilling in them a feeling of being inferior to whites. Some of the most forceful imagery came from psychologist Kenneth Clark, who conducted a series of tests on black children by showing them white and black dolls and asking them which ones they preferred. The children were much more likely to say that the white dolls were "good" or "nice" and to say that the black dolls were "bad."[16] Many critics dismissed such research as flimsy, but it presented an academic and empirical basis for the seemingly commonsense idea that state-enforced segregation harms the minority group.

SEPARATE CANNOT BE EQUAL

The Supreme Court based its decision in *Brown* on the Equal Protection Clause of the Fourteenth Amendment, stating that state-enforced segregation of students by race, no matter how equal the schools, would have an adverse effect on minority students, thus denying them equal benefits from the government that owns the schools. In ruling that the doctrine of separate but equal was unconstitutional with respect to public schools, the Court did not actually overturn *Plessy v. Ferguson*, but rather held that segregation, even if truly equal, had "no place" in public education. The Court did not provide any specific timeframe or guidelines for integration but instead invited the U.S. Attorney General and the states with segregated schools to return later with plans on how desegregation would be implemented.

The ruling in *Brown* was largely the work of Chief Justice Earl Warren. The former Governor of California, Warren came to expand the power of the federal courts dramatically during his tenure as Chief Justice; he was an incredibly able politician who understood how best to harness the power of the Court.[17] The Chief Justice made sure he spoke for a unanimous Court in order to give the *Brown* decision all possible authority and credibility. Warren deliberately framed the decision in the simplest of terms and made it short enough so that it could be run in its entirety in newspapers.[18] Inviting the states to participate in deciding how to integrate schools was another masterful gesture that Warren hoped would help minimize sentiment among Southerners that they were being shoved around by the federal government.[19]

BUT WAS IT CONSTITUTIONAL?

In making its decision in *Brown*, the Supreme Court relied on the Constitution's Equal Protection Clause, a much more vague description of constitutional rights than the Due Process Clause, the Fourteenth Amendment's other major definition of rights. The Court placed equal protection in the context of modern American education in order to find that segregation in public schools had a detrimental effect on black children, and thus denied them the same benefits, or equal protection, that their white neighbors received from the government that ran the schools.

The arguments made by the opposing sides in *Brown* were largely centered on determining whether the original intent of the framers of the Fourteenth Amendment had been to ban segregation in public schools. But Chief Justice Warren noted that inquiries into the original meaning of the Fourteenth Amendment had been inconclusive and circumstances had changed since the adoption of the Amendment, so the Court's ruling should instead focus on the role of education in contemporary America. "This discussion and our own investigation convince us that, although these sources cast some light, it is not enough to resolve the problem with which we are faced. At best, they are inconclusive. . . . What others in Congress and the state legislatures had in mind cannot be determined with any degree of certainty."[20]

What the Court doesn't explicitly say is that a close reading of the Fourteenth Amendment's original meaning and the court cases that followed it would likely have pointed to a position that state-commanded segregation was not unconstitutional.[21] Alexander Bickel, who was Justice Felix Frankfurter's law clerk at the time and went on to become one of the most respected constitutional commentators of the day, had prepared a memorandum for Frankfurter that found strong historical evidence that the Fourteenth Amendment had *not* been intended to outlaw segregation, instead leaving it as is for the States to determine.[22]

Furthermore, the same Congress that wrote the Fourteenth Amendment had passed laws supporting segregated schools in the District of Columbia and segregated schools run by the Freedman's Bureau, the federal agency that was largely responsible for the creation of a public education system in the South after the Civil War.[23] In 1896, the year that *Plessy* was decided, blacks in the South relied on the public schools established by the Freedman's Bureau as well as free schools established through the fund-raising efforts of black churches and Northern charities, but education was by no means universal or free.[24] Blacks in the North hardly had it any better. Despite the efforts of the Northern-dominated federal government to improve access to education for Southern blacks, Northern states still had widespread state-sponsored segregation in public schools in 1896.[25] Evidence such as this strongly suggests that the framers of the Fourteenth Amendment did not intend to ban segregated public schools.

Of course, the justices and a great many Americans knew in their hearts that segregation by the government was morally reprehensible because the schools for blacks could never be equal to the schools for whites and because governments violate the natural law when they treat people differently based on race, which is an immutable characteristic of birth. The justices chose to follow the natural law, which is color-blind, rather than remaining silent and allowing the positive law of segregation to continue. As Professor Michael J. Klarman of the University of Virginia School of Law has argued, "In *Brown* the law was reasonably clear: Segregation was constitutional. For the justices to reject that finding suggested that they had very strong personal preferences to the contrary. And they did."[26] Even Justice Hugo Black, a former KKK member and unrepentant segregationist who was appointed by President Franklin D. Roosevelt as a favor to Democrats in the Deep South, joined the majority opinion. Black had since turned away from his past views and actually advocated that the Court go further and overturn *Plessy* outright.

In finding that equal protection extended to cover the right to an integrated education, the Court looked to sociological and psychological data that suggested segregation harmed the minority group. Speaking of the "importance of education to our democratic society" and how "it is the foundation of good citizenship," Chief Justice Warren revealed that the Court saw education as too important a right to be forfeited, even if the Fourteenth Amendment does not specifically mention it.

The Court's emphasis on protecting rights not specifically mentioned in the Constitution is an implicit reference to the concept of natural law, a principle that identifies certain fundamental liberties that must be protected from government encroachment. The justices concluded that segregated government-owned schools, even when equal in all other respects, have a harmful effect on blacks and therefore they are simply unjust. *Brown* may not have been grounded in solid constitutional precedent, but the justices shattered the separate-but-equal doctrine that was the legal basis for the evils of Jim Crow, reaffirming the belief that, just as they have from time immemorial, courts may and should uphold the natural law.

A serious misgiving of *Brown* was its conscious deliberate instruction that schools begin to desegregate "with all deliberate speed." This marks the first time in Supreme Court history (but not the last) that the Court identified unconstitutional behavior by a state and permitted it to continue. All deliberate speed became an invitation for all intentional foot-dragging. It would take another generation of litigation in federal courts before *Brown*'s holding and Marshall's dream became reality.

THE SOUTH DIGS IN ITS HEELS

The Court tried its best to soften the impact of *Brown* by not setting a specific timeline or any guidelines for implementing the decision. And initially, it seemed as though the states that still supported segregation would accept the ruling, with prominent politicians such as Virginia Governor Thomas Stanley calling for "cool heads, calm study, and sound judgment."[27] Sadly, this honeymoon did not last long. Within a few months, Governor Stanley announced he would do everything in his power to prevent integration of the state-owned schools.[28]

Even more troubling was the reaction of President Dwight D. Eisenhower. President Eisenhower enjoyed immense popularity in the South and his endorsement of *Brown* would likely have done much to sway the views of moderate Southerners. This endorsement never came. Ike would only say that he was sworn to uphold the Court's decision and he would comply with it. Eisenhower's failure to support *Brown* was not because of any personal sympathy for segregationists but because he felt it was wrong for the federal government to address the issue.

Ike had spent a lifetime in the rigidly segregated U.S. Army. If it worked in the army, he reasoned, why couldn't it work in the schools? Having been born in Texas and raised in rural Kansas, perhaps Eisenhower had some grasp of the intense opposition many Americans had toward integrating the schools. As Eisenhower explained to Earl Warren right before the decision was handed down, "These are not bad people. All they are concerned about is to see that their sweet little girls are not required to sit alongside some big overgrown Negro."[29] Still, Eisenhower's reluctance to endorse the Supreme Court's decision was a devastating public relations blow to it. If the President was not going to speak in support of *Brown*, it was that much easier for segregationists to resist integrating the schools. Perhaps Roy Wilkins, executive secretary of the NAACP, was not so off the mark when he critiqued, "If [Eisenhower] had fought World War II the way he fought for civil rights, we would all be speaking German today."[30]

Faced with such a rising tide of opposition, it is perhaps unsurprising that the Supreme Court approached its delayed ruling on the strategy for integration with a great deal of caution. The Court's ruling, in what came to be known as *Brown II*, was a compromise designed to skirt the issue of a strict timeline. The justices knew that they could expect little support from Congress or the president—and active resistance from Southern states—and therefore aimed to give authorities some flexibility in desegregating the schools. But the Court delighted many segregationists by stating that local school boards need only comply with *Brown* "with all deliberate speed." Although the ruling also required that the school boards show good faith if they took extra time to comply, Southern states and local school boards used this vague statement as an excuse for digging in their heels against integration.[31] Never before or since had state unconstitutional behavior been given generations of time to be corrected, and the South took advantage of every excuse to avoid implementing integration in its public schools.

Southern state and local governments essentially sabotaged the two *Brown* decisions. Nearly all of the Southern senators and the majority of Southerners in the House of Representatives signed a manifesto accusing the Supreme Court of abusing its power and pledging to use all means possible to resist *Brown*.[32] Mississippi and Louisiana outlawed racially integrated schools, and Georgia banned state and local officials from using public funds on desegregated schools.

Much of the difficulty for those working to implement *Brown* was due to the number of incompliant school districts that had to be challenged individually in court. But when federal courts did attempt to intervene and order individual districts to be integrated, many states would abolish the school districts entirely, substituting private schools for white students, often with public funds. Mississippi and South Carolina actually went so far as to amend their constitutions to abolish public schools completely, substituting private schools for whites that were paid for with a mixture of public and private funds. Naturally, blacks were locked out of attending these alternate schools.[33]

In 1957, Arkansas Governor Orval Faubus called out his state's National Guard to block black students' entry to Little Rock High School. In the ensuing chaos, President Eisenhower responded by bringing in armed troops to protect the black students, but the symbol of a state governor thumbing his nose at the federal government over black children attending a public school attracted broad support. And to make matters worse, Faubus got in one last dig. After the federal troops left at the end of the school year, Little Rock schools were closed for the following school year.[34]

Even more potent was the symbolism of Alabama Governor George Wallace as he personally blocked the door of a building at the University of Alabama to prevent the enrollment of two black students. Wallace had delivered a speech at his inauguration earlier that year pledging "segregation now, segregation tomorrow, segregation forever." In what became known as the Stand at the Schoolhouse Door, Wallace moved aside only after being confronted by Deputy Attorney General Nicholas deB. Katzenbach, along with federal marshals and the now-federalized Alabama National Guard.

Due to the resistance of white-dominated school boards and local governments, it took at least ten years before even token integration occurred in the South and at least twenty years until states in the Deep South took the decision seriously.[35] Those who had fought so hard for desegregation clearly did not expect to come up against such fierce resistance. But ignoring the widespread support for segregation among white Southerners was a mistake on the part of the Supreme Court, Marshall, and the NAACP. Both Chief Justice Warren and Thurgood Marshall, who went on to become the first black Supreme Court justice in 1967, seem to have given little thought to the way in which the decision would be implemented, and this lack of planning for a backlash only made it easier for the opponents of integration.[36]

If it had not been for a number of courageous federal judges in the South who supported the *Brown* rulings, desegregation would have failed completely. The Fifth Circuit Court of Appeals, which then had jurisdiction over the Deep South, handed down a series of decisions in its 1965–1966 term that challenged the slow response by Southern state courts, government, and school districts; and the plans in many districts that sought to disguise segregation with token redistricting or token integration.[37] The judges of the Fifth Circuit, appointed during the 1950s and 1960s, were some of the most courageous talent ever assembled in the American courts. These men and their counterparts in the federal district courts were nearly all born in the South and many were avowed segregationists, but they all bravely ruled against segregation in the schools.[38] As Judge John Minor Wisdom stated in *U.S. v. Jefferson County Board of Education*, "the Constitution is both color-blind and color conscious. To avoid conflict with the equal protection clause, a classification that denies a benefit, causes harm, or imposes a burden must not be based on race. In that sense the Constitution is color-blind. But the Constitution is color conscious to prevent discrimination being perpetuated and to undo the effects of past discrimination. The criterion is the relevancy of color to a legitimate government purpose."[39] No one has more accurately or succinctly stated the role of the Fourteenth Amendment with respect to race before or since.

11

The Civil Rights Legislation of the 1960s and Afterward

The *Brown* decision and the loud and long opposition from Southern leaders may have filled the headlines in the 1950s, but the 1960s proved to be even more tumultuous. The decade was a period of immense social change for many Americans, and the violence and chaos that resulted from the push for civil rights saw this country nearly ripped apart. Church bombings, riots, and assassinations shocked the nation as civil rights activists pushed up against an often-unyielding South. During this chaotic time, the federal government made only feeble efforts at desegregation; it was not until television screens were flooded with images of civil rights marchers being attacked with whips, tear gas, and clubs by Alabama state police that Americans began to support federal intervention in great numbers.

The Eisenhower administration took only token steps toward protecting the rights of black people against hostile state and local governments. After failing to endorse the Supreme Court's decision in *Brown*, President Eisenhower largely ignored civil rights. He was spurred to action only when it seemed as though state governments in the South had completely rejected the racial neutrality required by the Fourteenth Amendment. Once again, the nation's most powerful man demonstrated that he was not willing to stand up to the monolithic white Southern establishment in opposing Jim Crow.

If the federal government failed to protect blacks from Jim Crow, it was not for lack of authority. The Constitution grants Congress the power to enforce the Thirteenth, Fourteenth, and Fifteenth Amendments "by appropriate legislation," but by the mid-1950s, after the *Brown* decision came down, Congress still had not passed a single civil rights bill since Reconstruction.[1]

Meanwhile, blacks in the South were still being kept from exercising their political will by state laws that imposed poll taxes, residency requirements, and literacy tests, and by police and court systems that looked the other way at outright threats of violence toward black voters. Congress passed the Civil Rights Act of 1957, which primarily sought to increase black access to the vote, but fierce opposition from Southern congressmen—including a record-breaking filibuster speech by South Carolina Senator Strom Thurmond—meant that the final bill was a watered-down version with no real bite. Another attempt by Congress in 1960 to pass a voting rights bill again came up against resistance from the South, this time including tactics like a filibuster by Southern senators that lasted for 125 consecutive hours, delaying a vote on the issue.[2] Although the 1960 Civil Rights Act did eventually pass, once again the foes of equality had made their voices known loud and clear, and the resulting bill once again did little to help advance civil rights.

JFK: A FLAWED HOPE?

John F. Kennedy was different from any president the country had ever elected. A member of one of America's wealthiest and most politically powerful families, who had been celebrated by the press since his decoration for actions in World War II, the forty-four-year-old Kennedy was also extremely telegenic and, even more singularly, he was Roman Catholic. Like Barack Obama in 2008, Kennedy struggled with allegations that his church spoke for him and controlled his decision making, going so far as to state, "I am not the Catholic candidate for president. I am the Democratic Party's candidate for president who also happens to be a Catholic. I do not speak for my church on public matters—and the church does not speak for me."[3] Civil rights activists had high hopes that this mold-busting new president would be the leader that finally turned the focus of the federal government toward eliminating Jim Crow once and for all.

Initially, it seemed like Kennedy would fulfill the hopes of those fighting for civil rights. In order to circumvent the powerful Southern forces in Congress, Kennedy used his executive authority to create a Commission on Equal Employment Opportunity, setting the stage for a series of efforts by his administration to combat segregation and discrimination based on race.[4] But for all his sympathy and understanding, Kennedy was an extremely shrewd politician. Kennedy and his vice president, Lyndon Baines Johnson, had won the South in the 1960 election by avoiding any mention of civil rights, and the new administration did not want to jeopardize Southern support by taking too strong a stand against official segregation.[5]

Kennedy also feared alienating the fierce Mississippi segregationist Senator James Eastland, who, as chairman of the Judiciary Committee, held the power to block the president's judicial appointments and who was a mainstay in the Democratic party.[6] It was perhaps only opponents of segregation, therefore, who were surprised when Kennedy refused to endorse a series of "freedom rides" organized by civil rights activists to challenge segregated buses and bus terminals in the South. With the federal government sending a clear message of indifference, segregationists brutally attacked the freedom riders and threw firebombs into the buses.[7] In Birmingham, Alabama, Public Safety Commissioner Eugene "Bull" Connor had his police officers stand by while a white mob beat freedom riders for over fifteen minutes before the police officers finally stepped in to intervene.[8]

The Kennedy administration also refused to offer any protection to voter registration efforts in the South. With hostile whites using threats, arson, and even gunfire to chase away volunteers from their attempts to educate blacks about their voting rights, these brave Americans should have been able to rely upon some sort of police protection.[9] Skeptics in the Kennedy administration claimed that state governments should be responsible for enforcing civil rights and protecting the activists and volunteers. But with local police regularly assisting the Ku Klux Klan in many areas of the South and arresting the activists on exaggerated or false charges, it was laughable to expect any support from state governments in the Deep South.[10]

Although Kennedy shrugged off any responsibility for aiding the embattled civil rights movement in the South, he possessed strong tools with which to do so. The Justice Department and the FBI could have exercised their authority to enforce the Thirteenth, Fourteenth, and Fifteenth Amendments by arresting and prosecuting those state government officials who harassed, threatened, and beat civil rights volunteers or who denied equal protection to blacks. Indeed, the FBI, and its dictatorial boss, J. Edgar Hoover, had no compunction about keeping files on millions of Americans and relentlessly pursuing suspected members of the Communist Party.[11] But Hoover was unwilling to provide any protection for the civil rights workers and, under his direction, the FBI undertook a campaign not to protect but rather to discredit Martin Luther King, Jr. by bugging his hotel rooms searching for evidence of extramarital affairs.[12]

The Justice Department was hardly any less interested in aiding the civil rights movement. Despite the fact that both the Justice Department and the FBI were on the scene during many of the clashes between civil rights workers and angry mobs, it was common that neither did anything to stop the violence or to prevent the arrest of hundreds of activists by local police on trumped-up charges.[13]

THE SOUTH EXPLODES

The chaos finally came to a peak in Birmingham, where Martin Luther King, Jr. and other civil rights workers intended to break down Jim Crow in the South's most segregated city with nonviolent actions that would incite Bull Connor to react violently. Imprisoned in the Birmingham city jail for a peaceful march that was in violation of a court order, King wrote a letter describing his intention of forcing the segregationists into a confrontation. "Nonviolent direct action seeks to create such a crisis and foster such a tension that a community which has constantly refused to negotiate is forced to confront the issue. It seeks so to dramatize the issue that it can no longer be ignored."[14]

King was the architect of the method of nonviolence that gripped the American civil rights movement during the final two decades of Jim Crow. Following what can only be described as a family tradition, King very early in his life became a Baptist pastor, leading the Dexter Avenue Baptist Church in Montgomery, Alabama, at the age of twenty-five. Reverend King tackled many of his achievements early in life, finishing high school at age fifteen and graduating from Morehouse College—a distinguished, historically black institution from which both his father and grandfather graduated—with a degree in sociology at nineteen. After three years of theological study at Crozer Theological Seminary in Pennsylvania, where he was elected president of a predominantly white senior class, he graduated with a Bachelor of Divinity degree in 1951. Immediately thereafter, King began doctoral studies in systematic theology at Boston University and received his Doctor of Philosophy on June 5th 1955. He was twenty-six years old.[15]

By this time, he was more than ready to accept the leadership responsibility of the "first great Negro nonviolent demonstration in the United States"[16]: The bus boycott in Montgomery, Alabama. Addressing the Holt Street Baptist Church on December 5th 1955, in response to Rosa Parks being taken from a bus, carried to jail, and arrested for refusing to give up her seat to a white woman, King stated:

> You know, my friends, there comes a time when people get tired of being trampled over by the iron feet of oppression. There comes a time when people get tired of being plunged across the abyss of humiliation, where they'd experience the bleakness of nagging despair. There comes a time when people get tired of being pushed out of the glittering sunlight of life's July and left standing amid the piercing chill of an alpine November. There comes a time. And we are here this evening because we are tired now.[17]

The boycott lasted 382 days. On December 21st 1956, the Supreme Court (in *Browder v. Gayle*) declared unconstitutional the laws requiring segregation on buses. During the Montgomery bus boycott, Martin Luther King Jr. was arrested, his house bombed, and he and his family subjected to personal abuse. At the same time, he emerged as the premiere civil rights leader in the United States.

In 1957, King was elected president of the Southern Christian Leadership Conference, an organization formed to provide new leadership for the civil rights movement. From then until his death, he traveled over six million miles and spoke in public more than twenty-five hundred times, appearing wherever there was injustice, protest, and action. He led a massive protest march in Birmingham, Alabama, that caught the attention of the entire world, providing what he called "a coalition of conscience."[18] It was this experience that inspired King's Letter from the Birmingham Jail in April 1963. In response to the notion that blacks should continue to wait for the government to come around, King explained:

We have waited for more than 340 years for our constitutional and God-given rights. Perhaps it is easy for those who have never felt the stinging dark of segregation to say, "Wait." But when you have seen vicious mobs lynch your mothers and fathers at will and drown your sisters and brothers at whim; when you have seen hate-filled policemen curse, kick and even kill your black brothers and sisters; when you see the vast majority of your twenty million Negro brothers smothering in an airtight cage of poverty in the midst of an affluent society; when you suddenly find your tongue twisted and your speech stammering as you seek to explain to your six-year-old daughter why she can't go to the public amusement park that has just been advertised on television, and see tears welling up in her eyes when she is told that Funtown is closed to colored children, and see ominous clouds of inferiority beginning to form in her little mental sky, and see her beginning to distort her personality by developing an unconscious bitterness toward white people; when you have to concoct an answer for a five-year-old son who is asking: "Daddy, why do white people treat colored people so mean?"; when you take a cross-county drive and find it necessary to sleep night after night in the uncomfortable corners of your automobile because no motel will accept you; when you are humiliated day in and day out by nagging signs reading "white" and "colored"; when your first name becomes "nigger," your middle name becomes "boy" and your last name becomes "John," and your wife and mother are never given the respected title "Mrs."; when you are harried by day and haunted by night by the fact that you are a Negro, living constantly at tiptoe stance, never quite knowing what to expect next, and are plagued with inner fears and outer resentments; when you are forever fighting a degenerating sense of "nobodiness" then you will understand why we find it difficult to wait.[19]

No matter how difficult it was to wait, Martin Luther King, Jr. stayed true to the method of nonviolent, direct action. His ideals were from the core of Christianity, as he embraced natural rights; techniques were taken from Mahatma Gandhi: Endure the most inhumane of treatment until the government decides to acknowledge natural law. Instead of honoring the natural law, the Federal Bureau of Investigation under J. Edgar Hoover tracked King by illegally placing wiretaps in his home and office phones, bugged his hotel rooms while he traveled across the country, named him the "most dangerous Negro leader in the country,"[20] and distributed reports of his private behavior to the executive branch, friendly reporters, and even King's family. He was assassinated in Memphis, Tennessee, on April 4th 1968.

On May 2nd 1963, the clash between King's natural law ideas and the government's outright legal (under positive law) racism led to violence that was a fulcrum for American racial and social history. On that day, nearly one thousand black children left school and attempted to march to the Sixteenth Street Baptist Church. Public Safety Commissioner Bull Connor had hundreds of them locked up, and when even larger numbers of children marched the next day, the police so brutally knocked them down with high-powered fire hoses that young women were thrown over the tops of cars and some people were sent skidding across the street.[21] That same day, Commissioner Connor instructed his men to start using ferocious police dogs to attack the protesters. Television, magazines, and newspapers spread images of young people being mauled and chased by German shepherds.[22] Even the most reluctant supporters of civil rights could not help but be disgusted when they opened *Time* magazine to read about Bull Connor yelling to his officers, "Let those people come to the corner, sergeant. I want 'em to see the dogs work. Look at those niggers run."[23]

The images from Birmingham destroyed the nation's idea that blacks in the South would just sit by and let state governments trample their constitutionally protected natural rights. In few bloody, chaotic days, the argument that the Jim Crow system was an indelible part of the Southern way of life seemed to be nothing more than a flimsy excuse for government-sponsored racism. Even the reluctant Kennedy administration seemed disgusted by the tactics of the Birmingham police. On seeing a photo of a police officer holding a young man's sweater as a dog tore at him, President Kennedy told reporters he felt "sick."[24]

As Alabama Governor George Wallace prepared to stand in the

schoolhouse door on June 11th 1963, President Kennedy addressed the nation on his plans for a new civil rights bill that would provide "the kind of equality of treatment which we would want for ourselves."[25] Kennedy stated that he recognized national opinion had turned firmly against any further appeasement of the segregationists. "The events in Birmingham and elsewhere have so increased the cries for equality that no city or state or legislative body can prudently choose to ignore them," the president stated.[26] Kennedy aimed for the new legislation to ban racial discrimination by businesses serving the general public and for it to empower the U.S. Attorney General to enforce the decision in *Brown* for desegregating schools. The administration hoped that if the federal government finally took a stand against segregation, it could provide an alternative to demonstrations, sit-ins, and further violence.

THE CIVIL RIGHTS LEGISLATION PASSES

Of course, John F. Kennedy never did get to see his civil rights act passed by Congress. Felled by an assassin's bullet on November 22nd 1963, Kennedy was succeeded by Lyndon B. Johnson as president. Johnson was the first Southern president since the Civil War, and many expected him to abandon the proposed civil rights legislation as he campaigned for election in 1964, but Johnson risked his political career by standing behind the legislation, telling Congress, "We have talked long enough in this country about equal rights. We have talked for one hundred years or more. It is time to write the next chapter, and to write it in the books of law."[27]

President Johnson signed the Civil Rights Act of 1964 on July 2nd 1964, after intense opposition from Southern members of Congress. As with earlier civil rights legislation, Southern senators launched a record-breaking filibuster in an attempt to kill the act. Senator Richard Russell of Georgia spoke of the unwilling-ness of the segregationists to bend when he said, "We will resist to the bitter end any measure or any movement which would have a tendency to bring about social equality and intermingling and amalgamation of the races in our states." Nonetheless, President Johnson and his supporters managed to gather enough votes to end debate and force a vote. Perhaps Johnson realized how much anger his behavior would incite when he predicted that "[The Democrats] have lost the South for a generation."[28] Make that two generations.

The 1964 Civil Rights Act prohibited discrimination based on race in public facilities and in the hiring of federally funded work-ers. It authorized the U.S. Attorney General to enforce school desegregation and made it easier for victims of discrimination at the hands of state governments to bring their cases in federal court, which helped shield imprisoned activists from unfair trials by politi-cally dependent state judges and all-white juries. Perhaps the most far-reaching of the Act's provisions was a ban on discrimination in hotels, theaters, and restaurants. Defining these as "public accom-modations," the Act went further than any previous federal law in eliminating discriminatory Jim Crow laws.

Integration of public accommodations was suddenly possible in even the most stubbornly segregationist parts of the South. The whole deck of cards holding up Jim Crow prohibitions collapsed. For the first time since Reconstruction, many Southern blacks found they could eat, drink, sleep, and see a movie wherever they liked, without regard for "Coloreds Only" signs.[29] A measure of person-hood, dignity, and natural rights that had been denied to so many for so long was suddenly restored.

Despite the possibilities the Act offered for blacks, the interven-tion of the federal government in the actions of private business and property owners troubled many. In his book *The Conscience of a Conservative*, Arizona Republican Senator Barry M. Goldwater argued that blacks and whites were equal before the law, but Goldwater opposed the dramatic encroachments on states' rights and property rights in the *Brown* decision and in the Civil Rights Acts. Arguing that "one of the foremost precepts of the natural law is man's right to the possession and the use of his property,"[30] Goldwater argued that the federal government was encroaching on the natural right of people to exclude whomever they pleased from their private property and that this right was no different for private business owners than it was for homeowners. Goldwater spoke for a great many in the country who worried that the Johnson administration had completely ignored constitutional restraints in pushing forward civil rights legislation that regulated private business owners.

If the federal government was overstepping its constitutional limits in finally addressing Jim Crow, it was a belated attempt to make up for a problem that it had been in large part responsible for abetting. Many of the Jim Crow laws were enacted by Southern state governments in the wake of Reconstruction, spiteful toward the federal government for treating them like a conquered people for over a decade. As state governments in the South attempted to undo the changes forced upon them by the North, white attitudes toward blacks hardened. Over the next half century, white discrimination toward blacks, whether government-sponsored or private, became a part of everyday life in Southern states and the federal government did nothing to stop it. For Southerners, the sudden demands in the 1950s and 1960s by the federal government for abrupt desegregation seemed like hypocrisy after so many years of silence and acquiescence. White Southerners could not help but bitterly compare this federal interventionism to the military rule the South experienced during Reconstruction.

The North was not immune to the migrations of blacks up from the South or to the forced integrations of formerly all-white suburban schools. Irish-Americans in Boston, Polish-Americans in Chicago, Italian-Americans in Brooklyn and Newark viewed themselves as innocent victims of an overly active federal system bent on forcing them into unwanted and undeserved lifestyle changes. Some feared the loss of blue-collar jobs to Northern-migrating Southern blacks.

The Northern resistance spawned notoriously contentious litigation in Boston and a bizarre construction-site blockade in Newark. In Boston, where the schools were controlled by blue-collar whites and segregated demographically and not by force of the government, litigation forcing school desegregation was resisted aggressively. The federal "interference" was personified by U.S. District Court Judge W. Arthur Garrity, who ran the public school system for a generation. In Newark in 1969, a developer had purchased land in a predominantly Italian neighborhood and secured a city permit to build a low-income high-rise residential dwelling, called Kawaieda Towers. Under cover of darkness, New Jersey State Senator Anthony Imperiale, a conservative Democrat, had himself welded to the closed gates of the Kawaieda construction site in such a manner as to make entry thereupon impossible without his dismemberment. With his body off the ground and his arms outstretched and immobile, the image of Jesus' sacrifice on the Cross was inescapable. Sen. Imperiale was eventually cut down from the chain link fence, and Kawaeida Towers was never built.

With such a loaded historical perspective, white Southerners were not willing to follow every command of the Civil Rights Act. Blacks may have been admitted to formerly segregated concert halls and lunch counters, but white discrimination continued in many other areas of life. Desegregation of the schools was a particularly slow and painful process, while the aim of ending unfair job advantages for whites was largely ignored. Whites were willing to share their diners and drinking fountains with blacks, but sharing schools and jobs was a very different matter. Even more of a failure was the provisions for increasing black access to the vote. The legislation may have stipulated that voting requirements be the same for all races, but it did not eliminate literacy tests, one of the most common methods for keeping blacks from the polls.[31]

BLOOD CONTINUES TO SPILL

The fight for black voting rights in the South was to make the violent summer of 1963 seem comparatively calm. Civil rights activists knew that further marches and demonstrations would almost certainly lead to bloodshed, but they were willing to accept the consequences if it meant turning national opinion toward a new bill on voting rights.

The battlefield selected was Selma, Alabama, a town with an openly racist sheriff who was backed by an equally racist state judge and the notoriously racist Governor George Wallace, who had so famously proclaimed, "Segregation today. Segregation tomorrow. Segregation forever." Martin Luther King, Jr. informed President Johnson of the planned campaign in Selma, and Johnson was almost certainly aware that the success of the campaign—meaning bloodshed and the public outrage it provoked—would help him get the new voting rights bill passed by Congress.[32] By silently allowing the Selma march to go forward, Johnson was not just a cynical politician; the president realized that major national support for civil rights would be needed if the voting rights bill were to stand a chance against Southern opposition.

Measured in terms of blood and violence, the Selma campaign

was an overwhelming success. On March 7th 1965, on what came to be called Bloody Sunday, six hundred civil rights marchers were attacked by state and local police with billy clubs, bullwhips, and tear gas. Televised images of the brutal attacks whipped up even more national outrage than the Birmingham violence two years earlier, and Johnson seized the moment to present his Voting Rights Act to Congress.[33] The new bill became law five months later, outlawing literacy tests, constitutional interpretation tests, and other requirements that had kept Southern blacks from the vote for nearly a century. Jim Crow was finally buried in law, if not completely in spirit.

NECESSARY BUT NOT NECESSARILY CONSTITUTIONAL

Congress had not passed a single piece of legislation aimed at eliminating racial segregation in private settings since 1883, when the Supreme Court struck down a civil rights act passed just after Reconstruction. In a consolidated set of cases challenging the 1883 law, the Court stated that the Fourteenth Amendment did not provide authority for the federal government to prevent discrimination by private actors. Although this and other Supreme Court cases clearly pointed to hotels and restaurants as private establishments that were immune from federal regulation against discrimination, the Supreme Court changed its tune in the 1960s, deciding that because hotels and restaurants effectively invited the public to them, they were a type of public place and were therefore subject to federal laws against segregation.[34]

To get around the restrictions on its authority created by the Supreme Court, Congress passed the 1964 Civil Rights Act under the Commerce Clause of the Constitution. Part of Article I, the clause seems quite clear in its meaning: "The Congress shall have power . . . to regulate commerce with foreign nations, and among the several states." The clause means exactly what it appears to say: any trade or passage of goods between merchants in two or more states should be kept regular, that is, free from interference by state governments. But Congress has often relied upon a broad definition of interstate commerce to give itself powers not intended by the framers of the Constitution, and the Supreme Court of the 1960s accepted even the most flimsy connections between federal legislation and interstate commerce to justify Congressional regulation of private businesses.[35]

Of course, even a lenient Supreme Court was going to have to stretch the definition of interstate commerce to uphold a federal law clearly aimed at private businesses and organizations that did not conduct business outside their respective states. Two cases, *Heart of Atlanta Motel v. United States* and *Katzenbach v. McClung* presented the Court with just this challenge. The Court ruled on both cases on the same day in 1964, using some of the most creative arithmetic in its history to find that the two stationary businesses fighting for their right to use their private property as they saw fit were engaged in interstate commerce. Both cases challenged the constitutionality of applying the Civil Rights Act of 1964 to private behavior on private property, rather than government behavior on public property.

In *Heart of Atlanta Motel*, the Court found that the motel was subject to the Act because a majority of its clientele were from out of state and because it advertised along interstate highways, even though none of these advertisements were outside the state. In *McClung*, the Court stretched the definition of interstate commerce even further by unanimously finding that a restaurant, Ollie's Barbeque Pit, was subject to the act because some of the food it served had come from out of state, even though it served an almost exclusively local clientele. In one swoop, the Supreme Court allowed the federal government to use the Commerce Clause more expansively than ever before in the country's history by permitting Congress to regulate and to control the private use to which private persons put their private property.

Even though Congress was grabbing powers not expressly granted or even implied to it by the Constitution, it exercised its moral authority in passing the Civil Rights Act of 1964. After the bloody events of the summer of 1963, President Lyndon Johnson and the public were clearly demanding federal action to end discrimination once and for all, whether that federal action was constitutional or not.

THE NORTH BURNS

The focus of the civil rights movement had always been discrimination in the South, but Northern blacks suffered their own indignities and obstacles to success. Just as the activists in the South seemed close to claiming victory against Jim Crow, black ghettos in the North exploded in a pattern of rioting that repeated itself throughout the second half of the 1960s.

Despite Supreme Court rulings and federal laws aimed at ending housing discrimination, segregated housing continued to be common throughout both the North and South throughout the 1960s. The federal government and state governments had allowed segregation to continue in the North, leaving black communities in urban areas cut off from many basic services and decent housing.[36] Blacks had flocked to Northern industrial cities like Newark, Detroit, Philadelphia, Chicago, and Cleveland in the first half of the century, but as the industrial economies of these areas deteriorated, urban-dwelling blacks increasingly found themselves out of work and with few options. White flight to the suburbs only increased segregation, leaving many Northern cities overwhelmingly black.

With such dire conditions in place, bitterness and resentment ran high—and it only took a spark to set off riots and looting. Alleged police brutality sparked race riots in a number of Northern cities throughout the second half of the 1960s. Rochester, New York, and Philadelphia suffered widespread chaos in 1964 after allegations of police brutality. In August 1965, an altercation over a traffic stop in the Watts neighborhood of Los Angeles escalated into a six-day riot involving more than thirty-five thousand people looting, burning, and shooting. The rioters laid waste to an area larger than Manhattan, causing over $200 million in damage; it took sixteen thousand national guardsmen and police officers to quell the violence.[37] More large-scale riots broke out in Cleveland and Omaha in 1966; Minneapolis, Newark, and Detroit in 1967; and Chicago, Washington DC, Baltimore, and Cleveland in 1968. Each time, Americans watched television footage of the devastation, shocked to see inner cities transformed into war zones.

Blacks also voiced their growing frustration with white discrimination as part of the black power movement. Led by Stokely Carmichael and others, supporters of black power proclaimed nonviolent protests and "accommodation" of racist policies as a failure and instead promoted racial separation, black nationalism, and even the use of violence to achieve equal rights for blacks. The Black Panthers were the group most likely to use violence and scare tactics to provoke white outrage. The Panthers often took advantage of a California law that permitted carrying a loaded rifle or shotgun as long as it was publicly displayed and pointed at no one. In 1967, the California State Assembly was scheduled to discuss a ban on public displays of loaded firearms. Thirty Black Panthers entered the Assembly chamber with their loaded weapons, an event reported nationwide on television and in newspapers to a shocked white audience.

The devastation wrought by the riots and, to a lesser degree, by the black power movement was not only felt in terms of lives lost and buildings burned, but in the dramatic turn of white opinion against the civil rights cause. In April 1965, whites who felt the federal government was moving too quickly and even unconstitutionally on integration stood at 28 percent. By August—after the Watts riots—the number had grown to 36 percent, and by September 1966, it was 52 percent.[38]

In response to the riots, President Johnson appointed a commission to find the causes of the riots and suggest measures to prevent future violence. In 1967, the commission presented its findings in the Kerner Report, concluding that the unrest was largely a response to racism and poverty.[39] But these governmental reports did little to mollify white opinion that the government had lost its grip on the inner cities, and it provided no immediate answers for the angry young black men in those cities who continued to riot and loot the following year.

One century after the Civil War tore this nation apart, America again was at war with itself. The drive for civil rights had accomplished much, but blacks in the South had still not achieved full recognition under the law and, increasingly, whites in the South and the North were turning against federal programs aimed at desegregation and racial equality. For many whites, what had begun as an attempt to right past wrongs by state governments and by the federal government had gone too far. This growing block of disenchanted voters was dismayed that the federal government was imposing its power on private businesses and property owners. They did not understand how public policy could mandate that the right of one person to eat a sandwich at a restaurant of his choosing was a greater right than the right of a restaurant owner to serve a sandwich to whomever he chose, and they utterly rejected the idea that the right to choose where to eat versus the right to chose to whom one serves food on private property was a matter for Congress to address.

Jim Crow was an immoral and harmful system that violated the natural law, but it had been allowed to flourish undisturbed by the federal government and promoted by state and local governments for half a century; white Southerners could not help but be shocked by the ferocity with which the federal government aimed to intervene in their way of life.

12

How Democrats and Republicans Use Racial Rhetoric to Get Elected

The Reverend Jeremiah Wright's congregation was accustomed to the occasional screeds delivered from his pulpit in the predominantly black Trinity United Church of Christ in southside Chicago, but the fiery rhetoric delivered on April 13th 2003, was hotter than most.

> The government gives [blacks] the drugs, builds bigger prisons, passes a three-strike law and then wants us to sing "God Bless America." No, no, no, *God damn America*, that's in the Bible for killing innocent people. *God damn America* for treating our citizens as less than human. *God damn America* for as long as she acts like she is God and she is supreme.[1]

The 2008 Democratic presidential primaries were tossed into a maelstrom when the words above came to light in March 2008. Wright's most famous parishioner was Barack Obama, a leading Democratic candidate for president, and when the media broadcast a series of Wright's incendiary sermons portraying the United States as a genocidal, racist superpower, the controversy was significant enough that many pundits asked whether Obama's campaign had been damaged beyond repair.[2] Wright's hateful words shocked many who thought that such bitter rhetoric was a thing of the past. In reality, racial rhetoric has been an integral part of the American political landscape for much of the past fifty years, exploited by both Democrats and Republicans for votes and power.

Beginning with the racist diatribes of George Wallace and other white Southern politicians in the mid-1960s, the rhetoric of race soon entered national politics. Though subtler than the outright hate of Wallace, racial rhetoric has become an inescapable and divisive part of the American political climate, abused by both parties in their quest to win votes. Republicans portray federal programs such as welfare and affirmative action as attempts by big government to take away rights and tax dollars from working class white Americans. The Democrats have shrewdly responded by playing on fears in the black community that welfare and other federal programs are under attack by the GOP. The effect? A political sideshow that rewards half-truths and exaggeration, distracting voters from the issues that really matter.

GEORGE WALLACE PREACHES
THE SERMON OF SEGREGATION

The 1968 presidential election was pivotal in American politics. Riots, assassinations, and differing stances on civil rights further polarized the voting habits of blacks and whites. The final nail was being driven into the coffin of the Southern Democrats. Richard Nixon ascended to the presidency on the strength of the so-called Silent Majority, a group of voters disenchanted after a decade of liberal interventionism and antiwar demonstrations. But perhaps the

most surprising part of the 1968 election was the astounding electoral success of presidential candidate George Wallace, the openly
segregationist by-then former governor of Alabama. Running as a
third party candidate openly opposed to civil rights, George
Wallace lost the election but shocked nearly everyone by grabbing
almost ten million votes, 40 percent of which came from outside the
South.[3] For an avowed segregationist to attract such widespread support was chilling proof that many people in the nation had turned
their backs on civil rights.

Wallace first came to national attention when he issued a challenge to the federal government in his inauguration speech as
governor of Alabama in 1962. In a now well-known passage he
proclaimed: "In the name of the greatest people that have ever trod
this earth, I draw the line in the dust and toss the gauntlet before
the feet of tyranny, and I say segregation now, segregation tomorrow, segregation forever."[4] The lines were written by his longtime
speechwriter, a member of the Ku Klux Klan. Wallace continued to
top headlines with his extremist views when he personally tried to
block black students from enrolling at the state-owned University of
Alabama, an event seen on television by millions.

Wallace cloaked much of his racist rhetoric in the language of
states' rights and opposition to federal interventionism. Voters outside the South began to support his opposition to civil rights in
growing numbers during the mid-sixties. Running against President
Lyndon B. Johnson in the 1964 presidential primaries, Wallace
attracted 43 percent of the vote in Maryland and 30 percent of the
vote in Indiana. Johnson recognized the symbolism that Wallace's
growing popularity signified when he said, "Alabama is coming into
Maryland, Alabama is coming into Indiana."[5] In the 1968 election,
Wallace added a law-and-order message to his rhetoric of states'
rights. On October 24th 1968, he packed Madison Square Garden

in New York City with twenty thousand screaming supporters as he railed against demonstrators, rabble-rousers, and the "sick Supreme Court."[6] The election two weeks later only demonstrated what many already knew: Many white Americans were disenchanted with the upheavals and chaos wrought during the decade-long fight for civil rights.

Wallace never managed to win the presidency, of course, but the immense public support for his openly segregationist platform caused many politicians to take notice. Senator Barry M. Goldwater, a principled, nonracist opponent of the 1964 Civil Rights Act, came very close to some of George Wallace's rhetoric in his support for states' rights. The Republican presidential candidate in 1964, speaking to a Southern crowd, instructed Republicans that it was time for the GOP to "go hunting where the ducks are," meaning that the party should exclusively focus on attracting white voters.[7]

Goldwater's so-called "Southern strategy" of abandoning the black vote to the Democrats became the defining aspect of Republican presidential candidates in the years to come. The 1968 election, coming in the midst of assassinations, the rise of the black power movement, and rioting in the inner cities, provided a perfect storm for exploiting racial rhetoric. Richard Nixon understood the fears of white middle America; fears that the government had lost control and the civil rights movement had unleashed more harm than good. Nixon mimicked Wallace by pledging a return to law and order, loudly opposing busing to expand school integration and promising to appoint a Southern conservative to the Supreme Court. Such statements were designed to appeal to Southerners, but Nixon's implicit criticism of the civil rights movement also won a great deal of support nationwide from his Silent Majority of white, working-class voters dissatisfied after a decade of widespread discord and chaos.[8] Nixon rarely mentioned race openly, but more than one hundred years after the end of the Civil War, it still paid dividends for him to exploit racial issues for electoral gain.

Nixon's success in polarizing the votes of the races in the 1968 election was to become a defining part of future Republican strategy. *The Emerging Republican Majority*, a book by Kevin Phillips that analyzed the 1968 race, quickly became required reading for Republicans. Phillip's book instructed politicians to capitalize on white fears of blacks as a means of eroding the traditional support the Democrats had among white working-class voters. The book noted how this core voting group increasingly saw the Democrats as aligned with black interests, a view that conservatives could easily exploit. Republicans, Phillips wrote, "can hardly ask for a better tactic than a national Democratic Party aligned with Harvard, Boston, Manhattan's East Side, Harlem, the *New York Times*, and the liberal Supreme Court."[9]

Nixon read the book and immediately recognized the promise that a strategy focused on regional and racial divides held for future elections. He instructed his advisors to "Use Phillips as an analyst—study his strategy—don't think in terms of old-time ethnics, go for Poles, Italians, Irish, must learn to understand Silent Majority . . . don't go for Jews & Blacks."[10] Unsurprisingly, Nixon's policy during his first term was a skillful mixture of public opposition to racial hiring quotas and busing, while he quietly allowed desegregation to continue in Southern schools. Nixon was committed to a color-blind interpretation of the law but knew it was crucial to retain Southern support by not appearing too conciliatory toward blacks.[11] This silent action by the Nixon administration was largely undertaken by Nixon's attorney general, John Mitchell, who had engineered Nixon's victory in 1968 as his campaign manager. Acting as the administration's enforcer, Mitchell met personally with segregationist representatives from local school districts, informing them that Nixon would not allow any further delays on school integration.[12]

Mitchell successfully enrolled two million black school children in integrated school districts in the South by 1970, and the Department of Justice under his leadership successfully litigated against local school boards that had resisted implementing the Supreme Court's order to integrate in *Brown*. But for all of its success at desegregation, the Nixon administration shrewdly maintained a public stance of suspicion toward the civil rights movement.

In the run-up to the 1972 election, Nixon loudly advertised himself as a racial conservative, proudly publicizing the NAACP's critiques of his civil rights policies. And just as Phillips' book had predicted, the Democratic candidate, Senator George McGovern of South Dakota, solidified his support among blacks by stridently supporting civil rights. The result? A landslide victory for Nixon, winning 70 percent of the Deep South and more than 60 percent of the states of the former Confederacy.[13]

THE DEMOCRATS BECOME
THE PARTY OF "SPECIAL INTERESTS"

The Democrats only reinforced their perception as liberal elitists by refusing to acknowledge the changing perceptions of the American public toward racial quotas and welfare. The late 1970s saw a dramatic rise in crime, birthrates of illegitimate children, and the number of households on welfare in black communities, but Democrats refused to adapt their policies to fit the changing landscape, arguing that federal programs such as busing for school integration, affirmative action, and welfare were a necessary part of achieving racial equality. This was code for a necessary part of winning votes: Keep blacks dependent on government programs, promise to enhance the programs, and the blacks will vote Democratic every time. Was this government-enforced dependence really just a form of slavery by another name? These attitudes among Democratic politicians only reinforced voters' perceptions of them as a party of elite academics, insulated from the real problems of American society and uninterested in truly helping to get blacks out of government dependency.[14]

Meanwhile, Republicans solidified their popularity among both white working-class voters of Nixon's Silent Majority and former segregationist Democrats of the Deep South by shifting their political platform to fit the growing disenchantment that many Americans had with the civil rights movement.[15]

The 1970s also saw the Democrats losing the allegiance of many white working-class voters as they allowed the party's structure increasingly to accommodate special interest groups. In 1968, the Democratic party rules were changed, allowing greater power in the presidential nominating process to the special interests at the expense of the white middle-class and lower-class voters who often had provided the crucial swing votes for the Democrats. White working-class Americans were most likely to feel that their schools, jobs, and communities were threatened by federal programs such as busing and affirmative action. As the Democrats focused their attention so heavily on minority groups, they ignored the very people who were most subject to the policies supported by the party.[16]

RACIALLY CHARGED RHETORIC BECOMES ENTRENCHED IN PRESIDENTIAL POLITICS

Conservative political rhetoric since 1968 has sought to portray the civil rights agenda, particularly welfare and affirmative action programs, as an attempt by liberals to redistribute wealth from hardworking Americans to special interest groups. Special interest, of course, is political code for minority. For over thirty years, Republicans have been very successful in using this rhetoric to forge a strange alliance between working-class whites and corporate interests.[17] Although these two groups may seem like odd bedfellows, conservatives have co-opted the antitax, antigovernment rhetoric in order to court votes among those opposed to expansion of civil rights programs. Republicans cynically noted the increasing gap in national polls during the 1970s between those who supported increased spending to aid blacks and those who felt blacks should help themselves.[18] By portraying New Deal–era programs like Social Security as "good welfare" and food stamps and Aid to Families with Dependent Children as "bad welfare," the Republicans effectively divided the remaining support Democrats had among white working-class voters in the 1980s.[19]

The two parties became increasingly polarized as they took different stands on issues involving race. The Republicans slammed Democratic support for quotas and racial preferences in hiring and government contracts as an attempt to take away private property rights from hardworking Americans and to impose federal control over school choice, hiring, public safety, and social mores.[20]

A sharp increase during the 1980s in the rate of crime, illegitimacy, and drug use among blacks only helped to sway public opinion away from liberal social welfare programs.[21] In 1980, there were 1,107,500 reports of serious violent crime nationwide; by 1990, this number had skyrocketed to 1,555,900.[22] The media increasingly tied these statistics to the explosion of crack use among young inner city blacks. News of a "crack epidemic" filled the headlines. The public perception of inner cities was of broken, immoral places that were beyond repair by government or society. By 1980, 65 percent of whites were opposed to the government giving special help to special interests.[23]

Unsurprisingly, politicians sensed the political capital to be made by opposing the welfare system. President Ronald Reagan hammered away at the need to reform welfare and to turn back the clock on federal aid programs with statements such as, "We don't have a trillion-dollar debt because we haven't taxed enough; we have a trillion-dollar debt because we spend too much." Reagan may have simply proposed reducing the bloated federal government, but it just so happened that the programs being cut were those previous administrations had enacted to win the loyalty, votes, and dependency of minorities.[24]

The connection to race was obvious enough. Speaking about what was wrong with welfare, Reagan described a woman from Chicago's Southside: "She has 80 names, 30 addresses, 12 Social Security cards, and is collecting veteran's benefits on four nonexisting deceased husbands. And she is collecting Social Security on her cards. She's got Medicaid, getting food stamps, and she is collecting welfare under each of her names."[25] The underlying image was that of a jobless, immoral black woman who was living at the expense of the hard-working majority. The actual facts of the case were less dramatic (the woman used only two identities and her take was $8,000, not the $150,000 Reagan claimed), but the cynical metaphor struck a chord with millions of voters.

Reagan opened his 1980 presidential campaign in the small town of Philadelphia, Mississippi, telling the crowd, "Programs like education and others should be turned back to the states and local communities with the tax sources to fund them. I believe in states' rights. I believe in people doing as much as they can at the community level and the private level."[26] Innocuous enough, right? But for those paying attention, the underlying symbolism was hard to miss.

On June 21st 1964, this small town had been the site of the vicious murder of three civil rights workers, an act that grabbed national headlines. James Chaney, Andrew Goodman, and Michael Schwerner had been stopped for an alleged speeding violation by the Neshoba county deputy (and Klansman) Cecil Price, who handed over the young men to the Klan to be killed. To open a presidential campaign with a speech about states' rights in a place with such a loaded history was hardly an accident.

Ronald Reagan was extremely successful in using the lessons of the 1968 election to build a conservative coalition of corporate interests and white working-class and middle-class voters. A constitutional originalist, his speeches routinely outlined the morbid growth of the federal government and the failures of the federal government to leave the individual alone. Reagan himself was no racist. But he was extremely successful at tapping into rising opposition toward big government among middle- and lower-class white voters. White and black Americans were becoming increasingly polarized between the Republican and Democratic parties, so Reagan suffered very little political cost from his base of white voters by backing cuts to welfare. The cuts to welfare affected just 2 percent of white households but 15 percent of black households.[27]

It was not just Republicans who called for an end to welfare. President Bill Clinton may have been called "the first black President" by novelist Toni Morrison, but he was also an adept politician who understood white voter antipathy toward welfare and other civil rights programs.[28] During the 1992 presidential campaign, Clinton promised to "end welfare as we know it."[29] Clinton's tactical awareness of public opposition to welfare helped him to win the election against President George H. W. Bush on the strength of such sentiment.

BLACK EXTREMISM AND POLITICAL POWER

Just as presidents have exploited white fear and anger toward blacks, leaders in the black community have made their own shrewd calculations in attempts to garner attention. Black leaders making statements intended to inflame and shock whites are nothing new. Beginning with Malcolm X and the black power movement of the 1960s, radicals spouting venom about white racism, lies, and conspiracies have tended to grab the headlines while more rational, measured voices such as Martin Luther King Jr. got pushed aside.

Perhaps one of the most successful black radicals of the past few decades has been Louis Farrakhan of the Nation of Islam. Farrakhan has successfully courted controversy with his demagogic remarks on race and religion. In 1984, he called Adolf Hitler a "wickedly great man."[30] Sensing the outrage and media attention caused by this remark, Farrakhan pressed forward with anti-Semitic remarks, repeating lines such as, "Many of the Jews who owned the homes, the apartments in the black community, we considered them bloodsuckers because they took from our community and built their community but didn't offer anything back to our community."[31] He knew sensationalism would secure him media coverage.

But for all the negative attention, Farrakhan receives great respect from the black community. Even his critics wanted to be a part of the Million Man March he organized in 1995 in Washington, DC. Farrakhan's demagoguery offers many blacks a chance to hear their anger and frustration toward perceived white racism aired to a national audience. Thus Farrakhan manages to position himself as venting black grievances against whites as he plays to the apprehensions and fears of whites.[32]

Jesse Jackson is another black leader who has cannily used racially explosive language to garner media attention. Though less explicit in his rhetoric than Farrakhan, in the 1984 Democratic primary Jackson repeatedly called up stereotypes and negative portrayals of Jews as "hymies" who controlled the media.[33] Jackson has also preyed on the position of blacks in the inner city by portraying Jews as slumlords who exploit poor blacks.[34]

Reverend Jeremiah Wright became the most recent black leader to come to national attention with his hateful speech. Wright's comments describing the United States as an oppressive nation founded on genocide were hardly new, but in March 2008 they were repeated endlessly in newspapers, radio, and television to national indignation. The controversy over Senator Barack Obama's relationship with his former pastor surfaced again a month later, when Reverend Wright made a series of appearances that seemed calculated at generating negative media coverage. Speaking to the National Press Club, Wright repeated many of his most outrageous claims, including comparing the U.S. Marine Corps to the Roman soldiers who killed Jesus and the conspiracy theory that the government created HIV to kill blacks.[35] That week, a nonpartisan media research group reported that 42 percent of all political stories in the media were focused on the controversy.[36]

The divisive rhetoric of black and white leaders only exacerbates the racial divide in this country. In many ways, the suspicions and fears that have divided Americans since the Civil War continue to be exploited by politicians in both major parties. After four decades of politicians' finding great success courting votes in this manner, racial rhetoric is now firmly entrenched in American politics. Sadly, little has changed in the relationship between the races since the 1960s.

13

Justice and Law Enforcement

Recently, radio shock jock Don Imus was once again attacked by those who desire a politically correct society where any mention of race is taboo when he speculated as to why Dallas Cowboy star Adam "Pac-Man" Jones is continually getting arrested. "What color is he?" Imus asked. After his hunch that Jones is black was proven right, he confirmed: "Well, there you go!"[1]

Imus's reaction is hardly remarkable. When word gets out that someone is arrested for a blue-collar crime, it seems that more often than not there is a preconception in our society that the person arrested is black. Don Imus wasn't saying that blacks are more likely to commit crimes, he was saying that the police—the government— most often go after blacks, regardless of evidence of guilt.

The urge in many to pin down Don Imus as a white person who has a problem accepting black people comes less from a fundamental belief that anyone who makes an unpopular remark about race is a racist, but more from our nation's unresolved obsession with race, fostered by the federal government, in which the truth is sooner pushed under the rug than meaningfully discussed.

The truth is that statistics show that 25 percent of all black males can expect to spend time in prison during their lifetimes, while only 4 percent of white males ever go to prison.[2] Blacks make up 13 percent of the U.S. population,[3] but they total 38 percent of all prison inmates.[4] Black men are incarcerated seven times more often than their white counterparts.[5] The disparities in drug punishment are even larger: Nearly 10 percent of America's black population use illegal drugs, compared to 8.1 percent of the white population.[6] Despite these similar figures, of every 100,000 black Americans, 359 are imprisoned on drug charges; of every 100,000 white Americans, only 28 have the same fate.[7] A third of all black males aged 20 to 29 are currently locked up, on probation, or on parole.[8] One-third! The question needs to be asked: Are these statistics proof of racism in the criminal justice system, or are there other causes?

CRIMINAL [IN]JUSTICE SYSTEM

"One of you two is gonna hang for this. Since you're the nigger, you're elected." These words were spoken by Texas Ranger Wesley Styles to Clarence Brandley, a black man charged with the murder of a white high school girl. Brandley was later exonerated in 1990 after ten years on death row.[9] Such outright racism by a government official is no isolated incident. In preparing for the penalty phase at the trial of Anthony Peek, a black defendant, a white judge in Florida said in open court, "Since the nigger mom and dad are here anyway, why don't we go ahead today instead of having to subpoena them back at cost to the state." Anthony Peek was sentenced to death, and the sentence was upheld by the Florida Supreme Court in 1986 after it rejected his claim of racial bias.[10] A prosecutor in Alabama used the fact that several potential jurors were affiliated with Alabama State University, a predominantly black institution, as the reason for striking them from the jury pool. This pretext was considered race-neutral by the trial court.[11]

In Missouri, Judge Earl Blackwell issued a signed press release announcing his new affiliation with the Republican Party while presiding over a death penalty case against an unemployed black defendant. The press release stated in part, "The Democrat party places far too much emphasis on representing minorities . . . people who don't want to work and people with a skin that's any color but white." The judge denied a motion to recuse himself from the trial, and the defendant, Brian Kinder, was convicted and sentenced to death. The Missouri Supreme Court affirmed in 1996.[12] Police, judges, and prosecutors, charged with the duty of upholding the law, routinely undermine the rights of black defendants.

The disproportional treatment of whites and blacks in the criminal justice system is no twentieth-century phenomenon. Race and crime have been linked since the earliest days of our nation's history. It is a link created by the federal government: When America's forefathers decided to deny slaves their humanity by treating them as property in a country founded on liberty, the founders controlled their new property by creating slave codes. These slave codes created two legal systems, one for whites and the other for blacks. Since the early days of the republic, blacks have routinely encountered this disparity in treatment under the law.

This attitude did not end after the Civil War. The idea of two different legal systems, one for blacks and one for whites, continued with black codes, legislation that virtually defined every former slave as criminal. Under these laws, vaguely defined acts such as mischief, vagrancy, and insulting gestures, were crimes only if they were committed by blacks. In many Southern states, free blacks over the age of eighteen were automatically considered criminals unless they could furnish written proof of a job at the beginning of each year.[13]

This criminalization of blacks was accelerated by the fee system. In the South in the late 1800s and the early 1900s, many police officers did not receive a salary; instead, they received a fee for each person they arrested. The judge who tried the accused then drew his pay from the court costs assessed against those he found guilty.[14] Though the Supreme Court of the United States condemned this practice in 1927 with its decision in *Tumey v. Ohio*, the mere fact that such a procedure would be allowed in the judiciary is preposterous. Fines were imposed which were impossible to pay. Those who could not pay their fines became leased convicts, meaning a private jailer guarded, disciplined, fed, housed, and worked the convicts as he saw fit. Sounds like slavery all over again. This convict lease system, which occurred across the South between 1883 and 1910, had a big advantage for the enslavers; since they did not own the convicts, they lost nothing by working them nearly to death. The usefulness of leased convicts did not even end with death, as their bodies were often sold for profit.[15]

Convict leasing was gradually replaced by other forms of prison slavery, including the state use system, whereby the state sold prison-made products and services.[16] The infrastructure of many Southern states was built and maintained by convicts under this system. Black women dug the campus of Georgia State College, while prisoners as young as twelve years old worked in chain gangs to maintain the streets of Atlanta.[17] The state went into business selling products made by convict labor.

The Fourteenth Amendment was enacted to correct these abuses. However, with the adoption of the Jim Crow laws in the South and Jim Crow culture in much of the North, law enforcement and prosecution procedures again cemented the idea of separate legal systems for whites and blacks. Police turned a blind eye to lynching, the most heinous of crimes committed by whites, while punishing blacks very harshly for even the most elementary offenses, even arresting them for no offense at all, such as looking white women in the eye.

In 1931, nine black boys aged from thirteen to twenty one were accused of raping two white women in Scottsboro, Alabama. The women made up the rape story to cover up their extramarital affairs with a couple of white men. After only three days of trial, all of the so-called Scottsboro Boys except the youngest were sentenced to die in the electric chair. After appeals, one of the two women recanted her story, admitting that no rape happened at all. Still, the new all-white jury decided to convict. Judge James Edwin Horton set aside the verdict and there was a third trial. Again, the Scottsboro Boys were convicted. In 1935, the Supreme Court overturned the convictions. Even though there was no doubt that the boys were innocent, the prosecutor, Charles Watts, again filed charges against the oldest five, and again, the retrial resulted in convictions for all of the defendants. The last Scottsboro defendant gained his freedom in 1948 after spending seventeen years behind bars.[18]

Some people like to believe that our long history of racist courts, prosecutors, and juries has been erased from the modern criminal justice system. It is an unrealistic belief. The laws and procedures controlling today's police, court, and corrections system still fail to ensure an identical outcome for blacks and whites accused of the same crime. Rather than outright discrimination, black defendants today must contend with disparities in numbers of arrests, prosecutions, and sentencing. Unlike discrimination, disparities are not always intentional, yet are just as crippling to a black defendant and to the community.

In April 2000, using state and national data compiled by the FBI, the Justice Department conducted a comprehensive study that documented huge racial disparities at every level of the juvenile justice system. Black children under the age of eighteen make up 15 percent of their national age group, but they currently represent 26 percent of all those who are arrested.[19] After entering the juvenile justice system, white and black juveniles with the same records are treated very differently. According to the Justice Department's study, among white youth offenders, 66 percent are taken to juvenile court, while only 31 percent of the black youths are offered the same leniency. Among those young people who have never been to prison before, blacks are nine times more likely than whites to be sentenced to juvenile prison. For those charged with drug offenses, blacks are forty-eight times more likely than whites to be sentenced to juvenile prison.[20]

How does this happen? Social status and relationships with powerful people influence how cases are handled. The drug-dealing child of a powerful, rich white business professional very likely would be sympathetically viewed as "in need of treatment," and an expensive treatment program would immediately be offered as an alternative to incarceration. The drug-dealing child of a poor, single, black woman on welfare, however, would be viewed as a menace to society and tossed, without hesitation, into the unforgiving jaws of the criminal justice system.

The police have become soldiers fighting an enemy rather than peace officers who solve street problems, serve the guilty and the innocent, and protect our freedoms. Blacks (and poor people in general) have become the enemy under assault. Arresting officers often lie. They get away with their lies because there is no process in place to verify their stories. If police officers don't like a person's attitude, they can drum up charges and make an arrest for obstruction of justice or disorderly conduct, just as in the days of the old black codes. Police tactics have reverted to harassment, threats, intimidation, violence, or worse. In 2003, a police officer in Pensacola,

Florida, approached a car in which two teenagers were kissing. The officer threatened to arrest them unless the girl jumped up and down topless for him.[21] The officer was given two years' probation and was later fired. A former Atlanta police officer admitted to lying routinely under oath in order to obtain search warrants.[22] In New York City, police regularly get away with firing their weapons upwards of fifty times at any one incident without even a reckless endangerment charge. The unwritten police code to protect and defend each other is well known and accepted by most, so those who abuse their authority often go unpunished and unchallenged.

The courtroom is no better. There is no per-case spending ceiling for prosecutors. However, states have statutory spending maximums for public defenders. In Alabama the maximum is $1,000 for a felony and $2,000 for capital cases. In South Carolina, it is $750. In Virginia, $350 is the most spent by the state in defense of most felonies. In Tennessee and Kentucky it is $1,000 for a noncapital felony and $2,500 for a capital case.[23] Most capital cases take between one thousand and fifteen hundred hours to prepare and to try. Public defenders, who often have dozens of cases at one time, can often be motivated by expediency rather than justice. Nearly three-quarters of all prison inmates have public defenders.[24] These underresourced and overextended public defenders, many of whom are great trial lawyers, almost always represent black defendants; because black defendants often lack the funds to afford private counsel. Handicapped, these public defenders and indigent defendants appear before judges who, faced with an overburdened docket themselves, prefer having no trial at all or the fastest trial possible. Fast trials often mean no justice for blacks who are already seen as a threat in our society.

If there is a trial, a black defendant will rarely face a jury of his peers. Until the United States Supreme Court decided *Batson v.*

Kentucky in 1986, lawyers had the right to request the removal of potential jurors without declaring any reason. Blacks are often seen as being in favor of the defense and were thus removed as jurors. Today, lawyers must articulate a nondiscriminatory reason for exercising their preemptory challenges when any racial pattern is discernable. However, this burden is extremely low and easy to get around.

During the 1997 election for Philadelphia's district attorney, it was revealed that one of the candidates, Jack McMahon, had produced a training video for new prosecutors when he was an assistant D.A. in which he instructed them on whom to exclude from the jury. "Young black women are very bad!" he said. He then continued, "Blacks from low-income areas are less likely to convict." His training tape also instructed the new recruits on how to hide the racial motivation for their jury strikes.[25]

Prosecutors across the country buy into the same scheme. If two individuals commit the same act, one can be charged with a greater or lesser crime at the prosecutor's sole discretion. The black suspect is often charged with the more serious crime, while the white suspect is offered a plea bargain that carries a lower penalty.[26] This is because prosecutors know it will be much easier to convict the black defendant. Throwing justice out the window, career-driven prosecutors jump at the opportunity to convict.

Until 2007, the federal mandatory sentencing regime put many more blacks in prison for cocaine possession than whites. Under federal mandatory sentencing guidelines adopted during the Reagan administration, "defendants convicted with just 5 grams of crack cocaine, the weight of 5 sugar packets, were subject to a five-year mandatory minimum sentence. The same penalty was triggered for powder cocaine only when an offense involved at least 500 grams."[27] This slanted punishment scheme resulted in thousands of blacks being imprisoned for possession of small amounts of crack cocaine while whites who were prosecuted for possession of greater amounts of the purer powder cocaine were given generally lighter sentences. Fortunately, the Supreme Court finally struck down mandatory sentencing in 2007, determining that the guidelines were incorrect when applied to two drugs that are essentially the same.[28]

Even without mandatory sentencing, prosecutors are less inclined to offer plea bargains to black defendants. In 1992, the *Los Angeles Times* reported that not one white offender had been convicted of a crack cocaine offense in federal court in Los Angeles since 1986, when Congress first enacted mandatory drug sentences. There were 222 white defendants charged with crack cocaine offenses in Los Angeles from 1990 to 1992, all prosecuted in state court, and all avoiding the harsher sentences required under federal sentencing mandates. The defendants in all twenty-four crack cocaine cases tried in federal court were black.[29] The initial reaction is to assume that the disparity is due to the fact that more blacks used crack cocaine than whites. However, reports indicate that at the time, 52 percent of crack cocaine users were white.[30]

While it existed, mandatory sentencing moved the discretion in sentencing from the judge to the prosecutor. When the judge had the power to use his or her discretion, the decision was made under public scrutiny. Prosecutors make their decisions behind closed doors. The decisions they make often reek of the ambition to create a public image for themselves. The result is blatant abuse of the death penalty. When sentencing decisions are made by judges, they are aided by presentencing reports created by probation officers. These reports include information on the defendant's prior record, family background, education, marital status, and employment history. Many blacks convicted of crimes come from deprived backgrounds. They have histories in their records—unemployment, trouble in school, deep family problems, and so on—that judges, who largely come from middle-class backgrounds, might otherwise have trouble understanding. Because prosecutors do not use these reports in deciding what charges to bring, they are much more likely to seek the death penalty.

From the days of slavery through the years of lynching and Jim Crow laws, capital punishment has always been deeply intertwined with race. Unfortunately, the days of racial bias in the death penalty are not over. Across the country the statistics are startling. Though blacks make up 13 percent of the national population, they comprise 42 percent of the inmates on death row.[31] Of the 845 individuals executed since the United States resumed capital punishment in 1977, 80 percent were put to death for killing whites, while only 13 percent were executed for killing blacks, this despite the fact that blacks and whites are murdered in almost equal numbers.[32] When federal death row inmate Louis Jones was executed in 2003, he became the one hundred eighty-third black person executed in the United States since 1977 for the murder of a white person. At the time of his death, only twelve whites had been put to death for the murder of a black person.[33]

The numbers are not limited to a particular state or region. Studies across our country show a consistent pattern of racial disparities in the application of the death penalty between blacks and whites. Examinations of the relationship between race and the death penalty have now been conducted in every major death penalty state. In 96 percent of these reviews, there was a pattern of either race-of-victim or race-of-defendant discrimination, or both.[34] The main question underscoring these pages of data is not if, but *why* race matters in the application of the death penalty. A study by Professor Jeffrey Pokorak and researchers at St. Mary's University Law School in San Antonio, Texas, provides part of the explanation.

Their study found that the key decision makers in capital cases around the country are almost exclusively white men. Of the chief district attorneys in states using the death penalty in the United States, nearly 98 percent are white and only 1 percent are black.[35] At least one in five blacks who are sentenced to die have their fate decided by an all-white jury. That number skyrockets when juries of eleven whites and one black are taken into account.

One should not at all be surprised by the disparities. Ever since July 4th 1776, federal and local governments in the independent United States have aided in the treatment of black Americans as chattel property or as second-class citizens. The federal government's repeated missteps (to put it lightly) and sometimes gross indifference in the area of race relations have fostered an environment in which abuses of power are accepted as normal. Still, the government refuses to do anything productive to remedy its failure. Instead, it enacts affirmative action laws that are both unconstitutional and disastrous to the idea of racial equality.

THE FEDERAL GOVERNMENT'S TRAGIC FAILURE

Virtually all racism in the twentieth century has official government behavior at its roots. But the apparent statistical inequalities in our criminal justice system have just as much to do with poverty as they do with race. The connection between poverty and crime has long been noted. During the 1930s, a much larger part of the white population was poor, and whites committed a greater percentage of street crime. Whites then accounted for nearly 80 percent of those incarcerated, compared to 45 percent today. Now, less than 7 percent of whites live in extreme poverty in the inner cities, compared to 38 percent of blacks.[36] Generally speaking, the white poor are dispersed, compared to black poor, who are more concentrated. Studies and common sense consistently demonstrate that residence in densely populated, dilapidated city environments with high levels of poverty, homelessness, unemployment, infant mortality, and substandard housing fosters criminal behavior.

The government tries to remedy these conditions through taxes, restrictive regulations, corporate subsidies, racial set-asides, and welfare programs. These measures encourage white Americans to adopt a group mentality that only perpetuates resentment and racism; because racism is simply an ugly form of collectivism, a mind-set that views humans strictly as members of particular groups rather than as unique individuals with immortal souls.[37] Further, such measures only weaken the criminal justice system. As suburban populations rapidly grow, political power in these poor city neighborhoods is diminished. Urban criminal justice systems become managed by suburban voters, state legislators, and state and federal appellate judges who neither reap the benefit of good decisions nor bear the cost of bad ones. A criminal justice system under the thumb of suburban voters and politicians is a system prone to act on majoritarian impulses and prejudices. Government officials will not do anything that will effect true change because the current system keeps them in power.

Before 1960, criminal procedure doctrines were, by contemporary standards, simple and spare. However, the Warren Court decisions of the 1960s, which added to the power of the state and national electorates at the expense of local communities, changed the politics of crime. For political conservatives, criminal punishment is an intrusive form of government regulation. Spending on criminal justice is redistributive: money spent to warehouse poor criminals comes disproportionately from the pockets of rich taxpayers. Conservative politicians dislike government regulation and redistributive spending—yet conservative politicians upended this tradition.

During his 1966 campaign for governor of California, Ronald Reagan's tough-on-crime rhetoric drew blue-collar Democrats across the partisan aisle in huge numbers, thus changing the nation's electoral configuration.[38] The Warren Court's criminal procedure decisions were crucial to that process in that they made street crime a national political issue for the first time in American history. For the first time, conservative national politicians could attack "soft" judges and talk about issues that were formerly the sole territory of local politicians.

Oddly, America's punitive turn did not come from the political right; it came from the left's response to the right's new rhetoric. Liberal politicians like President Johnson and Attorney General and later Senator Robert F. Kennedy embraced punitive politics—and the game of competing to see who could be tougher on crime commenced.[39]

In 1992 this competition was still in full swing. During the Democratic primaries, Arkansas Governor Bill Clinton, falling behind in the polls, returned to his State to supervise the execution of a mentally challenged black inmate named Ricky Ray Rector. His ploy worked. He finished a close second in the New Hampshire primary and went on to win the Democratic nomination and the White House. The important thing to realize is that there was no philosophical disagreement between opposing sides; rather, the politics of crime had developed into a game of can-you-top-this.[40] In 2002 the U.S. Supreme Court in *Atkins v. Virginia* outlawed executing the mentally challenged.

Both right and left supported criminal justice policies that, in principle, they found repugnant. The right disbelieved in big government, yet helped create a prison system of unprecedented scope and size. The left opposed racially discriminatory punishment, yet reinforced and expanded the most racially skewed prison population in American history. Crime policy was not a means of addressing crime; the policy's consequences for the poor blacks who were both victimized by crime and punished for it were, politically speaking, irrelevant. Each side supported punitive policies because the other side had done so and because changing course seemed politically risky.[41] There are only a few voices today in the public sphere more interested in upholding the Constitution, guaranteeing natural rights, and rejecting unfair prosecutions, no matter how unpopular the outcome. The paucity of these voices means they find very little political support.

The noncriminal sphere of government is no fairer. The inability of the government to get its own act together is the reason that in most litigation over workplace discrimination, the government itself is the defendant. Across the nation, violators of both state and federal antidiscrimination statutes are most often the ones we choose to enforce them.

New Jersey is one of the main culprits. In 2002, two white former New Jersey state troopers who admitted that they were trained to use racial profiling escaped jail time for shooting four boys (three blacks and one Hispanic) on a routine traffic stop. The officers, James Kenna and John Hogan, admitted in court that they stopped the van carrying the four boys because they were tactically encouraged by state and federal officials to practice racial profiling. The state agreed to pay $12.95 million to settle a lawsuit filed by the four young men.[42]

The release of ninety-one thousand pages of internal records by the State of New Jersey reveals a systematic policy of racial profiling. The statistics show that although minority drivers make up only 13 percent of motorists on state roadways, they account for 80 percent of those stopped by state troopers.[43] The State Police publicly prohibit racial profiling, but according to a 1999 memo from

Deputy Attorney General Debra Stone, "racial profiling exists as part of the culture." Stone, who is apolitical and a veteran prosecutor, reported that senior troopers served as coaches in showing new recruits how to carry out racial profiling; trooper after trooper has testified that coaches taught them how to profile minorities.

Even black state troopers were not immune from the treatment. If they were off duty, they were often pulled over for "DWB"—driving while black.[44] One such officer, a state police sergeant, wrote that he had been stopped forty times by fellow white state troopers while he was off duty.[45] He was never charged with a crime or motor vehicle violation.

New Jersey released the massive number of documents due to demands from lawyers representing drivers who sued the State on grounds of racial discrimination. One of the attorneys, William Buckman, said that much of this material had been denied him when he'd requested it five years prior. "There seems to be only one reason to withhold all of this: to conceal from the public how high up in the attorney general's office people were aware of the length and the breadth of the problem," he said. The mountain of official records constitutes the most damning evidence of crude official racism, fostered and accepted by top state officials of both the Democratic and Republican parties.[46]

The problem isn't limited to racial profiling. In 1998, the New Jersey Department of Corrections fired Edward O'Lone, a white man, after he refused to stop dating a black woman. What business is it of the state what the race is of those its employees date? Though Mr. O'Lone was a white man, he argued that he should be treated as if he belonged in a protected group because he was terminated for his refusal to stop dating a woman who is a member of the protected group. The New Jersey courts agreed.[47]

In 1998, a county sheriff's officer in New Jersey, Carrie Taylor, brought suit against her employer, the county sheriff, for creating a hostile work environment in violation of New Jersey's Law Against Discrimination.[48] The sheriff, Henry Metzger, called Taylor a "jungle bunny" while in the presence of his under-sheriff, Gerald Isham, triggering boisterous laughter from Isham in return. Taylor claimed the incident caused her emotional distress for which she consulted a psychiatrist on a periodic basis. The trial court found the basic issue of law to be whether the remark uttered by Metzger was, from the perspective of a reasonable African-American, sufficiently severe to have produced a hostile work environment. Still, the trial court entered summary judgment in favor of the defendant, ruling that a two-word phrase, uttered only once, did not and could not constitute a hostile work environment.

The New Jersey Supreme Court reversed and held that sometimes even a single utterance of an epithet can, under particular circumstances, create a hostile work environment and it was up to the jury, not the courts, to determine the severity of the situation.

In 2008, Barry Parker, an employee of Trenton Water Works, filed a complaint against the City of Trenton that alleged that his efforts to obtain promotions were frustrated and blocked by the City due to his race. Parker was initially hired in 1993; however, he did not receive his first promotion until 2000. In order to qualify for promotions, Parker tried to have his work schedule altered so he could take outside work-related classes. These schedule changes were repeatedly denied. Parker alleged that his white co-workers were permitted to change their schedules to attend classes. During his deposition, Parker recounted an incident in which he told his superior, John Martin: "I don't want you to take it personally or anything but you're looking at your first black mechanic." Parker testified that Martin responded, "There will never be a black mechanic here."[49] Martin was an official of the government of a major American city. There can be no moral duty versus private property rights argument here: This is the very behavior that the Fourteenth Amendment and all the civil rights laws enacted since its adoption were written to prevent.

After filing his complaint, Parker noticed a drawing of a hangman's noose on a building map in one of the plant's hallways. He was terminated soon thereafter. Following discovery, the City filed a motion for summary judgment. In his May 12th 2004, oral opinion, the motion judge found no genuine issues of material fact as to plaintiff's discrimination and hostile environment claims. He granted summary judgment to defendants. The appellate court reversed this judgment. It faulted the motion court judge for accepting as true the blanket denials offered by the City and accused the judge of failing to follow the proper principles that governed motions for summary judgment.[50]

It is no coincidence that—along with police departments—public school officials, hospital administrators, parks and recreation supervisors, municipal agencies, and other state agents and agencies are often in the defendant's chair facing charges of racial discrimination. If the government cannot heal itself, how can it possibly set out to heal the country?

Further, those who run the federal government are driven by the desire to remain in power. Government officials are very aware of the fact that as our society matures and black Americans continue to have an active role in state and federal governments, there is a real danger that electoral power may shift back to the inner cities, thus giving blacks in those cities more political power. If this happens, many of the policies that keep people in power at the expense of black Americans will be forced to change. It remains to be seen if the avalanche of American voters demanding change in the 2008 elections will result in any fundamental alterations to our flawed justice system.

14

Baseball

Throughout our nation's history, government officials, both federal and local, have too often cowered in the area of race relations: Even presidents have succumbed to the political powers of a racist electorate. Governors, mayors, and judges have set aside their oaths for a flawed belief that blacks could be treated as inferior. Police, military officers, physicians, and public servants have voluntarily abandoned their duty to uphold what is right and decided to stand on the wrong side of the battle between good and evil.

These decisions, made by hundreds of American government officials, set our country on a disastrous course of fear, misunderstanding, confusion, and uncertainty by which we are still overcome. In the midst of all this fear, misunderstanding, confusion, and uncertainty, one white man had the foresight to see what America could be and the fortitude to be the first to try and make it so, not because of political pressure, not because it was the popular move, but because it was right. Perhaps surprising to some but not surprising to most, he hailed from the world of sport. His name was Wesley Branch Rickey, and he, along with Jack Roosevelt Robinson, changed America forever.

The Rickey-Robinson story is compelling, even for those uninterested in baseball. Theirs is a wonderfully American story that reveals a great deal about twentieth-century America and it deserves the attention of Americans of all generations. It shows how the power of ideas and personal industry can overcome the culture of government.

Jackie Robinson, the grandson of a slave and son of two share-crop farmers, was born in Cairo, Georgia, on January 31st 1919, during the height of Jim Crow. As an infant, Jackie's father abandoned the family. His mother, seeking a better life for her four children, joined the "great migration" of black Americans out of the South. Her journey led them west to California.[1] Discrimination was not foreign to the West. Although few laws addressed the issue of black-white relations, widely accepted practices defined the limits of tolerance. Most hotels, restaurants, and recreational facilities refused to accept blacks, restrictive covenants (provisions in deeds that prohibited sales of real estate to blacks) barred blacks from living in certain neighborhoods, and job discrimination impeded economic advancement. As in the South, black Americans in pre-World War II California faced hostility at every turn.

Sustained only by a mother's unwavering spirit, Jackie Robinson turned to sports to escape both poverty and the local call of street gangs. And he excelled at sports. His abilities led him to college at UCLA.[2] While most black athletes of the time played for black colleges or in all-black leagues, Jackie Robinson achieved his initial fame on integrated playing fields. However, his athletic career was abruptly interrupted by World War II.

His army career typified the black military experience of the time. Drafted in 1942 and assigned to Fort Riley, Kansas, Robinson faced more racial discrimination than ever. He was barred from Officer Candidate School, barred from playing on his military unit's team, and restricted to segregated facilities. Still, he rose to the rank of second lieutenant and waged a campaign to improve the conditions for black soldiers at Fort Riley. After his transfer to Fort Hood, Texas, Robinson was court-martialed when he refused to move to the back of a military bus and then defied the officers who attempted to arrest him. A military tribunal acquitted Robinson of all charges, but the episode only intensified his commitment to realize racial justice.[3]

At the time of his release from the army, Jackie Robinson was at the peak of his athletic talents. Though good enough to star in any of the major American team sports, organized baseball, the professional football leagues, and major basketball teams refused to accept black players. Robinson's best alternative was to join baseball's Negro leagues. In the spring of 1945, he joined the Kansas City Monarchs.[4]

SOUL OF THE GAME

Like UCLA, professional baseball had integrated playing fields in the nineteenth century. The number of black players in professional leagues peaked in 1887 when Fleet Walker, Bud Fowler, George Stovey, Robert Higgins, and Frank Grant were on rosters of clubs in the International League, one step from the majors. Although they suffered harassment and discrimination off the field, they were reluctantly accepted by most of their teammates and opponents. At the turn of the twentieth century, separation of the races was the rule after the United States Supreme Court's decision in *Plessy v. Ferguson*. A "gentlemen's agreement" now ruled over organized baseball (the major and minor leagues) from the last years of the nineteenth century until 1946. The agreement, though never formally written, was understood by all owners and leaders to be a total ban on black players.

Black baseball players who wanted to play professionally had to join all-black teams (though several of the light-skinned black players made it to the big leagues by claiming they were Latin American). With the growing base of potential fans in the North due to the great migration, top-quality black teams appeared in the Northeast and Midwest: The Genuine Cuban Giants and Cuban X Giants of New York City (both made up of African-Americans, despite their names), the Cuban Stars and Havana Stars (both with real Cuban-Americans), the Lincoln Giants of New York City, the Newark Eagles, the Philadelphia Giants, the Bacharach Giants of Atlantic City, the Homestead (Pennsylvania) Grays, the Hilldale Club of Philadelphia, and the Norfolk (Virginia) Red Stockings. In the Midwest the leaders were the Chicago American Giants, the Chicago Columbia Giants, the Leland Giants of Chicago (formerly the Union Giants), the Kansas City (Missouri) Monarchs, and the Indianapolis ABCs. These teams vied for the mythical "colored championship of the world."[5]

Major league baseball teams often played black teams during the pre- and postseasons. In 1909, the Chicago Cubs won three close games in a series with the Leland Giants. In 1915, pitcher Smokey Joe Williams of the Lincoln Giants completed a five-hit shutout of the National League champion Philadelphia Phillies.

But in the late 1920s, Commissioner Kenesaw Mountain Landis forbade big league clubs from competing against all-black clubs in the off-season. Many believe his reasoning for doing so was frustration over how well the black clubs competed. The Negro National League and Negro Eastern League formed in 1920 and 1921, respectively. During that decade, a Negro World Series began and was held annually until the Negro leagues failed in 1931. A second Negro National League was founded in 1933, and the Negro American League was formed in 1936.

At their best, players from the Negro leagues played some of the best baseball America had ever seen. Leroy Robert "Satchel" Paige was a pitching legend. Born in 1906, his professional playing career lasted from 1926 until 1965. He appeared in the Major League Baseball All-Star Game in both 1952 and 1953, at the ages of forty-six and forty-seven respectively (without performance-enhancing drugs), and was the first Negro league player elected to the Major League Baseball Hall of Fame. James Thomas "Cool Papa" Bell was an American center fielder in Negro league baseball. He is considered by many baseball historians as being the fastest man ever to play the game, having been recorded as rounding the bases in only twelve seconds. As Satchel Paige noted in his autobiography, *Maybe I'll Pitch Forever*, "If Cool Papa had known about colleges or if colleges had known about Cool Papa, Jesse Owens would have looked like he was walking."[6]

Buck Leonard was a ten-time all-star in the Negro leagues. His dynamic talent as a hitter caused many to compare him to Lou Gehrig, though many thought he was superior to Gehrig as a fielder. In 1999, Leonard ranked forty-seventh on the *Sporting News* list of the 100 Greatest Baseball Players of all time. He was one of only five players so honored who played most of their careers in the Negro leagues. Then there was Josh Gibson, known as the "black Babe Ruth." He stood six-foot-one and weighed 210 pounds. Baseball historians consider Gibson to be among the very best catchers and power hitters in the history of baseball. His lifetime batting average, according to Hall of Fame official data, was .359. The *Sporting News* of June 3rd 1967, credits Gibson with a home run in a Negro league game at Yankee Stadium that struck two feet from the top of the wall circling the center field bleachers—about 580 feet from home plate. Although it has never been conclusively proven, it is rumored that he even slugged one over the third deck next to the left field bullpen in 1934, the only fair ball ever hit out of the old Yankee Stadium. His baseball Hall of

Fame plaque reads he hit "almost 800 homeruns" in his 17-year career.[7]

These players and many more saw the Negro leagues as an opportunity to showcase their amazing talents. They saw it as a vehicle for perhaps being discovered by white team owners in mainstream major league baseball, where true respect awaited. For Jackie Robinson, however, the Negro leagues proved a distasteful experience. Accustomed to the highly structured training and schedule of major college sports and hostile to all forms of segregation, Robinson considered the Negro leagues a step down. The long, hot bus rides, the degrading treatment at white-owned facilities, and the informal attitudes of his league-mates frustrated Robinson, who neither smoked, drank, nor enjoyed what Satchel Paige called the "social ramble" of baseball life.[8] Although Robinson performed well with the Kansas City Monarchs, batting .387 and starting at shortstop in the East-West All-Star Game, he always disparaged his stint in the Negro leagues. What Jackie didn't know was that his performance with the Monarchs attracted intense scrutiny.

Branch Rickey had secretly decided to bring blacks into the major leagues. Under the guise of forming a new Brooklyn Brown Dodger squad, he assigned his top scouts to evaluate Negro league talent. They were to look not only at playing ability, but also at the player's mental toughness, maturity, and capacity to withstand hostility. Rickey himself sought out Wendell Smith, the sportswriter for the *Pittsburgh Courier*, the nation's most popular black newspaper, and quizzed him about potential players for the Brown Dodgers. Smith, who might have suspected Rickey's true intentions, recommended Jack Roosevelt Robinson.[9]

Branch Rickey offered conflicting reasons for his decision to desegregate baseball. Often, he spoke of a need to erase the memory of the black college player whom he had coached in 1904 who had wept when barred from staying with his teammates at a midwestern hotel. Just as frequently, he denied any noble intent and invoked a desire to field the best team possible. "The Negroes will make us winners for years to come," he boldly predicted.[10] Clyde Sukeforth, Rickey's best scout, was to be Jackie Robinson's personal scout, trailing him and sending detailed reports back to Brooklyn.[11] Although players such as Paige and Gibson were more prominent, Robinson became Rickey's favorite because of his skills and personality. When Robinson was placed temporarily on the sidelines (after being injured), Sukeforth saw an opportunity for the first face-to-face meeting between two men that would soon change America forever.

The meeting took place in Rickey's office at 215 Montague Street, Brooklyn, New York. In the office were volumes of quotations, one of which stated the following:

> He that will not reason is a bigot.
> He that cannot reason is a fool.
> He that dares not reason is a slave.[12]

As Jackie Robinson and Clyde Sukeforth entered Branch Rickey's office, they were met only with a deep stare. Maintaining his silence, Rickey reached for a cigar before signaling his guests to take seats; the gesture implied that their meeting would not be a short one.

"Do you have a girl?" Rickey asked.[13] The question was not merely small talk. Rickey knew that if Robinson found the right girl, he should marry her, sooner rather than later, because he would need all the help he could get in the months and years to come. After shedding light on his true intentions for Jackie, Rickey added, "I don't know how you play, but my scouts do. If he says you're a good ballplayer,"—pointing to Sukeforth—"I'll take his word for it." He then posed the most important question. "What I don't know is whether you have the guts." Before Robinson could reply, Rickey cut him off: "I'm looking for a ball player with guts enough *not* to fight back. You've got to do this job with base hits and stolen bases and fielding ground balls, Jackie. Nothing else!"[14]

Before a stunned Robinson could respond, Rickey stripped off his sport jacket and started imitating what was in store for Jackie. He imitated a white hotel clerk refusing to give Robinson a room, after finding accommodations for all of his other teammates. He then imitated a waiter ordering him to leave a restaurant that kindly served the rest of the team. He imitated rowdy fans pushing and shoving Jackie the way he would be pushed and shoved in hotel lobbies and railroad stations throughout the country. In closing he summed up his point: "What I am saying to you, Jackie, is that you will have to be more than a good ballplayer." After a brief silence, Robinson finally spoke: "Mr. Rickey, I think I can play ball, and I promise you that I will do the second part of the job, although I can't be an obsequious, cringing fellow." If Branch Rickey had any remaining doubts, they were dispelled when he heard Jackie Robinson utter those words.[15] Rickey, the champion of courage and reason, could not condone anyone being obsequious or cringing.

Still, Ricky wasn't done. He went on to read a passage from Giovanni Papini's *The Life of Christ*, which spoke about the three answers that men can make to violence: Revenge, flight, and turning the other cheek. He wanted to stress to Jackie that only by utilizing the third of these answers could one truly grasp respect and approach greatness. "Only he who has conquered himself can conquer his enemies."[16]

"Can you do it?" Rickey asked, "Three years—can you do it?" Before Robinson could answer, Rickey continued to question, "What do you do when they call you a black son of a bitch?"

Without waiting for a response, Rickey threw a swing at Robinson. It missed, but the accompanying words did not. "What do you do?" he shouted at his target. Before Robinson could answer, Rickey answered for him, "You cannot strike back! So what do you do?" Jackie finally had his chance to answer, "Mr. Rickey, I've got two cheeks."[17]

The interrogation was over. And Jackie Robinson signed the first Major League Baseball contract offered to a black ballplayer. It was a great moment in American history, witnessed by only three people, but it would in a real sense begin social relations anew. It would do for human relations in America what no politician or public office holder ever did or could do.

A ONE-MAN CIVIL RIGHTS MOVEMENT

Branch Rickey swore Jackie Robinson to a vow of silence; if word got out too soon the whole thing could be ruined. He wanted to keep his meeting with and signing of Jackie Robinson entirely on the hush. Jackie found it hard to maintain this vow around his family, but they hardly wanted to listen to him, much less believe him, when he went on about being signed by the major league Brooklyn Dodgers. When Rickey finally broke *his* silence, the first people he told were his wife and six children. It was extremely important to him that they understand and share his dream. And they did.

But they would be alone. On October 23rd 1945, the world learned that Jack Roosevelt Robinson of the Kansas City Monarchs had signed a contract to play professional baseball for the Brooklyn Dodgers organization. The line from the Dodgers was that Robinson's signing had little to do with racial justice and everything to do with his being a fine player who could help Brooklyn win baseball games.[18] Branch Rickey wanted nothing negative about the unfolding Jackie Robinson story to appear in print; therefore any mention of his youthful brushes with the law, battles with the Army, or sometimes terrible temper were kept completely under wraps. His personal history was not paraded before the public, but his baseball credentials were openly criticized. New York *Daily News* columnist Jimmy Powers thought he was, at best, a "1,000-to-1 shot to make the grade." The *Sporting News* scouting report said that if Robinson were white, he would only be a "Class C" prospect. Cleveland Indian pitcher Bob Feller added: "If he were a white man, I doubt if they would consider him big league material."[19]

Friends in the Negro leagues failed to come to Jackie's defense. Perhaps it was resentment, perhaps jealousy, perhaps simply fear for Jackie and for themselves; many from the Negro leagues believed that Branch Rickey signed Jackie knowing he would fail, thereby quashing integration possibilities for the better Negro league players.

Admitted Buck Leonard about Jackie Robinson: "We didn't think he was that good."[20] Satchel Paige had the foresight to see the bigger picture. Not until much later did Paige go public with his feelings of rejection and resentment toward Robinson. An argument could be made that Satchel was the best pitcher in all of baseball, white or black, even though he was approaching forty years of age. He felt that he should have been chosen over Robinson, and many Negro league players agreed. Still, in public, Paige never belittled Robinson, calling him a "number one player" and stressing that Rickey "didn't make a mistake in signing Robinson."[21] On why he wasn't chosen over Robinson: "Those major league owners knew I wouldn't start out with any minor league team. . . ."[22]

Jackie would, and in February 1946, after marrying Rachel Isum in Los Angeles, the two headed to Florida for Robinson's first spring training camp as a Dodgers farmhand with the Montreal

Royals of the International League. From the moment of their arrival, the Robinsons encountered the evils of Jim Crow. In Pensacola, airline officials removed them from their scheduled flight. At Sanford, threats of violence forced them out of town. In Jacksonville and Deland, public officials refused to allow Jackie to play. On one occasion, a local sheriff stormed onto the field and demanded his ouster midgame.[23] You could not make this up: The government stops a black man from playing on a professional athletic team owned by a white man on a ball field owned by another white man. Robinson was ready to give up before his challenge truly had begun.

Gene Benson, a Negro league veteran, and Wendell Smith were hired by Branch Rickey to be unofficial tutors and confidantes to Jackie. They often had to convince him not to give up. It would be two years before President Harry S Truman would order the desegregation of the armed forces. Eight years would pass before the U.S. Supreme Court would issue its *Brown v. Board of Education* decision. Martin Luther King Jr. was a seventeen-year-old student at Morehouse College at the time, Barack Hussein Obama was not yet born, and Jackie Robinson was "a one-man civil rights movement."[24] The hopes of thirteen million black Americans were loaded onto Jackie Robinson's shoulders.

He would not disappoint. On opening day 1946, Jackie Robinson's Montreal Royals defeated the Jersey City Giants fourteen to one. Jackie Robinson got four hits, including a three-run home run, scored four times, stole two bases, and twice scored from third by inducing the opposing pitcher to balk. The trend remained for the rest of the season. Despite fastballs aimed at his head, spike attempts geared toward his knees, threats of race riots in Baltimore (the league's southernmost city), and vile harassment by opposing players, Robinson led the International League in batting average

(.349) and runs scored (113). He finished second in stolen bases and registered the highest fielding percentage (the percentage of times a defensive player properly handles a batted or thrown ball) of any second baseman. Led by Robinson, Montreal went on to win the league pennant by nineteen and a half games and the Little World Series minor league championship.[25]

Life away from the baseball diamond wasn't nearly as triumphant. The people of Montreal accepted the Robinsons on a superficial level only. They were objects, not neighbors. In the clubhouse, Jackie's teammates kept their distance. Despite his success, life as a Montreal Royal was desperately lonely. Branch Rickey embarked on a strategically planned blueprint for Jackie Robinson's road to the Dodgers. When spring training began in 1947, Rickey dispatched the Dodgers and Royals to Cuba and Panama in an effort to avoid the Jim Crow mentality of Florida. He also set out to transform Robinson into a first baseman, the Brooklyn club's greatest need.

Rickey believed that a demonstration of Robinson's skill would generate support from his Dodgers players, who would unanimously call for his promotion. Again, Robinson did not disappoint, ringing up a .429 batting average. Nevertheless, rather than demand his ascension, several Dodgers, led by Alabama-born Dixie Walker, circulated a petition to keep him off the team. The move was not unanticipated by Rickey; he was counting on his manager, Leo Durocher, to put down any player rebellion before it happened. People manipulated others in the 1940s the same way they do so now; by appealing to their pockets.

It was midnight when Durocher called a team meeting, and he made his case as bluntly as he could: "This fellow is a real great ballplayer. If he turns out to be half as great as he looks, every Dodger will make money. I don't care if the guy is yellow or black, I say he can make all of us rich. From everything I hear, he's only the first, boys, only the first."[26] Rickey and Durocher were not alone; several players, most notably Kentucky-born shortstop Harold "Pee Wee" Reese, refused to sign the protest and on April 10th 1947, Rickey elevated Robinson to the Brooklyn Dodgers club as its first baseman. Still, his damage control was far from over.

He also had to get major league baseball on board. Baseball's first commissioner, Kennesaw Mountain Landis, perpetuated the color line and prolonged the segregation of organized baseball. However, in 1944 Commissioner Landis died. His successor was Albert Benjamin "Happy" Chandler, a Kentucky-born Democrat. His commitment to the cause of baseball integration was unknown, and after an informal fifteen-to-one vote by club owners against permitting black players in the major leagues (Rickey being the lone yes vote), there was little evidence that he would support Rickey. Nevertheless, Commissioner Chandler told the Dodgers president to go ahead and "bring him in. He'll play if he's got the capacity to play."[27]

Another very important piece in Branch Rickey's elaborate puzzle was garnering the support of Dodgers play-by-play announcer, Walter "Red" Barber. Barber was a reassuring voice, trusted by Dodgers fans; his words and voice would be critical to advancing fan acceptance of Jackie Robinson. A son of Mississippi, when Red Barber was told that Jackie Robinson would be joining the Brooklyn club, he threatened to quit. Fortunately, Lila Barber, his wife, had other ideas about the economy of the Barber household. "Think about it," she told her husband. He did and agreed to stay on the job. Red Barber would soon grow to respect Robinson and became an effective ally for him. However, when asked, he was much more modest: "I didn't resent him and I didn't crusade him. I broadcast the ball [game]."[28]

Rickey then sought to address the black community. He

requested the presence of some thirty local black leaders at the Carlton Branch of the Brooklyn YMCA. His words were piercing:

> The biggest threat to [Jackie Robinson's] success, and the one enemy most likely to ruin that success, is the Negro people themselves! Every step of racial progress you have made has been won by suffering and often bloodshed. This step in baseball is being taken for you by a single person whose wound you cannot see or share. . . . And yet, on the day that Robinson enters the big leagues, every one of you will go out and form parades and welcoming committees. You'll strut. You'll wear badges. You'll hold Jackie Robinson Days and Jackie Robinson nights. You'll get drunk. You'll fight. You'll be arrested. You'll wine and dine the player until he is fat and futile. You'll transform his victory into a national comedy, and ultimately into a national tragedy, yes, a national tragedy! Don't spoil Jackie's chances.[29]

Branch Rickey knew his experiment's success depended not only on how well Jackie played, or how he dealt with bigotry, but also on how the black community reacted along the way. Rickey's audience members that night responded enthusiastically to his call. They understood their role. Black Americans, Southern and Northern, had a special obligation to do everything they could to avoid even the appearance of departing from the straight-and-narrow middle-class path.[30] This included how they dressed and carried themselves at games, how they cheered, how they booed, and even how they responded to the many hecklers Jackie would face in the stands. He really was his own "one-man civil rights movement."

ENDURE, PITY, AND EMBRACE

A few weeks later, while sharing an afternoon with a Dodger employee, Branch Rickey found himself reciting from Alexander Pope's *Essay on Man*:

> Vice is a monster of so frightful mien
> As to be hated, needs but to be seen;
> Yet seen too oft, familiar with her face,
> We first endure, then pity, then embrace.[31]

As he pondered those words, Rickey leaned back and stared into space for his twist on what Pope had written: "First they'll endure Robinson, then pity him, then embrace him."[32] Around the league, Robinson's arrival prompted undercurrents of dismay. Rumors circulated that the St. Louis Cardinals and Chicago Cubs would strike rather than compete against a black player. Opposing pitchers beaned Robinson seven times during the first half of the season. Hotels in Philadelphia and St. Louis barred him and a hotel in Cincinnati even made him take his meals to his room out of fear that his presence in the hotel dining room might offend other guests.

His worst day occurred on a windy April afternoon when the Dodgers faced the Philadelphia Phillies at Ebbets Field. Under the leadership of manager Ben Chapman, the Philadelphia ballplayers subjected Robinson to an unconscionable stream of racial abuse. The insults began in the first inning and continued until the last out was made. Dodgers traveling secretary Harold Parrot reported to Branch Rickey that he had never heard such "dugout filth to match the abuse that was sprayed on Robinson last night."[33] Robinson had to contend with such inflammatory speech as: "Hey, Nigger, why don't you go back to the cotton field where you belong?" and "They're waiting for you in the jungles, black boy" and "Hey, snowflake, which one of those white boys' wives are you dating tonight?"[34]

Robinson kept both his promise to Rickey and his unspoken pact with black fans; he never retaliated. His only response was a hit that scored the winning run as the Dodgers took a one-to-nothing victory. Jackie would later admit that that game against the Phillies was the closest he ever came to cracking up.

Something good came from that game. The true bond shared between teammates, regardless of one's views, showed itself as many of Jackie's Dodgers teammates were angered by the conduct of the opposing team. At one point, second baseman Eddie Stanky took matters into his owns hands by taunting back: "Listen, you yellow-bellied cowards. Why don't you yell at somebody who *can* answer back? There isn't one of you who has the guts of a louse."[35] Stanky was Robinson's major defender among the Dodgers. In Rickey's judgment, Stanky had little natural ability. He couldn't hit, run, field, or throw very well. But he was helping the team in another way, by embracing Jackie Robinson and by openly, courageously, and fearlessly defending him. Even Dixie Walker, the main culprit behind the petition to ban Jackie from the team, was angered by the behavior of the Philadelphia manager. He confronted Ben Chapman after the game, telling him that he'd crossed the line.

Jackie would need this rally of support around him, as death threats soon began coming in the mail, both to his hotel rooms and to the clubhouse. When the team played in Cincinnati, the abuse was particularly offensive. In the midst of the verbal abuse, Pee Wee Reese left his position on the field at shortstop and walked to Jackie at first base. He put his arm over his shoulder and started to talk for a few seconds, the way pals often do. Suddenly the hecklers in the stands and in the dugout grew silent. It was the first time a white player had touched a black player fondly and deliberately on a public baseball diamond. Another milestone had been reached. "That meant so much, so much," Jackie later recalled. "It was just a kind and incredible gesture." Reese later remembered catching a little heat over it when he returned home to Louisville, but this soon passed.[36]

Amid this backdrop of pressure and challenge, Robinson carved out not just an extraordinary rookie season, but a monument to courage. He batted over .300 for most of the season and led the league in stolen bases. He trailed just one other player in runs scored and paced the Dodgers in home runs, leading them to the pennant. Major league baseball awarded him with its first Rookie of the Year award.

In 1947 baseball fans came to see Jackie Robinson. Ebbets Field was home to huge crowds. Fans of every race were piling in to see Jackie play. According to Red Barber, Jackie Robinson was the "biggest attraction in baseball since Babe Ruth."[37] That attraction brought in a season attendance record of 1,807,526, a record the Brooklyn Dodgers would never break. Over his ten seasons in major league baseball, Jackie Robinson crafted a batting average of .311, an on-base percentage of .440, with 197 stolen bases (20 successful attempts stealing home plate), and a fielding percentage of .983. In addition to Rookie of the Year, he went on to garner the Most Valuable Player award in 1949, a world championship in 1955, and six consecutive All-Star Game nominations from 1949 to 1954.

These statistics place Jackie among the best players in baseball history and are Hall of Fame–worthy regardless of his race. Still, Robinson's statistics tell only half the story. By injecting major league baseball with the more aggressive and flashy base-running and batting style of the Negro leagues, Robinson transformed the game and, in the process, transformed the nation.

THE FIRST AND THE GREATEST

Branch Rickey knew Jackie Robinson was the one; and there could only be one. He could have selected two or three black players and positioned them to break the color barrier together, but this he deliberately chose not to do. In his mind it was crucial that one player be given the center stage. This individual did not necessarily have to be the best black baseball player, but he did have to be the best person. Jackie Robinson turned out to be both.

Not surprisingly, the federal government had no public reaction to Jackie Robinson's historical venture in 1947. As governments usually do, it failed to acknowledge the severity or magnificence of what was taking place. If government officials supported Jackie, they would offend a politically powerful South and quite possibly commit political suicide. If they didn't, they would offend the growing black community and quite possibly suffer the same consequence.

In 1947, two years after a second world war that left blacks and whites in our country more divided than ever before and in the midst of the horror of Jim Crow segregation, America's favorite pastime decided to integrate. The burden would fall to one man. He would face a variety of evils: Supposed fans of the game would spit at him, throw fruit at him as if he were a jungle animal, and scream reckless obscenities in his direction, all in the presence of their own and other children; local police authorities would remove him from the playing field; teams would threaten to strike; cities would threaten to riot; death threats would be sent to his home, his wife and child being put in harm's way—because of a belief that blacks and whites shouldn't play sports together. Through it all, Jackie Robinson's only recourse would be to take it, to endure. and endure he did.

If he had even by accident retaliated, where we would be today? The opposition against President Truman's signing the Executive Order desegregating the military would no doubt have been renewed; the lawyers who represented the Board of Education of Topeka, Kansas, in that landmark 1954 case would have had concrete evidence of the dangers of integration; and government officials who came together in 1964 to pass the Civil Rights Act might have never been convinced that it was the right thing to do.

By having nothing to do with his triumph, the government, albeit unknowingly, let Jack Roosevelt Robinson become a black hero with whom whites could identify. Without such a hero, white Americans may have never cared enough about black Americans to be bothered by racial injustice. Jackie Robinson did for his country what its federal government could not: he renewed the civil rights revolution.

Conclusion

I have written and published three books prior to this one. Each was about the role of the government in a free society.

In *Constitutional Chaos: What Happens When the Government Violates Its Own Laws,* I argued that we can all lose our freedoms if the government, and the people who run it and work for it, are not required to obey the same laws and comply with the same norms as the rest of us.

In *The Constitution in Exile: How the Federal Government Has Seized Power by Rewriting the Supreme Law of the Land,* I argued that Americans have slowly and inexorably permitted the federal government to grow to such enormous size, to seize such tremendous power, and to acquire such fantastic wealth that we are all in danger of losing the freedoms protected by the delicate balance and distribution of powers that the Constitution was written to maintain.

And in *A Nation of Sheep,* I made the case that the Orwellian vision of his terrifying masterpiece *1984* can happen here—and is happening here.

In all three works, I demonstrated that only by adherence to the natural law, by a rejection of positivism, and by upholding the Constitution can our freedoms remain secure.

CONCLUSION

In the book you have just finished reading, a history of black-white legal and political relations in America, you have had recalled for you the worst chapters, greatest abuses, and most indelible stains in American history. All the evils that whites have visited upon blacks were done by the power of a perverse idea that made its way into the government. For over two hundred years, the government, filled with collectivists and shielded by positivism, has believed that it could write any law, enact any policy, and enforce any cultural norm, so long as there was popular support for them.

But racism in America goes beyond popular support: It is, in essence, popular hatred. It is hatred based on skin color, and like most hatred, it is grounded in fear. And hatred is truly, as we have seen in the foregoing pages, the most destructive of human attributes. The pain of its sting knows no end.

Hatred based on race has animated American governments in every generation since the pilgrims first came here. This hatred has resulted in egregious personal loss for tens of millions and cultural destruction for all of us.

In my previous books, I argued that term limits would guarantee new blood and new ideas in government. I still believe that. New people and turnover in government can eventually eradicate old attitudes. In those pages and elsewhere, I have advanced the ideas that without a fundamental, obvious public rejection of positivism and embrace of the natural law by the government, the courts should presume that what the government seeks to do is unconstitutional; the government should be compelled to justify constitutionally, under the natural law and morally, whatever it wants to do, whenever and wherever it wants to do it.

I believe those arguments are now self-evident and must be considered seriously. But a recent event gives pause for hope.

If there is anyone out there who still doubts that America is a place where all things are possible, who still wonders if the dream of our founders is alive in our time, who still questions the power of our democracy, tonight is your answer.[1]

When Barack Obama, a man from a white mother and a black father, uttered those words on November 4th 2008, the entire country recognized that he would be the forty-fourth president of the United States. And listening, I said a prayer for the dawn of a new age in America. I agree with very few of his attitudes about the role of government in the lives of our people. But he is the last best hope, and now the best incarnate hope, for a post-racial America. On his shoulders—those of a big-government liberal Democrat—will rest the ironic task of wedding America again to the natural law, of shedding from America forever the vestiges of positivism, and of creating a black-white relationship that is color-blind from its core to its outermost limits.

I am hopeful for a post-racial society—one in which the government and accepted norms of behavior are color-blind—but not for one in which the government adheres fully to the natural law or the Constitution. As I write this, the nation is riveted by hearings on Capitol Hill at which the chief executive officers of General Motors, Ford, and Chrysler, and the president of the United Auto Workers Union are on national television literally begging the Congress for handouts, loans, loan guarantees—any form of taxpayer-generated cash that will postpone their self-induced day of financial reckoning. They will no doubt get the money, even though the Constitution nowhere authorizes such theft and in numerous places prohibits it.

The Constitution grants Congress only seventeen specific delegated powers. And it commands in the Ninth and Tenth

Amendments that the powers not articulated and thus not delegated by the Constitution to Congress be reserved to the states and the people.

The Constitution does not repose in the Congress the power to bail out individuals or private industry: Bailouts violate the equal protection doctrine because the Congress can't fairly pick and choose whom to bail out and whom to let expire; they violate the General Welfare Clause because they benefit only a small group and not the general public; they violate the Due Process Clause because they interfere with contracts already entered into; and they turn the public treasury into a public trough. Worse still, Congress lacks the power to let someone else decide how to spend the peoples' money.

It is clear that the framers wrote a Constitution as a result of which contracts would be enforced, risk would be real, choices would be free and have consequences, private property would be sacrosanct, and the natural law will be respected.

The new government will no doubt tax and spend, seize property and regulate industry, violate rights, and enact collectivist positivist laws.

But maybe, just maybe, a black president will make the American government forget to hate.

Acknowledgments

Writing a book about a part of American history as sweeping and emotional as this is a task that consumes one's energy, saps one's joy, and challenges one's sense of fairness. The expenditure of energy is in the research and reduction of ideas to writing. The loss of joy is in the realization of harms caused that can never be adequately redressed. The challenge to fairness is in the knowledge that one has with one's best effort written a case that needs to be made.

Needless to say, any work of this nature is not a product of just one person. My research assistants, Andrew C. Ellis, Keiyana Fordham, Maximillian S. Shifrin, and Adrian D. Stubbs, who at this writing are second-year law students anxious to get out into the world and right its wrongs, were invaluable in doing the raw research and drafting the initial version of many of the paragraphs, the ultimate versions of which you see printed here.

My friend and colleague, James C. Sheil, has generously edited every book I have written, including this one. His professional skills and intellectual honesty have sharpened and improved everything I have published. My personal assistant at Fox News, Tamara Gitt, and my Fox News personal producer, Kathryn Klein, have tolerated the impatience of a boss pulled in a variety of directions, but who still must produce an intellectually demanding and honest work. My radio partner, Brian Kilmeade, who challenges my ideas every day, helps to keep those ideas keen and relevant. My colleague Geraldo Rivera, who is one of the most intellectually honest persons I know, continually reminds me to defend freedom, even in its darkest hours, or we will lose it.

Finally, my boss at Fox, Roger Ailes, who has the brightest mind and is the greatest person in all of the media, has made possible all of my post-judicial work. Without his faith in my work and the bit of a gamble he took with me in 1998, you would not know me, and I would not have produced this book.

Whatever good, whatever insight, whatever lessons may come from this book are the result of the collaborative work of all those above who contributed to it. Whatever fault may be found or errors that may be discovered are mine and mine alone.

A Word About
Thomas Jefferson

No discussion about race and freedom in America would be complete without a few words on Thomas Jefferson. I am an un-apologetic admirer of Jefferson and believe that he was the greatest American president because his views on the primacy of the individual over the State, the States over the federal government, and his fidelity to the Constitution are second to none among our chief executives.

Yet, I began this book by criticizing the most famous line he wrote in his most famous work. I did so because, notwithstanding his authorship of the Declaration of Independence, he bought, sold, and owned slaves; and he most likely fathered seven children with one of those slaves, Sally Hemmings, who essentially was his mistress and concubine during his years in Paris, at the State Department, in the Vice Presidency, and during his eight years in the White House.

Jefferson, like many of his successors, was a product of a white racist culture. By all accounts, he was also a kind and gentle master who freed his slaves upon his own death. But, he accepted the power of the State to deny blacks their humanity, their person-hood, and their free will, a view truly and profoundly antithetical to everything else he stood for throughout his enormously productive life.

Shortly after he died, Jefferson was vilified by prominent slaveholders in the South, foremost among them Sen. John C. Calhoun, not for fathering children with Ms. Hemmings, but, incredibly, for having written that "[A]ll men are created equal." Calhoun called that uniquely Jeffersonian phrase the most dangerous of all political error. He feared that Jefferson, of all people, started the antislavery ball rolling with the "poisonous fruit" of the Declaration of Independence.

So, does Thomas Jefferson's personal behavior, reprehensible as it was, negate the wonderful statements he wrote into the Declaration of Independence or even neutralize him as the great icon of rugged individualism and personal freedom? My answer is an unqualified: NO.

Jefferson is still the standard against whom all presidents should be measured. The Declaration of Independence, which he wrote and shepherded through the Continental Congress, was the most radical, profound, uplifting written expression of human freedom in all of history. Here is what he accomplished and gave us: He turned the political world on its head in favor of the individual and against government. When Kings and potentates reluctantly acquiesced to the demands of their subjects, that was power granting liberty. But when the idea of personal inalienable rights was wedded to the soul of America, and that gave birth to the Constitution, it was liberty granting power; and power granted can be taken back. I am convinced that he knew in his heart that slavery was violative of all this.

With all his personal flaws, this American sphinx is the most indispensable man in American history.

Notes

CHAPTER 1

1. Gustave Glotz, *Ancient Greece at Work* (London: Georg Olms, 1926), p. 192.
2. David Brion Davis, *The Problem of Slavery in Western Culture* (Ithaca, NY: Cornell University Press, 1966), p. 35. This book, which won the 1967 Pulitzer Prize, is essential reading on the origins and development of slavery in the Americas.
3. Davis, *Slavery in Western Culture*, p. 35.
4. Jack Hayward, *Out of Slavery: Abolition and After* (London: Frank Cass, 1985), p. 17. Emphasis in original.
5. Keith Bradley, *Slavery and Society at Rome* (Cambridge: Cambridge University Press, 1994), p. 32.
6. Hayward, *Out of Slavery*, p. 18.
7. Bradley, *Slavery and Society at Rome*, pp. 32–33.
8. Davis, *Slavery in Western Culture*, pp. 36, 49.
9. Ibid., pp. 43–49.
10. Ibid.
11. Ibid., pp. 118–21.
12. At the end of 2006, 38 percent of all sentenced male inmates in state and federal jails were black, according to the annual report *Prisoners in 2006*, by the Bureau of Justice Statistics, a wing of the Department of Justice. Further statistics on prison populations by race can be found in the report, at www.ojp.usdoj.gov/bjs/pub/pdf/p06.pdf.
13. Robin Kelley and Earl Lewis, *To Make Our World Anew: A History of African Americans to 1880, Volume I* (Oxford University Press, 2005), p. 7.
14. Davis, *Slavery in Western Culture*, p. 43.
15. Clements R. Markham, ed., *The Journal of Christopher Columbus During His First Voyage, 1492–93* (London: Kessinger Publishing, LLC, 2007), p. x.
16. Christopher Columbus, journal entry, September 1498, quoted in Tzvetan Todorov and Richard Howard, *The Conquest of America: The Question of the Other* (Norman: University of Oklahoma Press, 1999), p. 47.
17. Kelley and Lewis, *To Make Our World Anew*, p. 9.
18. Herbert Klein, *The Atlantic Slave Trade* (New York: Cambridge University Press, 1999), p. 75.
19. Kelley and Lewis, *To Make Our World Anew*, pp. 11–13.
20. Ibid.
21. Ibid., pp. 11–12.
22. Benjamin Quarles, *The Negro in the Making of America* (New York: Collier, 1964), pp. 29–30.
23. Ibid., pp. 25–26.
24. Kelley and Lewis, *To Make Our World Anew*, p. 14.
25. For a detailed account of the appalling experiences aboard the vessels, see Marcus Rediker, *The Slave Ship: A Human History* (New York: Viking, 2007).
26. Kelley and Lewis, *To Make Our World Anew*, p. 15.
27. Ibid., pp. 14–15.

28. Ibid., p. 15.
29. Eric Foner, "Demon Cruelty," *London Review of Books*, July 31, 2008, quoting Marcus Rediker, *The Slave Ship: A Human History* (New York: Viking, 2007).
30. Kelley and Lewis, *To Make Our World Anew*, pp. 15–16.
31. Quarles, *The Negro*, p. 30.
32. Ibid., p. 31.
33. Ibid., pp. 36–37.
34. Ibid., p. 37.
35. Ibid., p. 39.
36. Ibid., p. 42.
37. Ibid., p. 43.
38. While the Northern colonies never had close to as many slaves as the South, there were still significant numbers of blacks held in slavery in the North. A more detailed discussion of this oft-forgotten part of American history follows in chapter 2.
39. Quarles, *The Negro*, p. 47.
40. Kelley and Lewis, *To Make Our World Anew*, p. 66.
41. Ibid., p. 67.
42. Quarles, *The Negro*, p. 47.
43. Ibid., p. 48.
44. The method by which white Southerners gradually tightened the laws to cement the status of slaves was part of the larger effort by whites to ensure they had a permanent labor source for plantation agriculture. An exceptional discussion of slavery as a system of labor, and not purely racial domination, can be found in Kenneth Stammp, *The Peculiar Institution* (New York: Vintage Books, 1956), pp. 6–7.
45. Kenneth Stammp, *The Peculiar Institution* (New York: Vintage Books, 1956), p. 5.
46. Quarles, *The Negro*, p. 46.
47. Ibid.

CHAPTER 2

1. Kenneth Stammp, *The Peculiar Institution* (New York: Vintage Books, 1956), pp. 8–10.
2. Stammp, *Peculiar Institution*, pp. 144–47.
3. Ibid., pp. 148–51.
4. Robin Kelley and Earl Lewis, *To Make Our World Anew: A History of African Americans to 1880* (Oxford: Oxford University Press, 2000), p. 175.
5. Kelley and Lewis, *To Make Our World Anew*, p. 175.
6. Ibid.
7. Stammp, *Peculiar Institution*, pp. 162–70.
8. Benjamin Quarles, *The Negro in the Making of America* (New York: Collier, 1964), p. 88.
9. Stammp, *Peculiar Institution*, pp. 171–76.
10. Ibid., pp. 190–91.
11. Ibid., p. 322.
12. Ibid., pp. 300–305.
13. Ibid., p. 333.
14. Ibid., p. 337.
15. Quarles, *The Negro*, p. 85.
16. Ibid., p. 86.
17. Stammp, *Peculiar Institution*, p. 341.
18. Quarles, *The Negro*, p. 93.
19. Ibid., p. 87.

NOTES

20. Stammp, *Peculiar Institution*, pp. 194–201.
21. Ibid., p. 194.
22. Quarles, *The Negro*, p. 88.
23. Stammp, *Peculiar Institution*, p. 208.
24. Ibid., p. 210.
25. Ibid., pp. 210–16.
26. Ibid., pp. 220–23.
27. Quarles, *The Negro*, pp. 78–80.
28. Stammp, *Peculiar Institution*, p. 271.
29. Kelley and Lewis, *To Make Our World Anew*, p. 171.
30. Stammp, *Peculiar Institution*, pp. 245–48.
31. Kelley and Lewis, *To Make Our World Anew*, p. 172.
32. Stammp, *The Peculiar Institution*, pp. 266–71.
33. Thousands of slaves were imported through Portsmouth and then smuggled into other colonies in order to avoid the import tariffs. A good overview of slavery in New Hampshire and the other New England and Mid-Atlantic colonies can be found at www.slavenorth.com/newhampshire.htm. See also "Town Unearths Colonial Slave Cemetery," CBS News, February 13, 2006, www.cbsnews.com/stories/2006/02/13/eveningnews/main1312816.shtml.
34. Oscar Reiss, *Blac ks in Colonial America* (Jefferson, NC: McFarland, Inc. 1997), p. 81.
35. Henry Scofield Cooley, *A Study of Slavery in New Jersey* (Baltimore: The Johns Hopkins Press, 1893), pp. 37–38.
36. Kelley and Lewis, *To Make Our World Anew*, p. 173.
37. Ibid., p. 182.
38. Stammp, *Peculiar Institution*, p. 89.
39. Ibid., pp. 109–111.
40. Ibid., p. 188.
41. Quarles, *The Negro*, p. 97.
42. Ibid.
43. *Habeas corpus* is an ancient right, recognized in the West since the Magna Carta was signed in 1215. It is the right of all persons confined by any government against their will to be brought before a neutral judge and to compel the government to justify the lawfulness of the confinement. In America, the federal government and the Southern states vehemently denied that the slaves were persons. The U.S. Supreme Court recently affirmed that this right belongs and has belonged to all persons, even those detained by the U.S. military at Guantanamo Bay, Cuba.
44. Frederick Pollock, *Essays on the Law* (London: Macmillan, 1922), p. 42.
45. Clarence Thomas, "Why Black Americans Should Look to Conservative Policies," Heritage Foundation Lecture, August 1, 1987, http://www.heritage.org/research/politicalphilosophy/h1119.cfm.
46. "Letter to John B. Colvin," *The Political Writings of Thomas Jefferson*, ed. Merrill D. Peterson (Chapel Hill: UNC Press, 1993), p. 162.

CHAPTER 3

1. Lawrence Goldstone, *Dark Bargain: Slavery, Profits, and the Struggle for the Constitution* (New York: Walker & Company, 2005), p. 101.
2. Thurgood Marshall, Commentary: Reflections on the Bicentennial of the United States Constitution, 101 *Harvard Law Review* 1, 2 (1987). It may seem like blasphemy to criticize the Founding Fathers, but Justice Marshall, as we will later see, had

very good reasons for finding fault with some of the decisions made at the Constitutional Convention.

3. Goldstone, *Dark Bargain*, p. 16.

4. Geoffrey R. Stone, Louis M. Seidman, Cass R. Sunstein, Mark V. Tushnet, Pamela S. Karlan, *Constitutional Law* (New York: Aspen Publishers, 2005), p. 448.

5. Robert Goldwin and Art Kaufman, *Slavery and Its Consequences: The Constitution, Equality, and Race* (Washington D.C.: AEI, 1988), p. 8.

6. D. Robinson, *Slavery in the Structure of American Politics 1765–1820* (New York: W. W. Norton & Co. Inc, 1971).

7. The delegates from the slaveholding and the free states were acutely aware of the mathematics of apportioning representatives to Congress.

8. Goldwin and Kaufman, *Slavery and Its Consequences*, p. 8.

9. Goldstone, *Dark Bargain*, p. 123.

10. *Prigg v. Pennsylvania*, 41 U.S. 539 (1842).

11. Stone, Seidman, Sunstein, Tushnet, Karlan, *Constitutional Law*, p. 453.

12. *Strader v. Graham*, 51 U.S. 82 (1841).

13. 55 Virginia 132.

14. An Act for the Gradual Abolition of Slavery, Trenton, New Jersey, 1804.

15. *State v. Post*, 20 N.J.L. 368 (Supreme Court of New Jersey 1845).

16. Ibid.

17. *Commonwealth v. Ames*, Mass. Supreme Court 79 Mass 26.

18. *State v. Post*, 20 N.L.J. 368 (Supreme Court of New Jersey 1845).

19. *Calder v. Bull*, 3 U.S. 386 (1798).

20. Ibid.

CHAPTER 4

1. "Thomas Jefferson to John Holmes" (transcription of letter), from the Thomas Jefferson Library of Congress Exhibition, U.S. Library of Congress, www.loc.gov/exhibits/jefferson/159.html.

2. Robert Pierce Forbes, *The Missouri Compromise and Its Aftermath* (Chapel Hill: University of North Carolina Press, 2007), p. 33.

3. Forbes, *Missouri Compromise*, p. 33.

4. Ibid., p. 34.

5. "Notes on the State of Virginia," 1781.

6. Ibid.

7. James Albert Woodburn, "The Historical Significance of the Missouri Compromise," *Annual report of the American Historical Association*, 1894, p. 255.

8. Ibid.

9. Ibid., pp. 256–57.

10. Ibid.

11. Ibid.

12. Ibid., p. 253.

13. Earl M. Maltz, *Dred Scott and the Politics of Slavery* (Lawrence: University Press of Kansas, 2007), p. 60.

14. Ibid.

15. Ibid., p. 61.

16. Ibid.

17. Ibid.

18. Ibid.

19. Ibid., p. 63.

20. *Dred Scott v. Sandford*, 60 U.S. 393 (1857).

21. Gloria Browne-Marshall, *Race, Law, and American Society* (New York: Routledge, 2007), p. 6.
22. *Dred Scott v. Sandford*, 60 U.S. 393 (1857).
23. *Scott*, 60 *U.S.* 393, 1857.
24. Maltz, *Dred Scott and the Politics of Slavery*, p. 140.
25. Ibid., p. 142.

CHAPTER 5

1. Abraham Lincoln, speaking at Springfield, Illinois, on June 16, 1858, quoted in Michael P. Johnson, *Abraham Lincoln, Slavery, and the Civil War: Selected Writings and Speeches* (Boston: Bedford/St. Martin's, 2001), p. 63. The rest of Lincoln's speech during the same debate makes clear that his overriding concern domestically was that the Union be preserved, slavery being only one of the issues contributing to the nation's sectionalism: "It will become all one thing or all the other. Either the opponents of slavery will arrest the further spread of it, and place it where the public mind shall rest in the belief that it is in the course of ultimate extinction; or its advocates will push it forward, till it shall become alike lawful in all the States, old as well as new—North as well as South."
2. Abraham Lincoln, in a letter to Horace Greeley dated August, 22 1862.
3. "1860 Presidential Election Results," © David Leip, 1999, www.uselectionatlas.org/USPRESIDENT/GENERAL/pe1860.html (accessed December 8, 2008). More information can be found in Kenneth M. Stammp, *And the War Came: The North and the Secession Crisis, 1860–1861* (Baton Rouge: Louisiana State University Press, 1950).
4. James McPherson, *Battle Cry of Freedom* (New York: Oxford University Press, 2003), p. 274.
5. Thomas J. DiLorenzo, *The Real Lincoln: A New Look at Abraham Lincoln, His Agenda, and an Unnecessary War* (Roseville, CA: Prima Publishing, 2002), pp. 119–22.
6. John Hope Franklin, *From Slavery to Freedom: A History of African Americans, Volume Two* (New York: The McGraw-Hill Co., 2000), p. 221.
7. William E. Gienapp, *Abraham Lincoln and Civil War America.* (New York: Oxford University Press, 2002), p. 47.
8. Ibid.
9. *Speeches and Writings, 1832-1858: Speeches, Letters, and Miscellaneous Writings, the Lincoln-Douglas Debates*, Don Edward Fehrenbacher, ed. (NY: Library of America, 1989), p. 167.
10. Franklin, *From Slavery to Freedom*, p. 229.
11. Eric Foner, *A Short History of Reconstruction* (New York: Harper & Row Publishers, 1984), p. 4.
12. The Proclamation gives some clue as to its purpose, stating it is being issued "upon military necessity." Emancipation was intended to cripple the economy of the South by undermining the region's major labor source. A further clue as to the real purpose of the Proclamation was that it did not free any of the slaves in the border states such as Kentucky and did not address slavery in the territory captured by the Union—the focus was squarely on those states that remained in rebellion against the Union. Further reading on the economic and military components of Lincoln's strategy can be found in John Hope Franklin's excellent *The Emancipation Proclamation* (New York: Doubleday, 1963).
13. Abraham Lincoln, Emancipation Proclamation, January 1, 1863, as recounted in Franklin, *From Slavery to Freedom*, p. 232.

14. It would seem that even today many blacks are aware that the Proclamation was more symbolic gesture than actual act of emancipation. Juneteenth, a holiday honoring the date of emancipation, does not refer to Lincoln's Emancipation Proclamation in 1863, but to June 19, 1865, when the slaves of Texas received their freedom at the close of the Civil War.

15. Douglas L. Wilson and Rodney O. Davis, eds., *Herndon's Informants: Letters, Interviews and Statements about Abraham Lincoln* (Urbana: University of Illinois Press, 1997), p. 164.

16. Robert Morgan, "The Great Emancipator and the Issue of Face: Abraham Lincoln's Program of Black Resettlement," *The Journal of Historical Review*, September 1993, vol. 13, number 5.

17. DiLorenzo, *The Real Lincoln*, p. 36.

18. Ibid., p. 43–45.

19. Morgan, "The Great Emancipator."

20. DiLorenzo, *The Real Lincoln*, pp. 35–37.

21. Jeffrey Rogers Hummel, *Emancipating Slaves, Enslaving Free Men: A History of the American Civil War* (Chicago: Open Court Publishing Co., 1996). Further reading on Lincoln's big government tendencies can be found in David Henderson's "Was Lincoln the Father of Big Government? Department of Historical Revisionism," Fortune (December 9, 1996), available at www.money.cnn.com/magazines/fortune/fortune_archive/1996/12/09/219359/index.htm (accessed December 8, 2008).

22. Franklin, *From Slavery to Freedom*, pp. 224–25.

23. Eric Foner, *Reconstruction: America's Unfinished Revolution* (New York: HarperCollins, 1988), pp. 58–59.

24. Ibid., pp. 55–60.

25. S. Mintz, "Conditions in the Contraband Camps," *Digital History*, 2007, www.digitalhistory.uh.edu/learning_history/children_civilwar/contra band_camps.cfm (accessed January 27, 2009).

26. Foner, *Reconstruction*, pp. 55–60.

27. Franklin, *Emancipation Proclamation*, p. 79.

28. Franklin, *From Slavery to Freedom*, pp. 238–39.

29. Ibid., pp. 227–28.

30. As noted in Leslie M. Harris, "The New York City Draft Riots of 1863," excerpted from *In the Shadow of Slavery: African Americans in New York City, 1626–1863* (University of Chicago Press, 2004): "In the month preceding the July 1863 lottery, in a pattern similar to the 1834 anti-abolition riots, antiwar newspaper editors published inflammatory attacks on the draft law aimed at inciting the white working class. They criticized the federal government's intrusion into local affairs on behalf of the 'nigger war.' Democratic Party leaders raised the specter of a New York deluged with Southern blacks in the aftermath of the Emancipation Proclamation." Leslie M. Harris, "The New York City Draft Riots of 1863," excerpted from *In the Shadow of Slavery: African Americans in New York City, 1626-1863*, www.press.uchicago.edu/Misc/Chicago/317749.html (accessed January 27, 2009).

31. Harris, "Draft Riots of 1863."

32. Franklin, *From Slavery to Freedom*, pp. 227–28. An example might be found in George W. Bush's tax policy, which reduced taxes from 33 percent to 26 percent for the top 1 percent of taxpayers while the middle 20 percent of taxpayers only saw their taxes reduced by 4 percent, according to a study released in 2004 by the Congressional Budget Office. "Study: Bush Tax Cuts Favor Wealthy, Congressional Study Finds Middle Class Paying More Of Tax Burden," CBS/AP, August 13,

2004, www.cbsnews.com/stories/2004/08/16/politics/main636398.shtml (accessed December 8, 2008).

33. Mark Neely, *The Fate of Liberty: Abraham Lincoln and Civil Liberties* (New York: Oxford University Press, 1991), pp. 68–72.
34. Franklin, *From Slavery to Freedom*, pp. 243–44.
35. John Hope Franklin, *Reconstruction After the Civil War* (Chicago: University of Chicago Press, 1961), p. 18.
36. Foner, *Reconstruction*, p. 36.
37. William Gienapp, *Abraham Lincoln and Civil War America: A Biography* (New York: Oxford University Press, 2002), p. 155.
38. Franklin, *Reconstruction*, p. 26.

CHAPTER 6

1. Thomas DiLorenzo, *The Real Lincoln: A New Look at Abraham Lincoln, His Agenda, an Unnecessary War* (Roseville, CA: Prima Publishing, 2002), pp. 15–16.
2. Ibid., p. 13.
3. Abraham Lincoln, speech on the Kansas-Nebraska Act at Peoria, Illinois, October 16, 1854, in Michel P. Johnson, *Abraham Lincoln, Slavery and the Civil War: Selected Writings and Speeches* (Boston: Bedford/St. Martin's: 2001), p. 45.
4. Abraham Lincoln, in a speech at Ottawa, Illinois (First Lincoln-Douglas Debate), August 21, 1858, in Johnson, *Slavery and the Civil War*, p. 72.
5. Abraham Lincoln, First Inaugural Address, March 4, 1861. Lincoln went on to state, "Apprehension seems to exist among the people of the Southern States that by the accession of a Republican Administration their property and their peace and personal security are to be endangered. There has never been any reasonable cause for such apprehension."
6. DiLorenzo, *The Real Lincoln*, p.14.
7. U.S. House of Representatives, 30th Congress, 2nd Session, The Constitution of the United States of America: Unratified Amendments, Doc. No. 106-214.
8. DiLorenzo, *The Real Lincoln*, p. 22.
9. Paul M. Angle and Earl Schenck Miers, eds., *The Living Lincoln: The Man in His Times, in His Own Words* (Fall River, MA: Fall River Press, 1992), p. 203.
10. Angle and Miers, p. 203.
11. Nathaniel Weyl and William Marina, *American Statesmen on Slavery and the Negro* (Arlington, VA: Arlington House, 1971), pp. 217–21.
12. James Mitchell, Commissioner of Emigration, to United States Ministers of the Colored Race, 1862, *The Robert Todd Lincoln Collection of the Papers of Abraham Lincoln* (Washington: Library of Congress, vol. 98).
13. "Mr. Lincoln and Freedom," The Lincoln Institute, quoting Ida M. Tarbell, *The Life of Abraham Lincoln*, Volume II (New York: The Lincoln History Society, 1903), p. 214, www.mrlincolnandfreedom.org/inside.asp?ID=56&subjectID=3 (accessed December 8, 2008). Mr. Lincoln and Freedom, a historical research project by the Lincoln Institute, provides extensive documents and analysis on Lincoln's involvement with the issue of slavery before and during the Civil War.
14. Ibid.
15. Ibid., quoting Carl Sandburg, *Abraham Lincoln, The War Years*, volume IV (New York: Harcourt Brace and Co., 1939), p. 6.
16. "Mr. Lincoln and Freedom," The Lincoln Institute, quoting John G. Nicolay and John Hay, *Abraham Lincoln: A History*, Volume X (New York: The Century Co., 1890), p. 76.
17. "Mr. Lincoln and Freedom," The Lincoln Institute.

18. Ibid., quoting Fawn M. Brodie, *Thaddeus Stevens: Scourge of the South*, (New York: W. W. Norton, 1959), p. 202.

19. "Mr. Lincoln and Freedom," The Lincoln Institute, quoting Sandburg, *Lincoln, The War Years*, pp. 5–6.

20. DiLorenzo, *The Real Lincoln*, quoting famed abolitionist Lysander Spooner, *Lincoln Unmasked: What You're Not Supposed to Know About Dishonest Abe*, p. 55.

21. Robert Morgan, "The Great Emancipator and the Issue of Face: Abraham Lincoln's Program of Black Resettlement," *The Journal of Historical Review*, September 1993, vol. 13, number 5.

22. DiLorenzo, *The Real Lincoln*, p. 12.

CHAPTER 7

1. John Hope Franklin, *Reconstruction After the Civil War* (Chicago: University of Chicago Press, 1961), pp. 1–13.

2. James E. Sefton, *The United States Army and Reconstruction* (Baton Rouge: Louisiana State University Press, 1967), p. 9.

3. Ibid., p. 55.

4. Ibid., p. 89–90.

5. Ibid., p. 55. General James H. Wilson, Military Commander of Georgia, observed that the general Southern attitude was "neither true loyalty and love for the Union nor hatred and desire for opposition, but some middle ground of willing acquiescence due to the thoroughness of the military defeat."

6. Eric Foner, *Reconstruction: America's Unfinished Revolution* (New York: HarperCollins, 1988), pp. 177–81.

7. Michael Vorenberg, *Final Freedom: The Civil War, the Abolition of Slavery, and the Thirteenth Amendment* (New York: Cambridge University Press, 2001), p. 77.

8. Foner, *Reconstruction*, pp. 67–70.

9. Franklin, *Reconstruction After the Civil War*, p. 28.

10. Foner, *Reconstruction*, p. 190.

11. Ibid., p. 192.

12. Ibid., p. 183.

13. Ibid.

14. "I say, as to the leaders, punishment. I also say leniency, reconciliation and amnesty to the thousands whom they have misled and deceived." Andrew Johnson, as quoted in George Fort Milton, *The Age of Hate: Andrew Johnson and the Radicals* (New York: Coward-McCann, Inc., 1930), p. 183.

15. Foner, *Reconstruction*, pp. 185–87.

16. Ibid., p. 189.

17. Ibid.

18. Ibid., pp. 173–74.

19. John Hope Franklin, *From Slavery to Freedom: A History of African Americans, Volume Two* (New York: The McGraw-Hill Co., 2000), p. 259.

20. Foner, *Reconstruction*, p. 203.

21. Ibid., pp. 203–05.

22. Ibid., p. 207.

23. Ibid., p. 210.

24. Ibid., p. 214.

25. Ibid., p. 228.

26. Franklin, *Reconstruction After the Civil War*, pp. 53–65, 70.

27. Eric Foner, *A Short History of Reconstruction* (New York: Harper & Row Publishers, 1984), p. 113.

28. Foner, *Reconstruction*, p. 106.
29. Ibid.
30. Ibid., p. 274.
31. Foner, *A Short History*, pp. 111–13.
32. Foner, *Reconstruction*, pp. 251–61.
33. Foner, *Reconstruction*, pp. 84–103.
34. Ibid., p. 105.
35. Franklin, *From Slavery to Freedom*, p. 44.
36. Franklin, *Reconstruction After the Civil War*, pp. 150–65.
37. Foner, *Reconstruction*, pp. 162–63.
38. Ibid.
39. Ibid., *Reconstruction*, p. 169.
40. Franklin, *From Slavery to Freedom*, p. x.
41. J. Morgan Kousser, *The Shaping of Southern Politics: Suffrage Restrictions and the Establishment of the One-Party South* (New Haven: Yale University Press, 1974), p. 39.
42. Foner, *Reconstruction*, p. 41, Table 1.5.

CHAPTER 8

1. Ronald L. F. Davis, "Creating Jim Crow," The History of Jim Crow (teacher resource produced by Thirteen/WNET New York), www.jimcrowhistory.org/history/creating.htm (accessed December 9, 2008). Davis, a professor at California State University, Northridge, offers an excellent account of the reasons the Jim Crow laws were created and how the power vacuum left by the end of federal Reconstruction allowed the laws to strip blacks of their rights.
2. Ibid.
3. C. Vann Woodward, *The Strange Career of Jim Crow, Third Revised Edition* (New York: Oxford University Press: 1974), p. 62.
4. 18 Stat. 335 § 1.
5. The Constitution of the United States, Amendment XIV, Section 1.
6. *Civil Rights Cases*, 109 U.S. 3 (1883), p. 25.
7. Davis, "Creating Jim Crow."
8. William Cohen, *At Freedom's Edge: Black Mobility and the Southern White Quest for Racial Control, 1861–1915* (Baton Rouge: Louisiana State University Press, 1991), p. 109.
9. Woodward, *Strange Career of Jim Crow*, p. 70.
10. Ibid.
11. *Plessy v. Ferguson*, 163 U.S. 537, p. 552.
12. Ibid., p. 551.
13. Not to be confused with his grandson, John Marshall Harlan, who held the same position decades later.
14. *Plessy*, p. 557.
15. Adam Fairclough, *Better Day Coming: Blacks and Equality, 1890–2000* (New York: Viking, 2001), p. 200.
16. Ibid., pp. 329–40
17. "Lynching," Slavery in America (teacher resource produced by Thirteen/ WNET New York), www.slaveryinamerica.org/scripts/sia/glossary.cgi?term=l&letter=yes (accessed December 9, 2008).
18. Richard Lacayao, "Blood at the Root," *Time*, April 2, 2000.
19. James Allen, *Without Sanctuary* (Santa Fe: Twin Palms Publishers, 2000), p. 95.
20. Lisa Cozzens, "The Murder of Emmet Till," African American History, © 1997, www.watson.org/~lisa/blackhistory/early-civilrights/emmett.html (accessed December 9, 2008).

NOTES

21. Albert W. Alschuler, "Racial Quotas and the Jury," *Duke Law Journal*, vol. 44 (February 1995).
22. A chilling account of the bombing can be found in John Archibald and Jeff Hansen, "Church bomb felt like 'world shaking," *Birmingham News*, September 15, 1997, at www.al.com/specialreport/?bombing/97-shaking .html (accessed December 9, 2008).
23. Earl Ofari Hutchinson, "Feds Must Also Answer for Lynchings," The Final Call online edition, May 28, 2002, www.finalcall.com/perspectives/lynchings05-28-2002.htm (accessed December 9, 2008).
24. Charles H. Smith, "Have Negroes Too Much Liberty," *Forum*, vol. XVI (October 1893), p. 181, as cited on "The Brute Caricature," The Jim Crow Museum of Racist Memorabilia, Ferris State University (Big Rapids, MI), www.ferris.edu/jim-crow/brute/ (accessed December 9, 2008).
25. George T. Winston, "The Relations of the Whites to the Negroes," *Annals of the American Academy of Political and Social Science*, vol. XVII (July 1901), p. 108, as cited on "Brute Caricature," Jim Crow Museum.
26. Charles Carroll, *The Negro Beast* (St. Louis: American Book and Bible House, 1900), p. 167, as cited on "Brute Caricature," Jim Crow Museum.
27. George M. Frederickson, *The Black Image in the White Mind* (New York: Harper & Row, 1971), p. 280, as cited on "Brute Caricature," Jim Crow Museum.
28. Ibid., p. 279.
29. Ibid., p. 280.
30. Ibid., p. 281.
31. "The Brute Caricature," The Jim Crow Museum of Racist Memorabilia, Ferris State University (Big Rapids, MI), www.ferris.edu/jimcrow/brute/ (accessed December 9, 2008).
32. Peter W. Bardaglio, *Reconstructing the Household: Families, Sex and the Law in the Nineteenth Century South* (Chapel Hill: University of North Carolina Press, 1998), pp. 197–99.
33. White fears of intermarriage with blacks were one of the overriding concerns behind Jim Crow. Fairclough, *Better Day Coming*, p. 26.
34. Fairclough, *Better Day Coming*, p. 26.
35. Ibid.
36. Ibid., p. 169.
37. Ibid., p. 203.
38. Ibid.
39. Ibid.
40. Peter Wallenstein, "Race, Policy, and K-12 Education: Segregated Schooling in Jim Crow Virginia," speech given September 21, 1999, at Virginia Tech, Blacksburg, VA, www.epi.elps.vt.edu/SYMPOSIUM/PW.htm (accessed December 9, 2008).
41. Fairclough, *Better Day Coming*, p. 170.
42. Richard Wormser, *The Rise and Fall of Jim Crow* (New York: Macmillan, 2003), p. 63.
43. Fairclough, *Better Day Coming*, p. 171.
44. Ibid., p. 172.
45. Ibid.
46. Thomas J. Sugrue, *Sweet Land of Liberty: The Forgotten Struggle for Civil Rights in the North* (New York: Random House, 2008).

CHAPTER 9
1. Woodrow Wilson, *A History of the American People* (New York: Best Books, 1918).
2. Richard Slotkin, *Lost Battalions: The Great War and the Crisis of American Nationality* (New York: Holt, 2006), p. 254.

3. Mary P. Motley, *The Invisible Soldier: The Experience of the Black Soldier in World War II* (Detroit: Wayne State University Press, 1987), p. 13.

4. For more about the service of the African-American soldier during World War I, read W. Allison Sweeney, *History of the American Negro in the Great World War: His Splendid Record* (New York: G. G. Sapp, 1919).

5. Quoted in Mary Penick Motley, *The Invisible Soldier* (Detroit: Wayne State University, 1975), p. 15.

6. Article provided by OldMagazineArticles.com;/www.oldmagazinearticles .com/pdf/Colored-Americans-in-France.pdf (accessed December 9, 2008).

7. Arthur E. Barbeau and Florette Henri, *The Unknown Soldiers: African-American Troops in World War I* (New York: Da Capo Press, 1996), p. 158.

8. Charles M. Dryden and Benjamin O. Davis, *A-Train: Memoirs of A Tuskegee Airman* (Tuscaloosa, AL: University of Alabama Press, 2003), p. 392.

9. Alan M. Osur, *Blacks in the Army Air Forces During World War II: The Problems of Race Relations* (Darby, PA: Diane Publishing, 1976), p. 5.

10. Ibid.

11. Motley, *Invisible Soldier*, p. 23, citing Trezzvant W. Anderson, *Come out Fighting: The Epic of the 761st Tank Battalion 1942–1945* (privately printed, 1945).

12. Motley, *Invisible Soldier*, p. 26.

13. Ira Lewis, editorial, *The Pittsburgh Courier*, February 7, 1942.

14. Beth Bailey, "The Double V campaign in World War II Hawaii: African Americans, racial ideology, and federal power," *Journal of Social History*, Summer 1993, available at www.findarticles.com/p/articles/mi_m2005/is _n4_v26/ai_14125267 (accessed December 8, 2008).

15. Stephen E. Ambrose, *Citizen Soldiers: The U.S. Army from the Normandy to the Bulge to the Surrender of Germany* (New York: Simon & Schuster, 1998), p. 345.

16. Dryden and Davis, *A-Train*, p. 176.

17. Charles F. Francis, *The Tuskegee Airmen: The Men Who Changed a Nation* (Boston: Branden Publishing Company, 1988), p. 237.

18. Ibid., p. 240.

19. Ibid., p. 25.

20. Jennifer Iversen, "Tuskegee Airmen Defied Hardships and Dared to Find Lifelong Success," *Metropolitan State College of Denver Department of Aviation and Aerospace Science Newsletter*, Vol. 3 No.1, Spring/Summer 2005, www.mscd-aviation-aerospace.org/news/newsletters/AESmetroflyervol3no1 .pdf (accessed December 9, 2008).

21. To read about other combat missions the Tuskegee Airmen engaged in, read *The Tuskegee Airmen: The Men Who Changed a Nation* by Charles F. Francis.

22. Francis, *The Tuskegee Airmen*, p. 206.

23. Ibid., p. 198.

24. Ibid.

25. Ibid., p. 222.

26. Ibid., p. 204.

27. The attacks on these soldiers as they spoke out against the institutionalized racism of the military was echoed in 1967, when Muhammad Ali refused to submit to the draft. He famously stated, "I ain't got no quarrel with them, no Viet-Cong ever called me Nigger." He was labeled an unpatriotic coward and threatened with jail for questioning why he should fight for freedoms that he had never known at home.

28. Francis, *The Tuskegee Airmen*, p. 208.

29. "The Tuskegee Syphilis Experiment," Infoplease, © 2000-2007 Pearson Education, publishing as Infoplease, www.infoplease.com/ipa/A0762136. html (accessed December 9, 2008).

30. Ibid.
31. Ibid.
32. Ibid.
33. James H. Jones, *Bad Blood* (New York: The Free Press, 1993), p. 8.
34. Ibid., pp. 10–12.
35. Ibid., p. 8.
36. "The Tuskegee Syphilis Experiment," Infoplease.
37. Jones, *Bad Blood*, p. 11.
38. Ibid., p. 13.

CHAPTER 10

1. James T. Patterson, *Brown v. Board of Education: A Civil Rights Milestone and Its Troubled Legacy* (New York: Oxford University Press, 2002), p. 12.
2. Melvin I. Urofsky and Paul Finkelman, *A March of Liberty: A Constitutional History of the United States, Volume II, From 1877 to the Present*, second edition (New York: Oxford University Press, 2002), p. 779.
3. Adam Fairclough, *Better Day Coming: Blacks and Equality, 1890–2000* (New York: Viking, 2001), p. 218.
4. James D. Anderson, *The Education of Blacks in the South, 1860–1935* (Chapel Hill: University of North Carolina Press, 1988), pp. 154–56.
5. Ibid., pp. 236–37.
6. Patterson, *Brown v. Board of Education*, p. 11.
7. A government observer described the ramshackle state of one black school as a "small and dilapidated shack without windows, in which investigators on opening the door found the school in absolute darkness and the teachers and pupils asleep." Fairclough, *Better Day Coming*, p. 174, citing Clark Foreman, *Environmental Factors in Negro Elementary Education* (New York: W. W. Norton, 1932), p. 40.
8. Patterson, *Brown v. Board of Education*, p. 10.
9. Ibid., citing Stephan Thernstrom and Abigail Thernstrom, *America in Black and White: One Nation, Indivisible* (Simon & Schuster, 1999).
10. "Jim Crow Laws," American RadioWorks, © 2008 American Public Media (Minnesota Public Radio), www.americanradioworks.publicradio.org/features/remembering/laws.html (accessed December 10, 2008).
11. Ibid.
12. Anderson, *Education of Blacks*, p. 157.
13. Ibid., p. 155.
14. Patterson, *Brown v. Board of Education*, p. 38.
15. Ibid., p. 35.
16. Ibid., pp. 43–44.
17. Urofsky and Finkelman, *A March of Liberty*, p. 779.
18. Ibid.
19. Ibid., p. 782.
20. Brown v. Board of Education of Topeka, United States Supreme Court, 1954, 357 U.S. 483.
21. Michael J. Klarman, "*Brown v. Board*: 50 Years Later," *Humanities*, March/April 2004, p. 1.
22. Raoul Berger, *Government by Judiciary: The Transformation of the Fourteenth Amendment*, second edition (Indianapolis: The Liberty Fund, 1997), p. 143.
23. Patterson, *Brown v. Board of Education*, p. 39.
24. John Hope Franklin, *Reconstruction After the Civil War*, second edition (Chicago: University of Chicago Press, 1961), p. 38. An extended discussion on black education

in the South in 1868 can be also found in chapter 1 of James D. Anderson's *The Education of Blacks in the South, 1860–1935.*

25. Davison M. Douglas, *Jim Crow Moves North: The Battle over Northern School Segregation, 1865–1954* (New York: Cambridge University Press, 2005), pp. 146–47. In the years following the Civil War, most Northern states abolished segregation in public schools but there were still numerous laws on the books as of 1868 that kept white and black students separate.
26. Klarman, "50 Years Later," p. 2.
27. Urofsky and Finkelman, *A March of Liberty,* p. 783.
28. Ibid., p. 785.
29. Patterson, *Brown v. Board of Education,* p. 81.
30. Ibid., p. 82.
31. Urofsky and Finkelman, *A March of Liberty,* p. 787.
32. Patterson, *Brown v. Board of Education,* p. 98.
33. Urofsky and Finkelman, *A March of Liberty,* p. 789.
34. Fairclough, *Better Day Coming,* p. 224.
35. Ibid., p. 225.
36. Urofsky and Finkelman (*A March of Liberty*), tell us, "Warren's strategy assumed that the states would accept the inevitability of desegregation by the time the Court handed down the implementation decree," while Patterson (*Brown v. Board of Education*) adds, "It was clear, however, that neither Marshall nor others on his team had thought deeply about this question, which was to prove so painful to answer."
37. Patterson, *Brown v. Board of Education,* p. 142.
38. J. W. Peltason, *Fifty-Eight Lonely Men: Southern Federal Judges and School Desegregation* (Urbana-Champaign: University of Illinois Press, 1961), p. 4.
39. *United States v. Jefferson County Board of Education,* United States Court of Appeals for the 5th Circuit, 1968, 396 F. 2d 44.

CHAPTER 11

1. Melvin I. Urofsky and Paul Finkelman, *A March of Liberty: A Constitutional History of the United States, Volume II, From 1877 to the Present,* second edition (New York: Oxford University Press, 2002), p. 795.
2. Ibid.
3. Address to the Greater Houston Ministerial Association, September 12, 1960.
4. Melvin I. Urofsky and Paul Finkelman, *A March of Liberty: A Constitutional History of the United States, Volume II, From 1877 to the Present,* second edition (New York: Oxford University Press, 2002), p. 796.
5. Jeremy D. Mayer, *Running on Race: Racial Politics in Presidential Campaigns 1960–2000* (New York: Random House, 2002), pp. 35–36.
6. Adam Fairclough, *Better Day Coming: Blacks and Equality, 1890–2000* (New York: Viking, 2001), p. 266.
7. Howard Zinn, "The Student Nonviolent Coordinating Committee," *Civil Rights Since 1787: A Reader on the Black Struggle,* Jonathan Birnbaum and Clarence Taylor, eds. (New York: NYU Press, 2000), pp. 472–73. Zinn's article is one of many essays in this informative and insightful collection.
8. Fairclough, *Better Day Coming,* p. 253.
9. Ibid., p. 262.
10. Ibid., p. 265.
11. Ibid.
12. Ibid., p. 281.
13. Ibid., p. 263.

NOTES

14. Martin Luther King Jr., "Letter From Birmingham Jail, April 16, 1963," MLK Online, www.mlkonline.net/jail.html (accessed December10, 2008).
15. Frederick W. Haberman, ed., *Nobel Lectures, Peace 1951–1970* (Amsterdam: Elsevier Publishing Company, 1972), online at www.nobelprize.org/nobel_prizes/peace/laureates/1964/king-bio.html (accessed December 10, 2008).
16. Haberman, *Nobel Lectures*.
17. Martin Luther King Jr., speech at the MIA Mass Meeting at Holt Street Baptist Church, Montgomery, Alabama, December 5, 1955, www.mlkonline.net/mia.html (accessed January 27, 2009).
18. Martin Luther King Jr., *The Trumpet of Conscience* (New York: Harper & Row, 1968), p. 67.
19. Martin Luther King Jr., "Letter from Birmingham Jail."
20. Jen Christiansen, "FBI Tracked King's Every Move," CNN, April 7, 2008, www.cnn.com/2008/US/03/31/mlk.fbi.conspiracy/index.html (accessed December 10, 2008). It should come as no surprise the FBI was interested in a figure so well known as King, but they also went to great lengths to discredit and humiliate him.
21. Diane McWhorter, *Carry Me Home: Birmingham, Alabama, the Climactic Battle of the Civil Rights Revolution* (New York: Simon & Schuster, 2001), pp. 270–71.
22. Fairclough, *Better Day Coming*, p. 278.
23. "Dogs, Kids, and Clubs," *Time*, May 10, 1963, www.time.com/time/magazine/article/0,9171,830260,00.html (accessed December 10, 2008).
24. Taylor Branch, *Parting the Waters; America in the King Years 1954–63* (New York: Simon & Schuster, 1988), p. 764.
25. "Radio and Television Report to the American People on Civil Rights" (transcript of radio address given from the White House on June 11, 1963), John F. Kennedy Presidential Library & Museum Historical resources,www.jfklibrary.org/Historical+Resources/Archives/Reference+Desk/Speeches/JFK/003POF03Civil Rights06111963.htm (accessed December 10, 2008).
26. Ibid.
27. Urofsky and Finkelman, *A March of Liberty*, p. 796.
28. Clay Risen, "How the South Was Won," *Boston Globe*, March 3, 2005.
29. Fairclough, *Better Day Coming*, p. 282.
30. Barry Goldwater, *The Conscience of a Conservative* (New York: Victor Publishing Co., 1960), p. 60.
31. Fairclough, *Better Day Coming*, p. 282.
32. Ibid., p. 288.
33. Ibid., pp. 290–91.
34. Urofsky and Finkelman, *A March of Liberty*, p. 804.
35. For more background on how the Supreme Court has expanded the federal government and eroded civil liberties, very often by relying on the Commerce Clause, I encourage you to take a look at Robert A. Levy and William Mellor's *The Dirty Dozen: How Twelve Supreme Court Cases Radically Expanded Government and Eroded Freedom* (New York: Penguin, 2008), and Thomas E. Woods' and Kevin R. C. Gutzman's *Who Killed the Constitution?* (New York: Crown Forum, 2008), and my own *The Constitution in Exile: How The Federal Government Has Seized Power by Rewriting the Supreme Law of the Land* (Nashville: Nelson Current, 2006).
36. Fairclough, *Better Day Coming*, p. 299.
37. Gerald Horne, "The Watts Uprising," *Civil Rights Since 1787: A Reader on the Black Struggle*, Jonathan Birnbaum and Clarence Taylor, eds. (New York: NYU Press, 2000), p. 555.

38. Fairclough, *Better Day Coming*, p. 302.

39. Jack E. Davis, *The Civil Rights Movement* (Boston, MA: Blackwell Publishing, 2001), pp. 298–99.

CHAPTER 12

1. Excerpted in Brian Ross and Rehab El-Buri, "Obama's Pastor: God Damn America, U.S. to Blame for 9/11," ABC News, March 13, 2008, www. abcnews.go.com/Blotter/Story?id=4443788 (accessed December10, 2008).

2. Jodi Kantor, "Obama Denounces Statements of His Pastor as 'Inflammatory,'" *New York Times*, March 15, 2008, www.nytimes.com/ 2008/03/15/us/politics/15wright.html?scp=20&sq=%22reverend%20wright%22&st=cse (accessed December 10, 2008).

3. Jeremy D. Mayer, *Running on Race: Racial Politics in Presidential Campaigns 1960–2000* (New York: Random House, 2002), p. 95.

4. Quoted in Michael J. Klarman, "*Brown v. Board*: 50 Years Later," *Humanities*, March/April 2004, p. 1.

5. Mayer, *Running on Race*, p. 48.

6. Dan T. Carter, *The Politics of Rage: George Wallace, the Origins of the New Conservatism, and the Transformation of American Politics*, second edition (Baton Rouge: Louisiana State University Press, 2000), p. 367.

7. Mayer, *Running on Race*, p. 46.

8. Ibid., p. 69.

9. Cited in Carter, *Politics of Rage*, p. 379.

10. These were notes taken by H. R. Haldeman, Nixon's chief of staff, during a meeting with Nixon on January 8, 1970, with Nixon (Box 2, H. R. Haldeman Papers, Nixon Presidential Materials). Cited in Carter, *Politics of Rage*, p. 381.

11. In a memo to White House counsel John Ehrlichman and H. R. Haldeman, Nixon wrote, "I am convinced that while legal segregation is totally wrong, forced integration of housing or education is just as wrong." Quoted in Kevin L. Yuill, *Richard Nixon and the Rise of Affirmative Action* (Lanham, MD: Rowman & Littlefield Publishers, 2006), p. 226.

12. James Rosen, *The Strong Man: John Mitchell and the Secrets of Watergate* (New York: Doubleday, 2008), p. 143. Further information on the immense success of Nixon and Mitchell's policy in desegregating Southern schools can be found on pages 139–145.

13. Mayer, *Running on Race*, pp. 96–97.

14. Thomas B. Edsall and Mary D. Edsall, *Chain Reaction: The Impact of Race, Rights, and Taxes on American Politics* (New York: W. W. Norton, 1991), p. 14.

15. Ibid., p. 15.

16. Ibid., p. 14.

17. Ibid., p. 144.

18. The Edsalls (on p. 152 of their book *Chain Reaction*), citing Warren Miller and Susan A. Traugott, *American National Election Studies Data Sourcebook* (Cambridge: Harvard University Press, 1989), p. 163, go on to say, "The percentage of respondents in 1980 saying that blacks and other minorities should help themselves, 41 percent, versus those saying that government should improve the social standing and economic position of blacks, 19 percent, was at an all-time high, compared to 37–29 in 1976, and 38–31 in 1972."

19. Edsall and Edsall, *Chain Reaction*, p. 152.

20. Ibid., p. 11.

21. Ibid., p. 156.

22. "Four Measures of Serious Violent Crime," Bureau of Justice Statistics, U.S. Department of Justice, www.ojp.usdoj.gov/bjs/glance/tables/ 4meastab.htm (accessed December 11, 2008). Each year, the FBI puts out the Uniform Crime Reports, a compilation of nationwide reports of serious violent crimes (rape, robbery, aggravated assault, and homicide). Of course, only some of these crimes are committed by blacks, but media reports frequently focus on black aggressors, leading to a perception in the public that blacks, particularly black men, are overwhelmingly responsible for violent crime.

23. Edsall and Edsall, *Chain Reaction*, p. 143.

24. http://thinkexist.com/quotes/ronald_reagan/3.html

25. "'Welfare Queen' Becomes Issue in Reagan Campaign," *New York Times*, February 15, 1976.

26. Edsall and Edsall, *Chain Reaction*, p. 158.

27. Ibid., p. 163.

28. Toni Morrison, "Comment," *The New Yorker*, October 5, 1998. Morrison's characterization of Clinton was adopted by both supporters and critics as reflective of his immense support among blacks. Interestingly, Morrison came to clarify her comments after the negativity expressed by Clinton toward Obama during the 2008 Democratic primaries.

29. Jodie Allen, "Working out Welfare," *Time*, July 29, 1996, www.time.com/ time/magazine/article/0,9171,984900,00.html?promoid= googlep (accessed December 11, 2008).

30. Robert Singh, *The Farrakhan Phenomenon: Race, Politics, and the Paranoid Style in American Politics* (Washington, D.C.: Georgetown University Press, 1997), p. 2.

31. "Farrakhan Remarks Stir Anger," *New York Times*, October 15, 1995.

32. Ibid.

33. Mayer, *Running on Race*, pp. 183–84.

34. Ibid., p. 184.

35. Wright spoke at the National Press Club on April 28, 2008. In response to the question, "In your sermon, you said the government lied about inventing the HIV virus as a means of genocide against people of color. So I ask you: do you honestly believe your statement and those words?" Wright answered, "Based on this Tuskegee experiment and based on what has happened to Africans in this country, I believe our government is capable of doing anything." And in response to the question on his earlier comparison of the U.S. Marines to the Roman soldiers who executed Jesus, "It sounds like some other governments I know . . . [Y]es, I can compare that. We have troops stationed all over the world, just like Rome had troops stationed all over the world, because we run the world." Transcript provided by the New York Times, April 28, 2008, www.nytimes.com 2008/04/28/us/ politics/28text-wright.html?pagewanted=1&sq (accessed December 11, 2008).

36. "PEJ Campaign Coverage Index: April 28–May 4, 2008: The Pastor's Press Tour is the Week's Big Newsmaker," The Project for Excellence in Journalism, Pew Research Center, www.journalism.org/node/10928 (accessed December 11, 2008). The same report found that 37 percent of the campaign coverage was focused on the Wright–Obama relationship during the week of March 17–23, when Wright's first comments began to appear in the media.

CHAPTER 13

1. Calvin Watkins, "Dallas Cowboys' Adam Jones upset with Imus' Comments," *Dallas Morning News*, June 24,2008,www.dallasnews.com/sharedcontent/dws/spt/ football/cowboys/stories/062408dnspocowbrief.31b5ac75.html (accessed December 11, 2008).

2. "American Indicators: Civil Liberties, Crime, & Drugs," © 2008, The Progressive Review, www.prorev.com/statscl.htm (accessed December 11 2008).

3. "2007 Statistical Abstract," Bureau of the Census, U.S. Department of Commerce, www.census.gov/compendia/statab/2007/2007edition.html (accessed December 11, 2008).

4. William J. Sabol, Heather Couture, and Paige M. Harrison, "Prisoners in 2006," Bureau of Justice Statistics, U.S. Department of Justice, www.ojp.usdoj.gov/bjs/pub/pdf/p06.pdf (accessed December 11, 2008). It is worth noting that the report also sees a slight decline in the percentage of black prisoners, but such a trend still does not change the troubling fact that the number of black men in jail is far out of balance to that of white males.

5. "2007 Statistical Abstract," note 2.

6. Substance Abuse and Mental Health Services Administration, *Results from the 2005 National Survey on Drug Use and Health: National Findings* (Rockville, MD: Office of Applied Studies, NSDUH Series H-30, DHHS Publication No. SMA 06-4194), 2006, www.oas.samhsa.gov/nsduh/2k 5nsduh/2k5results.pdf (accessed December 11, 2008).

7. "2007 Statistical Abstract," note 2.

8. Michael B. Katz, "The New Black Inequality," *Journal of American History*, June 2005.

9. Richard C. Dieter, "The Death Penalty in Black and White: Who Lives, Who Dies, Who Decides," © 2008, Death Penalty Information Center, www. deathpenaltyinfo.org/article.php?did=539&scid (accessed December 11 2008).

10. Ibid.

11. Ibid.

12. Ibid.

13. "Analysis of Racism in the Criminal Justice System," September 8, 2001, Justice Works, www.justiceworks.info/index.php?module=pagemaster &PAGE_user_op=view_page&PAGE_id=41&MMN_position=54:4 (accessed December 11, 2008).

14. Ibid.

15. Ibid.

16. Ibid.

17. Ibid.

18. Dan T. Carter, *Scottsboro: A Tragedy of the American South*, revised ed. (Baton Rouge: Louisiana Tech University Press, 1979), p. x.

19. "Analysis of Racism," Justice Works.

20. Ibid.

21. Associated Press, "Florida City Pays Girl Who Says Cop Made Her Do Topless Jumping Jacks $35K," January 27, 2007, www.foxnews.com/story/0,2933,247442,00.html (accessed December11, 2008). The city of Pensacola did not take action against the officer, Shawn Patrick Shields, for over six months, requiring the victim and her companion to undergo polygraph tests. The city finally settled with the victim for $35,000.

22. Steve Visser, "Ex Cop: Officers routinely Lied to Obtain Search Warrants," *Atlanta Journal Constitution*, May 5, 2008.

23. David Kairys, *The Politics of Law: A Progressive Critique* (New York: Basic Books, 1998), p. 414.

24. "Analysis of Racism," Justice Works.

25. "Former Philadelphia Prosecutor Accused of Racial Bias," *New York Times*, April 3, 1997, www.query.nytimes.com/gst/fullpage.html?res=9B07E7D7143DF930A

35757C0A961958260&sec=&spon=&pagewanted= 1 (accessed December 11, 2008).

26. An excellent study on the prevalence of plea bargains for low-level drug offenses that result in prison sentences was done by the Rand Corporation, a nonprofit research organization working in conjunction with Arizona State University: Riley, Rodriguez, Ridgeway, et al., "Just Cause or Just Because? Prosecution and Plea-Bargaining Resulting in Prison Sentences on Low-Level Drug Charges in California and Arizona," www.rand.org/ pubs/monographs/2005/RAND_MG288.sum.pdf (accessed December 11, 2008). See also: Jack Katz, "Legality and Equality: Plea Bargaining in the Prosecution of White-Collar and Common Crimes," *Law & Society Review*, Vol. 13, No. 2, Winter, 1979, pp. 431–59, and Clayton Sims, "The Historical and Racial Implications of Plea Bargaining" (research paper), MIT Open Courseware, Massachussetts Institute of Technology, www.ocw.mit.edu/NR/rdon-lyres/Political-Science/17-908Spring-2007/70220922-8A31-470C-8889-6097B38F09A4/0/plea_ bargaining.pdf (accessed December 11, 2008).

27. Marc Mauer, "The Disparity on Crack-Cocaine Sentencing," *Boston Globe*, July 5, 2006.

28. *Kimbrough v. U.S.*, 128 S. Ct. 558 (2007). See also Robert Barnes, "Justices Reinforce Leeway on Sentences," Washington Post, December 11, 2007, www.washington-post.com/wp-dyn/content/article/2007/12/10/AR2007121000558.html?hpid= topnews (accessed December 11, 2008).

29. Richard Berk, "Preliminary Data on Race and Crack Charging Practices in Los Angeles," 6 *Federal Sentencing Reporter* 36–37 (1993).

30. Ibid.

31. "USA: Death by Discrimination—the Continuing Role of Race in Capital Cases" (white paper), Amnesty International, AI Index AMR 51/046/ 2003, April 24, 2003, www.amnesty.org/en/library/asset/AMR51/046/2003/en/dom-AMR 510462003en.pdf (accessed December 11, 2008).

32. "Death Penalty Discriminates Against Black Crime Victims," *USA Today*, April 28, 2003.

33. "USA: Death by discrimination," Amnesty International.

34. Dieter, "Death Penalty in Black and White."

35. Ibid.

36. "The Color of Justice" (online lesson), © 2008 Constitutional Rights Foundation, www.crf-usa.crf-usa.org/brown50th/color_of_justice.htm (accessed December 11, 2008).

37. Ron Paul, "Government and Racism," LewRockwell.com, April 18, 2007, www.lewrockwell.com/paul/paul381.html (accessed December 11, 2008).

38. William S. Stuntz, "Unequal Justice," *Harvard Law Review*, vol. 121 (June 2008), p. 2005.

39. Ibid., p. 1997.

40. Ibid., p. 2010.

41. Ibid., p. 1997.

42. "Blacks Criticize Sentences of White New Jersey State Troopers After Plea Bargain in Racial Profiling and Shooting Case," *Jet*, February 4, 2002, www.findarticles.com/p/articles/mi_m1355/is_7_101/ai_83040497 (accessed December 11, 2008).

43. David Barstow and David Kocieniewski, "Records Show New Jersey Police Withheld Data on Race Profiling," *The New York Times*, October 12, 2000, www.query.nytimes.com/gst/fullpage.html?res=950CE0D7173FF931A25753C1A 9669C8B63&sec=&spon=&pagewanted=all (accessed December 11, 2008).

44. Ibid.
45. Ibid.
46. Ibid.
47. *O'Lone v. New Jersey Dept. of Corrections*, New Jersey Superior Court, 712 A.2d 1177.
48. *Taylor v. Metzger*, Supreme Court of New Jersey, 1998, 706 A.2d 685.
49. *Parker v. City of Trenton*, NJ App 2110, New Jersey Court of Appeals www.precydent.com/citation/NJ+App/a3647-06.
50. Ibid.

CHAPTER 14
1. Jules Tygiel, *Extra Bases: Reflections on Jackie Robinson, Race, & Baseball History* (Lincoln: University of Nebraska Press, 2002), p. 4.
2. Ibid., p. 5.
3. Ibid.
4. John C. Chalberg, *Rickey & Robinson* (Wheeling, IL.: Harlan and Davidson, 2000), p. 5.
5. Robert W. Peterson, "Baseball," *Encyclopedia Britannica* (Chicago: Encyclopedia Britannica Inc., 2008).
6. Satchel Paige, *Maybe I'll Pitch Forever* (Lincoln, NE: Bison Books, 1993), p. 50.
7. Kevin Holder, "Josh Gibson vs Barry Bonds: Who Is Baseball's True King?," Associated Content, Inc., October 1, 2007, www.associatedcontent.com/ article/395376/josh_gibson_vs_barry_bonds_who_is_baseballs.html?page=2 (accessed January 27, 1009).
8. Tygiel, *Extra Bases*, p. 5.
9. Ibid., p. 6.
10. Ibid.
11. Chalberg, *Rickey & Robinson*, p. 3.
12. Ibid., p. 6.
13. Ibid.
14. Ibid., p. 8.
15. Ibid., p. 9.
16. Ibid.
17. Ibid., p. 11.
18. Ibid., p. 105.
19. Ibid.
20. Ibid., p. 106.
21. Ibid.
22. Ibid.
23. Tygiel, *Extra Bases*, p. 7.
24. Ibid.
25. Ibid., p. 8.
26. Chalberg, *Rickey & Robinson*, p. 119.
27. Ibid., p. 113.
28. Ibid., p. 115.
29. Ibid.
30. Ibid.
31. Ibid., p. 121.
32. Ibid.
33. Ibid., p. 124.
34. Ibid.
35. Ibid.

36. Maury Allen, "Jackie Robinson: An American Hero," © 1999, www.evesmag. com/robinson.htm (accessed December 12, 2008).

37. Chalberg, *Rickey & Robinson,* p. 123.

CONCLUSION

1. Barack Obama, 2008 presidential acceptance speech at Grant Park, Chicago, Illinois, November 4, 2008.

Bibliography

James Allen, *Without Sanctuary* (Santa Fe: Twin Palms Publishers, 2000).

Stephen E. Ambrose, *Citizen Soldiers: The U.S. Army from the Normandy to the Bulge to the Surrender of Germany* (New York: Simon & Schuster, 1998).

James D. Anderson, *The Education of Blacks in the South, 1860–1935* (Chapel Hill: University of North Carolina Press, 1988).

Trezzvant W. Anderson, *Come out Fighting: The Epic of the 761st Tank Battalion 1942–1945* (privately printed, 1945).

Paul M. Angle and Earl Schenck Miers, eds., *The Living Lincoln: The Man in His Times, in His Own Words,* (Fall River, MA: Fall River Press, 1992).

St. Thomas Aquinas, *Summa Theologica* (Grand Rapids, M.I.: Christian Classics, 1981).

Peter W. Bardaglio, *Reconstructing the Household: Families, Sex and the Law in the Nineteenth Century South* (Chapel Hill: University of North Carolina Press, 1998).

Raoul Berger, *Government by Judiciary: The Transformation of the Fourteenth Amendment,* second edition (Indianapolis: The Liberty Fund, 1997).

Keith Bradley, *Slavery and Society at Rome* (Cambridge: Cambridge University Press, 1994).

Taylor Branch, *Parting The Waters; America in the King Years 1954–63* (New York: Simon & Schuster, 1988).

Gloria Browne-Marshall, *Race, Law, and American Society* (New York: Routledge, 2007).

Dan T. Carter, *The Politics of Rage: George Wallace, the Origins of the New Conservatism, and the Transformation of American Politics,* second edition (Baton Rouge: Louisiana State University Press, 2000).

Dan T. Carter, *Scottsboro: A Tragedy of the American South,* revised ed. (Baton Rouge: Louisiana Tech University Press, 1979).

John C. Chalberg, *Rickey & Robinson* (Wheeling, I.L., Harlan and Davidson).

William Cohen, *At Freedom's Edge: Black Mobility and the Southern White Quest for Racial Control, 1861–1915* (Baton Rouge: Louisiana State University Press, 1991).

Henry Scofield Cooley, *A Study of Slavery in New Jersey* (Baltimore: The Johns Hopkins Press, 1893).

David Brion Davis, *The Problem of Slavery in Western Culture* (Ithaca: Cornell University Press, 1966).

Jack E. Davis, *The Civil Rights Movement* (Boston: Wiley-Blackwell, 2000).

Thomas J. DiLorenzo, *The Real Lincoln: A New Look at Abraham Lincoln, His Agenda, and an Unnecessary War* (Roseville, CA: Prima Publishing, 2002).

Frederick L. Downing, *To See the Promised Land: The Faith Pilgrimage of Martin Luther King, Jr.* (Macon, GA: Mercer University Press, 1986).

Charles W. Dryden and Benjamin O. Davis, *A-Train: Memoirs of a Tuskegee Airman* (Tuscaloosa: University of Alabama Press, 2003).

BIBLIOGRAPHY

Thomas B. Edsall and Mary D. Edsall, *Chain Reaction: The Impact of Race, Rights, and Taxes on American Politics* (New York: W. W. Norton, 1991).

Adam Fairclough, *Better Day Coming: Blacks and Equality, 1890–2000* (New York: Viking, 2001).

Eric Foner, *A Short History of Reconstruction* (New York: Harper & Row Publishers, 1984).

Eric Foner, *Reconstruction: America's Unfinished Revolution* (New York: Harper Collins, 1988).

Robert Pierce Forbes, *The Missouri Compromise and its Aftermath* (Chapel Hill: University of North Carolina Press, 2007).

Clark Foreman, *Environmental Factors in Negro Elementary Education* (New York: W. W. Norton, 1932).

Charles F. Francis, *The Tuskegee Airmen: The Men Who Changed a Nation* (Boston: Branden Publishing Company, 1988).

John Hope Franklin, *From Slavery to Freedom: A History of African Americans, Volume Two* (New York: The McGraw-Hill Co., 2000).

John Hope Franklin, *The Emancipation Proclamation* (New York: Doubleday, 1963).

John Hope Franklin, *Reconstruction After the Civil War* (Chicago: University of Chicago Press, 1961).

George M. Frederickson, *The Black Image in the White Mind* (New York: Harper & Row, 1971).

William Gienapp, *Abraham Lincoln and Civil War America: A Biography* (New York: Oxford University Press, 2002).

Gustave Glotz, *Ancient Greece at Work* (London: Georg Olms, 1926).

Lawrence Goldstone, *Dark Bargain: Slavery, Profits, and the Struggle for the Constitution* (New York: Walker & Company, 2005).

Barry Goldwater, *The Conscience of a Conservative* (New York: Victor Publishing Co., 1960).

Robert Goldwin and Art Kaufman, *Slavery and its Consequences: The Constitution, Equality, and Race* (Washington D.C.: AEI, 1988).

Frederick W. Haberman, ed., *Nobel Lectures, Peace 1951–1970* (Amsterdam: Elsevier Publishing Company, 1972).

Jack Hayward, *Out of Slavery: Abolition and After* (London: Frank Cass, 1985).

Jeffrey Rogers Hummel, *Emancipating Slaves, Enslaving Free Men: A History of the American Civil War* (Chicago: Open Court Publishing Co., 1996).

Michael P. Johnson, *Abraham Lincoln, Slavery, and the Civil War: Selected Writings and Speeches* (Boston: Bedford/St. Martin's, 2001).

James H. Jones, *Bad Blood* (New York: The Free Press: 1993).

David Kairys, *The Politics of Law: A Progressive Critique* (New York: Basic Books, 1998).

Robin Kelley and Earl Lewis, *To Make Our World Anew: A History of African Americans* (New York: Oxford University Press, 2005).

Martin Luther King Jr., *The Trumpet of Conscience* (New York: Harper & Row, 1968).

Michael J. Klarman, "*Brown v. Board*: 50 Years Later," *Humanities*, March/April 2004.

Herbert Klein, *The Atlantic Slave Trade* (New York: Cambridge University Press, 1999).

BIBLIOGRAPHY

J. Morgan Kousser, *The Shaping of Southern Politics: Suffrage Restrictions and the Establishment of the One-Party South* (New Haven: Yale University Press, 1974).

Robert A. Levy and William Mellor, *The Dirty Dozen: How Twelve Supreme Court Cases Radically Expanded Government and Eroded Freedom* (New York: Penguin, 2008).

Earl M. Maltz, *Dred Scott and the Politics of Slavery* (Lawrence: University Press of Kansas, 2007).

Clements R. Markham, ed., *The Journal of Christopher Columbus During His First Voyage, 1492–93* (London: Kessinger Publishing, LLC, 2007).

Jeremy D. Mayer, *Running on Race: Racial Politics in Presidential Campaigns 1960–2000* (New York: Random House, 2002).

James McPherson, *Battle Cry of Freedom* (New York: Oxford University Press, 2003).

Diane McWhorter, *Carry Me Home: Birmingham, Alabama, the Climactic Battle of the Civil Rights Revolution* (New York: Simon & Schuster, 2001).

Warren Miller and Susan A. Traugott, *American National Election Studies Data Sourcebook* (Cambridge: Harvard University Press, 1989).

George Fort Milton, *The Age of Hate: Andrew Johnson and the Radicals* (New York: Coward-McCann, Inc., 1930).

Robert Morgan, "The Great Emancipator and the Issue of Face: Abraham Lincoln's Program of Black Resettlement," *The Journal of Historical Review*, September, 1993, vol. 13, number 5.

Alan M. Osur, *Blacks in the Army Air Force During World War II: The Problem of Race Relations* (Washington: Office of Air Force History, 1977).

Mary Penick Motley, *The Invisible Soldier* (Detroit: Wayne State University, 1975).

Mark Neely, *The Fate of Liberty: Abraham Lincoln and Civil Liberties* (New York: Oxford University Press, 1991).

John G. Nicolay and John Hay, *Abraham Lincoln: A History*, Volume X (New York: The Century Co., 1890).

James T. Patterson, *Brown v. Board of Education: A Civil Rights Milestone and Its Troubled Legacy* (New York: Oxford University Press, 2002).

J. W. Peltason, *Fifty-Eight Lonely Men: Southern Federal Judges and School Desegregation* (Urbana-Champaign: University of Illinois Press, 1961).

Frederick Pollock, *Essays on the Law* (London: Macmillan, 1922).

Benjamin Quarles, *The Negro in the Making of America* (New York: Collier, 1964).

Marcus Rediker, *The Slave Ship: A Human History* (New York: Viking, 2007).

Oscar Reiss, *Blacks in Colonial America* (Jefferson, NC: McFarland, Inc. 1997).

D. Robinson, *Slavery in the Structure of American Politics 1765–1820* (New York: W. W. Norton & Co. Inc, 1971).

James Rosen, *The Strong Man: John Mitchell and the Secrets of Watergate* (New York: Doubleday, 2008).

Carl Sandburg, *Abraham Lincoln, The War Years*, volume IV (New York: Harcourt Brace and Co., 1939).

James E. Sefton, *The United States Army and Reconstruction* (Baton Rouge: Louisiana State University Press, 1967).

Robert Singh, *The Farrakhan Phenomenon: Race, Politics, and the Paranoid Style in American Politics* (Washington, D.C.: Georgetown University Press, 1997).

BIBLIOGRAPHY

Richard Slotkin, *Lost Battalions: The Great War and the Crisis of American Nationality* (New York: Holt, 2006).

Kenneth M. Stammp, *And the War Came: The North and the Secession Crisis, 1860–1861* (Baton Rouge: Louisiana State University Press, 1950).

Kenneth Stammp, *The Peculiar Institution* (New York: Vintage Books, 1956).

Geoffrey R. Stone, Louis M. Seidman, Cass R. Sunstein, Mark V. Tushnet, Pamela S. Karlan, *Constitutional Law* (New York: Aspen Publishers, 2005).

Thomas J. Sugrue, *Sweet Land of Liberty: The Forgotten Struggle for Civil Rights in the North* (New York: Random House, 2008).

W. Allison Sweeney, *History of the American Negro in the Great World War: His Splendid Record* (New York: G. G. Sapp, 1919).

Ida M. Tarbell, *The Life of Abraham Lincoln*, Volume II (New York: The Lincoln History Society, 1903).

Tzvetan Todorov and Richard Howard, *The Conquest of America: The Question of the Other* (Norman: University of Oklahoma Press, 1999).

Jules Tygiel, *Extra Bases: Reflections on Jackie Robinson, Race, & Baseball History*, (Lincoln: University of Nebraska Press, 2002).

Melvin I. Urofsky and Paul Finkelman, *A March of Liberty: A Constitutional History of the United States, Volume II, from 1877 to the Present*, second edition (New York: Oxford University Press, 2002).

Michael Vorenberg, *Final Freedom: The Civil War, the Abolition of Slavery, and the Thirteenth Amendment* (New York: Cambridge University Press, 2001).

Nathaniel Weyl and William Marina, *American Statesmen on Slavery and the Negro* (Arlington, VA: Arlington House, 1971).

Douglas L. Wilson and Rodney O. Davis, eds., *Herndon's Informants: Letters, Interviews and Statements about Abraham Lincoln* (Urbana: University of Illinois Press, 1997).

C. Vann Woodward, *The Strange Career of Jim Crow, Third Revised Edition* (New York: Oxford University Press: 1974).

Richard Wormser, *The Rise and Fall of Jim Crow* (New York: Macmillan, 2003).

Kevin L. Yuill, *Richard Nixon and the Rise of Affirmative Action* (Lanham, MD: Rowman & Littlefield Publishers, 2006).

Howard Zinn, "The Student Nonviolent Coordinating Committee," *Civil Rights Since 1787: A Reader on the Black Struggle*, Jonathan Birnbaum and Clarence Taylor, eds. (New York: NYU Press, 2000).

Index

INDEX

INDEX

Emerson, John, 58–59
England, control of slave trade, 11
English colonists, acceptance of slavery, 13
Enlightenment, 4
equality, 1

F
families of slaves, 19, 22–23
Farrakhan, Louis, 208
Faubus, Orval, 175–176
federal budget, and tariffs, 75–76
Federal Bureau of Investigation, 185
    Uniform Crime Reports, 271n22
federal interventionism, opposition to, 200
federal mandatory sentencing, 217–218
fee system, for police arrests, 213
Feller, Bob, 236
Ferdinand (King of Spain), 6
Ferguson, John Howard, 127
Fifth Circuit Court of Appeals, 176–177
"fighting grandfather" clauses, 119
filibuster, 179
Florida, 74, 77, 120
folklore, 19
forced plantation labor, in Reconstruction, 110–112
foreman, 18
Fort Sumter, South Carolina, 73
Fowler, Bud, 229
France in WWI, and U.S. black soldiers, 143–145
free states
    vs. slave states, 54
    slaves transported to, 57
free will, xii
freedmen, status in Reconstruction, 107
Freedmen's Bureau, 107–108, 171
freedom, 1, 49
    pursuit of, 24–28
    ripping slave from natural state of, 15
    in state of nature vs. in society, 45
freedom of speech, xiii
"freedom rides", 180–181
French Legion of Honor, 143–144
Fugitive Slave Act of 1793, 42
Fugitive Slave Act of 1850, 91, 92
Fugitive Slave Clause, 35, 42
fugitive slaves, article of war on, 76

G
Gandhi, Mahatma, 185
Garrison, William Lloyd, 35

Garrity, W. Arthur, 190
Georgia, 74, 77, 175
German POWs, treatment in U.S., 148
Gibson, Josh, 231–232
Glass, Carter, 129
God-created human nature, as source of law, 48–49
Goldwater, Barry M., 201
    The Conscience of a Conservative, 189
"good character" clauses, 119
Goodman, Andrew, 207
government
branches of, 36–37
    failure of, 220–226
    failure to provide relief for freed slaves, 81
    federal inability to prohibit slavery, 62–63
    funding in mid-1800s, 75
    role in racism, xv–xvi
    role in slave trade, 7
    as source of law, 48–49
    workplace discrimination by, 223–226
government behavior, in black to white relationship, xi
government officials, desire to remain in power, 226
Graham, Christopher, 42–43
Grant, Frank, 229
Grant, Ulysses S., 117, 118, 125
Greeks, 1–2
Greeley, Horace, 93

H
habeas corpus, 28, 118, 255n43
Haiti, 86
    slave revolt, 108–109
Harlan, John Marshall, 129
Harvey, James III, 151
Hastie, Willaim H., 149
hatred, 247
Hayes, Rutherford B., 120
Hayward, Jack, 2
Heart of Atlanta Motel v. United States, 193–194
Heller, John R., 159–160
Henderson, John Brooks, 99, 100
Henderson Act of 1943, 157
Henry the Navigator, 6
Higgins, Robert, 229
Hispaniola, 7

INDEX

Hogan, John, 223–224
Holmes, John, 51
Homer Adolph Plessy v. State of Louisiana,
    127
Hoover, J. Edgar, 181–182, 185
Horton, James Edwin, 214
hostile work environment, 225
House of Representatives, 37
housing discrimination, 194
Houston, Charles, 163
Houston, Texas, race riot involving black soldiers, 145
Howard, Jacob, 100
Howard, William, 134
humane slaveholders, 16
Hunter, David, 76
Hunter, Frank, 153–155
Huxman, Walter, 168

I

Ile a Vache, 97
Illinois State Register, 65–66
Imperiale, Anthony, 190
Importation Clause, 35
Imus, Don, 210
income tax, 84–85
indentured servants, 11
India, slaves in, 3
individual in society, xiv–xv
individual liberties, 46
inferior race, 14
Innocent VIII (pope), 6
interracial marriages, banned, 125
interstate commerce, 193–194
Iredell, James, 46–47
Irwin, James B., 143
Isham, Gerald, 225

J

Jackson, Andrew, 27
Jackson, Jesse, 208–209
Jamestown, Africans as indentured servants,
    11
Jefferson, Thomas, 51, 53
    Declaration of Independence, xi, xii
    on Missouri Compromise, 51
    on natural law, 31
Jersey City American Standard, 73
Jim Crow laws, 104, 189, 213
    eliminating, 188
    failure of resistance to, 126

legal justification, 127–130
    and Marshall, 163
    Supreme Court and, 122–127
Johannsen, Robert W., 92
Johnson, Andrew, 107, 108–109
Johnson, Lyndon Baines, 180, 187, 191,
    196, 200
Johnson, Reverdy, 100
Jones, Louis, 219
judiciary, inconsistency in 19 c., 50
jury pool, 212
jury selection, 217
Justice Department
    and civil rights movement, 182
    study of racial disparities, 214–215
juvenile justice system, racial bias in, 215

K

Kansas City Monarchs, 229
Kansas-Nebraska Act, 57, 66, 94
Kansas, segregation laws, 163
Katzenbach, Nicholas deB., 176
Katzenbach v. McClung, 193–194
Kenna, James, 223–224
Kennedy, John F., 84, 179–182, 186
Kennedy, Robert F., 222
Kentucky, 74, 77, 137
Kerner Report, 196
Kindelberger, James H., 147
Kinder, Brian, 212
King, Martin Luther, Jr., 182–184, 191
    assassination, 186
    "Letter from a Birmingham Jail", 31–32,
    184–185
Klarman, Michael J., 172
Kock, Bernard, 97
Kruttschnitt, E.B., 129
Ku Klux Klan, 118, 181

L

labor regulations, bias against blacks, 111
Landis, Kenesaw Mountain, 230, 239
law and order, 201
laws
    origin, 48–49
    unjust and constitutional, 48
    unjust, duty of disobedience to, 31, 65
legal positivism, 45–46
    Taney's adherence to, 64
Leonard, Buck, 231, 236
Liberia, 86, 96, 97